WOMEN
IN INDONESIA

The **Research School of Pacific and Asian Studies (RSPAS)** at **The Australian National University (ANU)** is home to the **Indonesia Project**, a major international centre of research and graduate training on the economy of Indonesia. Established in 1965 in the School's **Division of Economics**, the Project is well known and respected in Indonesia and in other places where Indonesia attracts serious scholarly and official interest. Funded by ANU and the **Australian Agency for International Development (AusAID)**, the Project monitors and analyses recent economic developments in Indonesia; informs Australian governments, business and the wider community about those developments and about future prospects; stimulates research on the Indonesian economy; and publishes the respected *Bulletin of Indonesian Economic Studies*.

The School's **Department of Political and Social Change (PSC)** focuses on domestic politics, social processes and state–society relationships in Asia and the Pacific, and has a long-established interest in Indonesia. Together with PSC and RSPAS, the Project holds the annual **Indonesia Update conference**, whose proceedings are published in the **Indonesia Assessment series**. Each Update (and resulting Assessment volume) offers an overview of recent economic and political developments, and devotes attention to a significant theme in Indonesia's development.

The **Institute of Southeast Asian Studies (ISEAS)** in Singapore was established as an autonomous organization in 1968. It is a regional research centre for scholars and other specialists concerned with modern Southeast Asia, particularly the many-faceted problems of stability and security, economic development, and political and social change.

The Institute's research programmes are the Regional Economic Studies (RES, including ASEAN and APEC), Regional Strategic and Political Studies (RSPS), and Regional Social and Cultural Studies (RSCS).

The Institute is governed by a twenty-two-member Board of Trustees comprising nominees from the Singapore Government, the National University of Singapore, the various Chambers of Commerce, and professional and civic organizations. An Executive Committee oversees day-to-day operations; it is chaired by the Director, the Institute's chief academic and administrative officer.

INDONESIA ASSESSMENT SERIES

WOMEN IN INDONESIA
Gender, Equity and Development

edited by

Kathryn Robinson
Sharon Bessell

ISEAS

Institute of Southeast Asian Studies
Singapore

First published in 2002 in Singapore by
Institute of Southeast Asian Studies
30 Heng Mui Keng Terrace
Pasir Panjang
Singapore 119614

Internet e-mail: publish@iseas.edu.sg
World Wide Web: http://www.iseas.edu.sg/pub.html

Acknowledgement
The publisher gratefully acknowledges the artists for permission to reproduce their material on various pages in this book. On the front cover is a mixed media on canvas titled "Penganten Jawa" (Javanese Bride and Bridegroom) by Astari Rasjid, 2000; on the back cover is a work of bronze titled "Resistante" (Resistance) by Dolorosa Sinaga, 1996.

The responsibility for facts and opinions in this publication rests exclusively with the editors and contributors and their interpretations do not necessarily reflect the views or the policy of the publishers or their supporters.

ISEAS Library Cataloguing-in-Publication Data

Women in Indonesia: gender, equity and development/ edited by Kathryn Robinson and Sharon Bessell.
    (Indonesia assessment series ; 2001)
    1. Women—Indonesia.
    2. Women in development—Indonesia.
    3. Women—Indonesia—Social conditions.
    I. Robinson, Kathryn.
    II. Bessell, Sharon.
    III. Series.
DS644.4 I41 2001   2002   sls2002003619

ISBN 981-230-158-5 (soft cover)
ISBN 981-230-159-3 (hard cover)

Copy-edited and typeset by Beth Thomson, Japan Online.
Indexed by Angela Grant.

Printed in Singapore by Seng Lee Press Pte Ltd.

CONTENTS

TABLES

FIGURES

CONTRIBUTORS

Sri Moertiningsih Adioetomo
Researcher, Demographic Institute, Faculty of Economics, University of
Indonesia, Jakarta

Edward Aspinall
Research Fellow, Department of Political and Social Change, Research School
of Pacific and Asian Studies, Australian National University, Canberra

Zohra A. Baso
Chairperson, Consumers' Association Foundation of South Sulawesi (YLK-
SS), Makassar

Sharon Bessell
Director, Social Protection Facility, Research School of Social Sciences,
Australian National University, Canberra

Carla Bianpoen
Freelance Journalist and Art Critic, and Researcher, Insan Hitawasana
Sejahtera, Jakarta

Susan Blackburn
Senior Lecturer, School of Political and Social Inquiry, Monash University,
Melbourne

Tom Boellstorff
Assistant Professor, University of California – Irvine, and Southeast Asian
Studies Postdoctoral Fellow in 2001, Australian National University, Canberra

Lisa Cameron
Senior Lecturer, Department of Economics, University of Melbourne,
Melbourne

Ria Gondowarsito
Member, Nusa Tenggara Association, and independent consultant, Canberra

Barbara Hatley
Head, School of Asian Languages and Studies, University of Tasmania, Launceston

Graeme Hugo
Professor of Geography and Director, National Key Centre for Social Application of Geographical Information Systems, University of Adelaide, Adelaide

Terence H. Hull
Associate Director and Senior Fellow in Demography, Research School of Social Sciences, Australian National University, Canberra

Nurul Ilmi Idrus
Lecturer, Department of Anthropology, Faculty of Social and Political Sciences, Hasanuddin University, Makassar, and Research Scholar, Anthropology, Research School of Pacific and Asian Studies, Australian National University, Canberra

Khofifah Indar Parawansa
Former Minister for Women's Empowerment and former Head of the National Family Planning Coordination Agency (BKKBN), Jakarta

Gavin W. Jones
Professor, Demography Program, Research School of Social Sciences, Australian National University, Canberra

Lies Marcoes
Senior Researcher, Insan Hitawasana Sejahtera, Jakarta

Edriana Noerdin
Member, KaPAL Perempuan, Jakarta

Mayling Oey-Gardiner
Executive Director, Insan Hitawasana Sejahtera, and Professor, Faculty of Economics, University of Indonesia, Jakarta

Mari Pangestu
Director, Centre for Strategic and International Studies, Jakarta

Sudjadnan Parnohadiningrat
Ambassador of the Republic of Indonesia, Canberra

Kathryn Robinson
Senior Fellow, Anthropology, Research School of Pacific and Asian Studies, Australian National University, Canberra

Mohammad Sadli
Emeritus Professor, Faculty of Economics, University of Indonesia, Jakarta

Saparinah Sadli
Chair, National Commission on Violence against Women (Komnas Perempuan), Jakarta

Krishna Sen
Coordinator of Research and Postgraduate Studies, School of Media and Information, Curtin University, Perth

Soerdati Surbakti
Director General, Central Statistics Agency (BPS), Jakarta

ACKNOWLEDGMENTS

The Indonesia Update is held every year at The Australian National University (ANU) in Canberra with financial support from the Australian Agency for International Development (AusAID). The theme of the 2001 Update, held on 21–22 September, was 'Gender, Equity and Development in Indonesia'. The Ford Foundation, Jakarta, the Asia Foundation, Jakarta, and the Australia–Indonesia Institute in Canberra provided funding for additional Indonesian speakers, further enhancing the level of expertise we were able to bring to this topic.

We would like to thank all the speakers/authors for their thoughtful contributions to the debate, and their imaginative responses to the tasks we set them. The Indonesian Ambassador to Australia, H.E. Mr Sudjadnan Parnohadiningrat, opened the conference with a speech that reflected his engagement with issues of gender equity in international negotiations. We are also grateful to him for the logistic support provided by the Indonesian Embassy in Canberra in organising the large number of speakers from Indonesia. The former Minister for Women's Empowerment in the Abdurrahman Wahid cabinet, Khofifah Indar Parawansa, gave the keynote speech to the conference, and provided us with the unique perspective of a politician involved in the everyday business of policy and social change. Professor Saparinah Sadli, who is well known as a scholar and women's activist and who has won the respect of several generations of Indonesian women, provided a unique perspective on an activist's life. Dr Soerdarti Surbakti, as head of the Indonesian Central Statistics Agency (BPS), gave us an insight into the key role she has played in developing the information infrastructure necessary for policies to bring about gender equity.

In the spirit of gender equity, the political and economics updates were presented by women – Associate Professor Krishna Sen and Dr Mari Pangestu. We would like to acknowledge our gratitude to them for pulling together summaries of the year's events in difficult and rapidly changing times. Professor Mohammad Sadli and Dr Edward Aspinall provided discussant's comments, leading to lively debate.

Professor Mayling Oey-Gardiner gave us her 'insider's view' of recent political events. We thank her also for facilitating the participation of Ms Lies Marcoes and Ms Carla Bienpoen from Insan Hitawasana Sejahtera, and of Ms Zohra Andi Baso from YLK Makassar. Non-government organisations were well represented, with Ms Yanti Muchtar, Ms Edriana Noerdin and Ms Luguna Setyawati from KaPAL Perempuan presenting papers on issues arising in the context of regional autonomy, and Dr Ria Gondowarsito speaking about the development experience of the Australian-based Nusa Tenggara Association. We thank our Australian Indonesianist colleagues who responded to our request to write about gender and equity in Indonesia's reform period: Dr Susan Blackburn, Dr Terence Hull, Professor Gavin Jones, Professor Graeme Hugo, Dr Lisa Cameron, Dr Barbara Hatley, Ms Nurul Ilmi Idrus and Dr Tom Boellstorff. Many thanks also to the colleagues who chaired sessions and facilitated such lively debate.

The Update Conference is a major logistical feat. It is always carried off without apparent hitch, thanks to the professionalism of the staff of the Indonesia Project, who always give more than one could expect. We would like to thank the Indonesia Project 'team' of Karen Nulty, Liz Drysdale and Trish Van der Hoek, as well as Allison Ley of the Department of Political and Social Change; their organisational skills and enthusiasm make organising the Update a joy for the program convenors. Thanks are due also to Ann Bell, and to the ANU students who acted as volunteers.

We are grateful to the Indonesia Project, in particular Professor Hal Hill, who first raised the possibility of an update on the theme of gender, equity and development, the Project Director, Dr Chris Manning, and Dr Ross McLeod, who has been Director in Chris's absence. Chris Manning and Trish van der Hoek helped enormously in the production of the volume, for which we also must give warm thanks to the copy editor, Beth Thomson. Finally, we would like to thank Triena Ong, Managing Editor of the Institute for Southeast Asian Studies, who has done all she can to ensure speedy publication of this volume.

Kathryn Robinson and Sharon Bessell
February 2002

GLOSSARY

ADB	Asian Development Bank
adat	custom, tradition
Aisyiyah	women's organisation associated with Muhammadiyah
ASEAN	Association of Southeast Asian Nations
AusAID	Australian Agency for International Development
BIKN	Badan Informasi dan Komunikasi Nasional (National Information and Communication Board)
BAKMP	Badan Administrasi Kependudukan dan Mobilitas Penduduk (Administration Board for Population and Population Mobility)
Baknas	Badan Kependudukan Nasional (National Population Board)
Bappenas	Badan Perencanaan Pembangunan Nasional (National Development Planning Board)
belis	bridewealth
Bhineka Tunggal Ika	Unity in Diversity (the national slogan under the New Order)
BKKBN	Badan Koordinasi Keluarga Berencana Nasional (National Family Planning Coordination Agency)
BKN	Badan Kepegawaian Negara (State Civil Service Board)
BKPM	Badan Koordinasi Penanaman Modal (Investment Coordinating Board)
BPD	Badan Perwakilan Desa (Village Representative Body)

BPS	Biro Pusat Statistik (Central Statistics Agency)
Bulog	national food logistics agency
BUMN	Badan Usaha Milik Negara (state-owned enterprise)
camat	*kecamatan* (subdistrict) officer
CETRO	Centre for Electoral Reform
CGI	Consultative Group on Indonesia
CIDA	Canadian International Development Agency
Dati I	Daerah Tingkat I (first-level region, that is, province)
Dati II	Daerah Tingkat II (second-level region, that is, *kabupaten/kotamadya*)
desa	village
Dharma Pertiwi	Armed Forces Wives Association
Dharma Wanita	Civil Service Wives Association (principal official women's organisation under the New Order)
DPA	Dewan Pertimbangan Agung (Supreme Advisory Council)
DPD	Dewan Perwakilan Daerah (Regional Representative Council)
DPR	Dewan Perwakilan Rakyat (People's Representative Council – Indonesia's parliament)
DPRD	Dewan Perwakilan Rakyat Daerah (provincial level of parliament)
dwifungsi	the army's 'dual function' (military and socio-economic) in New Order Indonesia
Fatayat	women's organisation associated with the NU
fiqh	(Islamic) jurisprudence and law
FN-P3M	Fiqh An-Nisa Perhimpunan Pengembangan Pesantren (Organisation for the Development of Pesantren and Society)
Forhati	Forum Alumni Kohati
FPMP	Forum Pemerhati Masalah Perempuan (Women's Forum)
FWPSS	Forum Wartawan Perempuan Sulawesi Selatan (Women Journalists Forum of South Sulawesi)
GAYa Nusantara	national network of *gay* and *lesbi* organisations
GBHN	Garis-garis Besar Haluan Negara (Broad Guidelines on State Policy)
GDP	gross domestic product

GEM	gender empowerment measure
Gerakan Sayang Ibu	Cherish Mothers' Movement
Gerwani	mass women's organisation affiliated to the PKI
GMIT	Gereja Majelis Injili Timur (the main Calvinist church in West Timor)
Golkar	Golongan Karya (Functional Groups), state political party under the New Order, and now second largest in parliament
hadis	reports of the words and actions of the Prophet, regarded as a second scripture in Islam, ancillary to the Qu'ran
Haj	pilgrimage to Mecca
Hari Ibu	Mothers' Day
Hari Kartini	Kartini Day
harkat	dignity
HMI	Himpunan Mahasiswa Islam (Islamic Students' Association)
IAIN	Institut Agama Islam Negeri (State Institute for Islamic Studies)
IBRA	Indonesian Banking Restructuring Agency
IPPSS	Ikatan Perupa Perempuan Sulawesi Selatan (South Sulawesi Women Artists Association)
IKJ	Institut Kesenian Jakarta (Jakarta Institute of Arts)
ILO	International Labour Organisation
IMF	International Monetary Fund
Inheemsche	native Indonesian
Inpres	Presidential Instruction
Inpres Desa Tertinggal	Special Presidential Program for poor villages
IPPS	Ikatan Perupa Perempuan Sulawesi Selatan (South Sulawesi Women Artists Association)
jilbab	head covering for Muslim women
kabupaten	district
Kajian Wanita	Graduate Women's Studies Program, University of Indonesia
kampung	hamlet
KB Mandiri	Keluarga Berencana Mandiri (Self-reliant Family Planning)
KDRT	*kekerasan dalam rumah tangga* (domestic violence)

kecamatan	subdistrict
Kejaksaan Agung	attorney-general's office
kelurahan	village administrative unit (below *kecamatan*)
kepala desa	village head (elected by the people)
Keppres	Keputusan Presiden (Presidential Decree)
kesejahteraan	welfare
KH	Kyai Haji, a religious leader (*kyai*) who has completed the pilgrimage to Mecca (Haj)
KKN	*korupsi, kolusi, nepotisme* (corruption, collusion and nepotism)
KNKWI	Komisi Nasional Kemajuan Wanita Indonesia (Indonesian National Commission on the Advancement of Women)
kodrat	biological determination, one's inherent nature
Kohati	Korps HMI Wati
Komisi Pemantau Pemilu	Commission of General Election Observers
Komnas HAM	National Human Rights Commission
Komnas Perempuan	National Commission on Violence against Women
Konstituante	Constituent Assembly (the body responsible for reviewing the constitution)
Kowani	Kongres Wanita Indonesia (Indonesia Women's Congress), federation of women's organisations
KPI	Koalisi Perempuan Indonesia (Indonesian Women's Coalition)
KPKPN	Komisi Pemeriksa Kekayaan Penyelenggara Negara (Audit Commission on Wealth of State Officials)
KPPT	Konsorsium Perempuan Peduli Toraja (Consortium of Concerned Torajan Women)
krismon	the Indonesian monetary crisis
kyai	Islamic scholar or community leader
LBH-P2I	Lembaga Bantuan Hukum Pemberdayaan Perempuan Indonesia (Law Service for Indonesian Women's Empowerment)
Lekmas	Lembaga Kajian Masyarakat (Centre for Community Research)
LIN	Lembaga Informasi Nasional (Institute of National Information)

LP3M	Lembaga Pengkajian Pedesaan Pantai dan Masyarakat (Institute for the Study of Coastal Communities)
LKP2	Lembaga Konsultasi dan Pemberdayaan Perempuan (Institute for Women's Consultation and Empowerment)
LPP	Lembaga Pemberdayaan Perempuan (Centre for Women's Empowerment)
lurah	village head (selected by the *camat*, or subdistrict officer)
Majlis Tarjih	Assembly for Decisions on Islamic Law
MPR	Majelis Permusyawaratan Rakyat (People's Consultative Assembly), Indonesia's supreme sovereign body
Muhammadiyah	modernist wing of Indonesian Islam
Muslimat	women's organisation associated with the NU
New Order	the Soeharto era, 1965 to 1998
NGO	non-government organisation
NU	Nahdlatul Ulama (Revival of the Religious Scholars), Indonesia's largest traditionalist Islamic organisation
OCW	overseas contract worker
otonomi daerah	regional autonomy
P3EL	Women's Empowerment through Local Economic Development
PAN	Partai Amanat Nasional (National Mandate Party)
Pancasila	the five guiding principles of the Indonesian state under the New Order
pansus	special committee
Paris Club	informal group of creditor countries whose role is to find solutions to the repayment difficulties of debtor nations
pastor	Roman Catholic priest
PDI	Partai Demokrasi Indonesia (Indonesian Democratic Party)
PDI-P	Partai Demokrasi Indonesia – Perjuangan (Indonesian Democratic Party of Struggle)
pendamping suami	companion to the husband
pendeta	Protestant minister
Pengadilan Agama	religious court

peran ganda	dual role
pesantren	traditional Islamic boarding school
PJTKI	Perusahaan Jasa Tenaga Kerja Indonesia (Indonesian Overseas and Domestic Employment Agency)
PK	Partai Keadilan (Justice Party)
PKB	Partai Kebangkitan Bangsa (National Awakening Party)
PKI	Partai Kommunis Indonesia (Communist Party of Indonesia)
PKK	Pembinaan Kesejahteraan Keluarga (Family Welfare Movement), now Pemberdayaan Kesejahteraan Keluarga (Family Welfare Empowerment Movement)
Posyandu	Pos Pelayanan Terpadu (Integrated Health Post)
PPI	Perikatan Perempuan Indonesia (Indonesian Women's Association)
PPII	Persatuan Perkumpulan Isteri Indonesia (Union of Indonesian 'Wives' Associations)
PPP	Partai Persatuan Perbangunan (United Development Party)
PRD	Partai Rakyat Demokratik (People's Democratic Party)
preman	stand-over boys, thugs
Propenas	Program Perencanaan Nasional (National Planning Program)
PT	Perseroan Terbatas (limited liability company)
Puskesmas	Pusat Kesehatan Masyarakat (Community Health Centre)
reformasi	reform
Repelita	Rencana Pembangunan Lima Tahun (Five-year Development Plan)
Rukun Tetangga	neighbourhood association
Sakernas	Survei Angkatan Kerja Nasional (National Labour Force Survey)
SBI	Sertifikat Bank Indonesia (Bank Indonesia Certificate)
Sekretaris Negara	Secretary of State
SIP	Suara Ibu Peduli (Voice of Concerned Mothers)
SPKAM	Solidaritas Perempuan Komunitas Anging Mammiri' (Anging Mammiri' Community for Women's Solidarity)

SPSI	Sarekat Pekerja Seluruh Indonesia (All Indonesia Workers' Union), the authorised workers' union under the New Order
Susenas	Survei Sosio-ekonomi Nasional (National Socio-economic Survey)
SVD	Societas Verbi Divini (Society of the Divine Word), Roman Catholic missionary organisation of priests and brothers
syariah	Islamic law
Tim P2W	Tim Peningkatan Peranan Wanita (Women in Development Management Team)
TNI	Tentara Nasional Indonesia (Indonesian National Army)
TVRI	Televisi Republic Indonesia (Indonesian Public Television)
ulama	Muslim religious scholar
umma	followers of the Muslim religion
UNDP	United Nations Development Program
UNFPA	United Nations Fund for Population Activities
UNICEF	United Nations Children's Fund
UU	Undang Undang (Law)
Walhi	Wahana Lingkungan Hidup (Environmental Forum)
wali nagari	regional representative
waria	male-to-female transvestite
warung	small store
yayasan	foundation
YLKI	Yayasan Lembaga Konsumen Indonesia (Indonesian Consumers' Association Foundation)

PROLOGUE

H.E. Mr Sudjadnan Parnohadiningrat, *Ambassador of the Republic of Indonesia*

The role of Indonesian women in shaping the very fabric of our society is integral to the history of our nation. The struggle by Kartini to promote women's rights in education in the early 1900s and the holding of the first women's congress, Kongres Perempuan, in Yogyakarta on 22 December 1928, as well as many other women's activities in the following decades, have exemplified their contributions in building our society.

In 1952, shortly after independence, Indonesia ratified the UN Convention on Political Rights for Women through Law No. 68/1958. This law gives Indonesian women the right to vote and to be appointed to the legislature. It also assures women's right to assume any position in the government. The general election laws, No. 15/1969, No. 4/1975, No. 29/1980 and No. 3/1985, allow women to participate actively in the political arena and ensure women's right to participate in the decision-making process in Indonesia.

The ratification by the government of Indonesia of the Convention on the Elimination of All Forms of Discrimination against Women (the Women's Convention) by Law No. 7/1984, and of the Optional Protocol to the Convention in 1999, has added to the sanctity of the rights of Indonesian women to share in the development of the nation.

The ratification of these conventions obliges the government to adopt measures to eliminate all forms of discrimination against women. In keeping with both the letter and the spirit of the conventions, the government established a National Commission on Violence against Women on 15 July 1998, on the basis of Presidential Decree No. 181/1998 and with reference to the Women's Convention. The objectives of this commission include promoting public awareness of all forms of violence against women. It is also intended to create a conducive environment for the elimination of violence against women, to defend the human rights of women and to improve preventive measures pertaining to the elimination of violence against women. Its activities are directed towards empowering women and society in general, strengthening the capacity of organisations which defend women against violence, and influencing the government to take the necessary steps to ensure that all forms of violence against women are eliminated. The membership of the commission includes women's rights activists, academics, professionals and religious leaders.

Another important step taken by the government of Indonesia was the launching of the National Action Plan for the Elimination of Violence against Women. This establishes a policy of zero tolerance of violence against women. With the support of the Ministry for Women's Empowerment, the number of women's studies centres has grown in both public and private universities and institutes. Today there are more than 80 such centres conducting research on the situation of women, including topics such as traditional or local practices which hamper the implementation of the different women's conventions, traditional practices curtailing the advancement of women as well as many other issues related to Indonesian women. These centres also identify specific problems faced by women in particular provinces and propose recommendations to the provincial authorities on practical measures to address them.

Despite the various steps taken, and notwithstanding the active participation of women in the promotion of their rights, much remains to be done to improve the situation of women in Indonesia. In many respects Indonesian women are not treated as the equals of men, particularly in terms of rights and opportunities. Various traditional and cultural practices, as well as certain laws that are contrary to the principle of equality between men and women, remain to be dealt with by our society in order to rectify the situation.

By way of illustration, let me refer to the Marriage Law, which stipulates that the rights and position of the wife are equal to the rights and position of the husband, both in family and in society. However, by the same token, the roles of the husband and the wife are clearly delineated: the husband is the head of the family while the wife is responsible for the household. Therefore, by law, the husband becomes the master of the family while the wife's role is confined to the management of the family.

Let me in this connection offer you another example of flawed legislation which gives rise to concern. Domestic violence, which may involve a flagrant violation of the rights of women, is not specified distinctly under the Indonesian criminal code. This code sets forth the general crime of maltreatment and establishes penalties for it; cases of domestic violence could be, but rarely are, prosecuted under this legislation. Domestic violence is generally regarded by local police as a private matter. In most cases, law enforcement personnel are not responsive to the plight of women victims. In cases of rape and other forms of violence against women, unless there are witnesses the police generally refuse to bring the case to the court. The government is now planning to address this problem through both law reform and gender sensitisation training for the police in modern methods of dealing with incidents of violence against women.

As time goes on, the government of Indonesia, with the participation of women activists, is bringing domestic law into harmony with international norms governing the rights of women. In November 1998, the People's Consultative Assembly (MPR) passed several decrees pertaining to the promotion of the rights of women. They set out the principles to be observed by the government in undertaking legal reform, focusing on laws that are disadvantageous to the situation of women.

Reform has taken effect with regard to the following legislation:

- Manpower Law No. 25/1997 has been amended to eliminate discrimination in work promotion and training; provide equal payment for equal work; ensure social security rights and rights to occupational health and safety, non-discrimination on grounds of marital status or pregnancy, and menstruation and maternity leave.
- The following laws, while not specifically targeting gender equity, have been fundamental to the political reform process and have the potential to deliver benefits for women: the law governing freedom to express opinions in public has been replaced by Law No. 9/1998; a law on the freedom and independence of the press was adopted in 1998; the law on general elections has been replaced by Law No. 3/1999, which sets out both the right to vote and the right to be appointed, and states that women and men are equal in these matters; and the UN Convention on the Elimination of Racial Discrimination has been ratified by Law No. 29/1999.

To sum up, women in Indonesia have been actively promoting the rights of women, including gender equality, through their engagement in various political processes. Their actions have led to the adoption of a number of measures, and the promulgation of legislation by the Indonesian government. It cannot be denied, however, that women's struggle for gender equality faces cultural hurdles. Certain traditions, values and norms – such as the entrenched myth of the unequal relationship between men and women – are being upheld by many in opposition to the quest for gender equality. Today, when greater opportunities exist, I am convinced that Indonesian women can overcome these challenges through the application of long-term strategies and common endeavours involving different segments of society. The abolition of gender-biased myths that impede the promotion of the rights of women should be included in the national agenda, in order to encourage discourse, bring about greater gender awareness and eradicate gender bias. Only by words and deeds that are shared by all members of society can the rights of women be promoted. The contributors to this book will surely be able to register their accomplishments in this noble goal.

1 INTRODUCTION TO THE ISSUES

Kathryn Robinson and Sharon Bessell

In 2001, Indonesia appointed its fifth president – a woman. The politicking surrounding the elevation of Megawati Sukarnoputri to high office brought issues of gender and politics into public focus. It was prescient that the 2001 Indonesia Update – the first of the new millennium – had been organised around the issue of gender equity in the transition to democracy in Indonesia.

This book, published, like its predecessors, as part of the *Indonesia Assessment* series, presents the papers from the Indonesia Update – an annual conference held by the Indonesia Project and the Department of Political and Social Change in the Research School of Pacific and Asian Studies at The Australian National University in Canberra. The Indonesia Update brings together scholars, civil servants, community activists and members of the general public who share a deep interest in political, economic and social developments in Indonesia, to hear an update on the state of politics and the economy, and a series of papers by experts on a chosen theme.

In the political update presented in Chapter 2, media analyst Krishna Sen analyses the elevation of Megawati to the presidency through the lens of Indonesia'a media (media freedom being one of the touchstones of democracy frequently invoked by Abdurrahman Wahid in defence of his presidency). In Sen's view, and in a manner not unfamiliar in feminist analyses of representations of women, the Indonesian media principally presented Megawati in terms of 'lack'. She is uneducated, not an intellectual, and a woman. But Sen is optimistic about the future of Indonesian democracy, and outlines some provocative views of what the transition to the Sukarnoputri–Hamzah Haz team has meant: the locus of power appears to have shifted away from a previously entrenched political elite and has broadened beyond Java.[1]

In his response to Sen's update (Chapter 3), Edward Aspinall looks at the events leading up to President Abdurrahman's forced departure from office, and questions whether the Megawati presidency marks a return to authoritarianism. He identifies some risk to further democratisation if political uncertainty and economic problems continue unabated.

In the economics update in Chapter 4, Mari Pangestu notes how far the Indonesian economy has rebounded since the 'total crisis' of 1998, but reminds us of the severe problems still confronting the nation. The accession of Megawati to the presidency initially restored confidence after a period of uncertainty and paralysis in the final months of the Abdurrahman presidency. In particular, Megawati's economic team won international applause for its inclusion of professionals and experienced bureaucrats with pro-market and outward-looking approaches. But, as Pangestu notes, the honeymoon is now over and the sombre reality of Indonesia's economic circumstances has already resurfaced. Last year witnessed a slowdown in growth from 2000, and inflation has steadily increased. The government and private debt burden remains enormous, despite rescheduling of repayments. Pangestu shows that total government debt has tripled since 1996, largely as a result of the issuing of government bonds as a means of recapitalising the banking system. At present, repayments on interest alone account for 25 per cent of domestic revenue. In 2002 Indonesia must begin to make repayments on the principal, which will place further demands on the budget. The debt is undoubtedly an immense problem for President Megawati and her government but, as Pangestu argues, there are also other pressing issues that the government must confront. Tackling corruption, overseeing sweeping economic – as well as political – reforms, and restructuring remain monumental challenges for the new president and her team. As Pangestu points out, these challenges are compounded by decentralisation and ongoing social problems, including 30 million people (22 per cent of the population) living below the poverty line and widespread underemployment. She concludes that there are no magic formulas or short-cuts in resolving Indonesia's economic woes.

Mohammad Sadli suggests, in his response to Pangestu (Chapter 5), that in the current climate Megawati must show leadership and not remain silent and aloof. As the government embarks on its path of economic reform and – one hopes – restoration, it must, he argues, take the public with it, clearly communicating its policies, intentions and programs. Ultimately, Sadli argues, two issues are of utmost importance: the fight against corruption and poverty alleviation.

Although Indonesia enters a new era and a new millennium under the leadership of a woman, greater gender equity is by no means assured. Like Pakistan's Benazir Bhutto, the Philippines' Corazon Aquino and Gloria Macapagal Arroyo, and several other female leaders in Asia, Megawati has a solid family pedigree. Her father was Indonesia's charismatic first president, the man who led the nation during its transition from colonialism to parliamentary democracy and then ushered in the authoritarian shift to so-called 'Guided Democracy' in the late 1950s. Yet Megawati does have a political track record as the populist leader of the Indonesian Democratic Party of Struggle (PDI-P), which won the largest share of votes in the 1999 elections. In Chapter 5, Mohammad Sadli points out that Megawati has survived three critical tests to her leadership within her party and has consolidated her leadership. She is not, however, known to be an activist on gender issues. As Sadli points out, women's organisations had little success when they lobbied the new president to increase the number of women in cabinet.

The special theme of the 2001 Indonesia Update – gender, equity and development in Indonesia – emphasises the crucial links between the political agendas of gender equity and democratisation. During the New Order period, gender relations and gender roles were an important dimension of state control. Men and women had clearly defined roles that reinforced particular constructions of identity. Importantly, the public and private spheres were clearly – and artificially – separated, with women's roles confined largely to the private sphere. The ideal New Order woman was a mother, wife and household manager. This ideology has been captured by the term 'state ibuism' (Suryakusuma 1996).

When students occupied the parliamentary building in Jakarta in May 1998, it signalled the end of the dictatorial grip of the Soeharto regime on political authority. Among the protestors were representatives of the women's organisations that had developed in Indonesia in the latter part of the New Order. These women organised themselves into a group called the Indonesian Women's Coalition (KPI) and began issuing bulletins demanding that Soeharto resign and be brought to trial. Women activists consider themselves to have been central in bringing down the New Order, but feel they have not been adequately rewarded politically through formal representation.

In Chapter 9, Mayling Oey-Gardiner discusses the role women played in the downfall of Soeharto. Oey-Gardiner is best known for her work on the Indonesian economy, labour force and demography. Here, however, she writes in a very different voice, expressing her role as a feminist and political activist, involved in the events she discusses.

One legacy of the New Order is the ideal image of the domesticated woman. Sen (Chapter 2) and Boellstorff (Chapter 8) observe the ways in which New Order hegemony constructed and confined gender roles. The dominant image gave less focus to women's economic roles and marginalised groups that did not comply: working women,[2] unmarried women, lesbians and gay men were just some of those excluded by New Order constructions of gender roles. However, this dominant ideology has been used creatively by activists in a counter-hegemonic turn. In February 1997, several months before the dramatic student protests that saw the end of the Soeharto regime, activist women formed a group called Voice of Concerned Mothers (SIP) to protest the negative effects of the monetary crisis on women in their roles as housewives and mothers. At the time, the spiralling prices of basic commodities were a primary concern. In a much publicised *demo susu* (milk demonstration), these women took over the round-about outside the Hotel Indonesia in central Jakarta on 23 February and distrib-uted vouchers for powdered milk. The arrest of three of the women received an extraordinary amount of national and international publicity, with TV pictures broadcast around the world. During their trial, they drew attention not just to the effects of the economic crisis but also to the 'crisis in trust' in the government, most poignantly symbolised by the denial of their constitutional right to free speech. This gained them more publicity and triggered a spontaneous growth of the organisation, with women establishing local chapters and setting up *warung sembako* (stalls selling basic commodities) to help deal with the effects of the *krismon* (economic crisis).

The SIP has now grown into an organisation of mainly lower middle class women, and the elite women who established it have been somewhat sidelined. The development of the SIP has been paralleled by the growth of a large num-ber of women's organisations, many in the regions, concerned with issues such as violence against women and women's political representation.

In post-New Order Indonesia we have seen not so much the dismantling of New Order gender ideology as the opening up of space for a diversity of images and representations. These include those that are regional (Baso and Idrus, Chap-ter 16) and Islamic (Marcoes, Chapter 15) in character. The political transition has allowed far greater opportunity to recognise and celebrate the diversity and complexity of the lives and roles of women and men.

The New Order image of the ideal woman has always been under challenge from independent women's organisations and feminist activists. In the post-New Order period, official policy is also beginning to challenge existing stereotypes, at least to some extent. Under President Abdurrahman Wahid, Khofifah Indar Parawansa was appointed Minister for Women's Affairs. She was a new type of minister for a new era. A long-time political activist, her efforts to increase the status of women sit comfortably alongside her strong Muslim identity. One of her first actions as minister was to change the name of her ministry from the State Ministry for the Role of Women to the State Ministry for Women's Empowerment.

In her keynote address to the 2001 Indonesia Update – see Chapter 6 – Indar Parawansa grounds current women's activism in Indonesian history, traces the position of Indonesian women over time, outlines recent efforts to empower women and presents something of her own vision for gender equality in Indone-sia. She argues that there has been considerable progress in advancing women's rights and interests since the transition to democracy began, although challenges remain. Foremost among these are the male-biased bureaucracy, gender-biased interpretations of religious teachings, and value systems and cultural attitudes that discriminate against women. Her chapter is complemented by a brief dis-cussion piece by Susan Blackburn, a noted historian of the women's movement in Indonesia. Blackburn commends the radically new agenda that Indar Parawansa put into action during her time as Minister for Women's Empowerment. As she notes, the minister's vision and the new policy directions she instigated are central to the momentum for change that now exists in Indonesia. Blackburn sees Indar Parawansa as embodying the potential of Indonesian society today – a symbol of change for the better after three decades in which women and gender issues were subordinate to the New Order authoritarian project.

Several of the Indonesian speakers (including Khofifah Indar Parawansa and Saparinah Sadli) invoke the name of Raden Ajeng Kartini, widely acknowledged as a leading figure in the history of the Indonesian struggle for gender equity. Indonesia celebrates a national day to commemorate her as a nationalist heroine. Kartini was a 19th century Javanese woman who overcame the confinement of her solitude in seclusion as a high-born woman by writing to a number of Dutch women, including the feminist Stella Zeehandelaar, to whom she poured out her dreams of a world where women could be educated and autonomous. She was destined (it eventuated) for an arranged marriage and tragically died in childbirth in 1904 at the age of 25. She became a public figure when these private letters were published, first in their original Dutch in 1911.[3] Sylvia Tiwon (1996) has discussed the reworking of Kartini's life story in the official accounts in the New Order period in order to dilute her feminist credentials. Her renouncing of marriage, for example, becomes merely an expressed wish not to have an arranged marriage. The national day in her honour is celebrated with Kartini 'look-alike' competitions, where young women don the conservative *sarong–kebaya* symbolising the restrictive femininity of the New Order. Her transformation into a model for the contemporary Indonesian woman was completed by her designation as Ibu Kartini – *ibu* (literally, mother) being the term by which adult (married) women were known under the New Order. By contrast, Kartini's own letters present a young intellectual who reflected on social inequity, a kind of Indonesian Mary Wollstonecraft. The contemporary saintly myth presents her as a mother who died in suffering rather than as an important intellectual figure who was the first in a long line of Indonesian women to have contributed to international feminist debate.

In her highly personal contribution to this volume (see Chapter 7), the inspirational feminist scholar and activist Saparinah Sadli reflects on her own history of activism, and refers to generational differences in contemporary women's politics – older women who were part of an internationalist tradition of women's rights and gender equity versus a newer generation who see themselves as part of the second wave of feminism (as Kartini was squarely part of the first). Saparinah Sadli draws our attention to the difficulty – and the importance – of feminist scholars maintaining the flexibility to accept and even embrace different interpretations of feminism.

Today, the impetus for policy change and greater gender equality is being driven largely from within Indonesia, including by several contributors to this volume. Yet the international human rights and gender policy frameworks remain influential (Robinson 1998). The prologue to this volume, by H.E. Mr Sudjadnan Parnohadiningrat, the current Indonesian Ambassador to Australia, situates current policies in this international context.

The Convention on the Elimination of All Forms of Discrimination against Women (the Women's Convention) was ratified by the Indonesian government under former President Soeharto. Saparinah Sadli discusses the importance of the Women's Convention as an instrument for lobbying for change during the New Order period. She also provides insights into the role of the Convention Watch Working Group, which was established in 1994 by a group of feminists (including herself) to promote women's rights and advocate for the full implementation of the Women's Convention. In 1999, the Habibie government ratified the Optional Protocol to the Women's Convention, which allows individuals to take complaints to the UN committee responsible for overseeing state compliance with it.

In recent years the Indonesian government has also taken steps to adopt measures promoted as best practice in gender policy, in particular gender mainstreaming, which is an important strategy of the Beijing Platform for Action. Presidential Instruction No. 9/2000 directs all sections of the Indonesian government to implement gender mainstreaming. Indar Parawansa notes the potential of this policy to advance gender equality in Chapter 6, while Soedarti Surbakti (head of BPS, the Indonesian statistical bureau) discusses the importance of reliable, sex-disaggregated data to effective gender mainstreaming in Chapter 17. Gender mainstreaming has not to date been reinforced by policy instruments such as gender budgets and, as Surbakti points out, monitoring remains weak. Nevertheless, conscious efforts to address the gender dimensions of all policies – including those traditionally seen as being gender-neutral, and beginning with a gender analysis of the National Planning Program for 2000–04 (Propenas) – are a positive step.

International influences are not automatically progressive, however. Terence H. Hull and Sri Moertiningsih Adioetomo note in Chapter 19 that well-intentioned international donors who rushed to support and subsidise contraceptives at the outset of the financial crisis inadvertently undermined the self-sufficiency of the state-sponsored family planning program.

Serious questions remain about the extent to which international human rights and gender policy complement or contradict local values. Saparinah Sadli (Chapter 7) reminds us that the terms 'feminism', 'feminist' and even 'gender' are still questioned by most Indonesians. Indeed, where there is support for an agenda for gender equity, it is often restricted to women's organisations and a small group within key ministries. Government policies on women are directed from a state ministry, with no direct representation in the regions, as has been the case with the sectoral ministries. This has created problems for the implementation of government policies and programs for women. In 1995, a presidential instruction established multisectoral teams in provinces and districts (Tim P2W) to coordinate the activities of sectoral ministries with regard to women's policy and programs.

With the move to regional autonomy (*otonomi daerah*), the capacity of the Ministry for Women's Empowerment to implement its programs has declined. The Tim P2W have formally been 'revitalised' under a ministerial instruction that each district have a *biro* (bureau) or *badan* (agency) for women's affairs, but whether or not this will happen is up to the political will and, very importantly, the budget, of each region.

Regional autonomy is also meant to revitalise *adat* or local custom as a counter to the 'uniformisation' that characterised the New Order.[4] Regional autonomy is intended to support democratisation in accord with the spirit of *reformasi*: that is, not a return to old hierarchical structures, and not gender-biased. Noerdin discusses in Chapter 14, however, the manner in which many regions have been planning local ordinances that will delimit women's civil rights, in particular dress codes and curfews for women (sometimes, but not always, linked to an agenda to introduce *syariah* law). These regional regulations (*perda*) need to be ratified by the national parliament (DPR). So far none have been, but in many districts enforcement has been introduced, albeit informally, before the laws are on the books. Baso and Idrus (Chapter 16), Boellstorff (Chapter 8) and Noerdin (Chapter 14) all raise the worrying issue of local violence (often gender-based), which must be confronted by local authorities. Violence against women is now high on the agenda of many women's organisations. As Marcoes (Chapter 15) points out, these groups want justice for women in the public and domestic spheres.

Along with her position as Minister for Women's Empowerment, Indar Parawansa also headed BKKBN, the National Family Planning Agency. As Hull and Adioetomo point out, she played a central role in placing firmly on the agency's agenda human rights and other issues that were in the past too sensitive to broach. Notably, she has called for recognition of the rights of adolescents to reproductive health care; somewhat controversially she has argued that teenage girls who become pregnant should be allowed to continue with their education. That a minister should raise such issues publicly is a sign of real change in Indonesia. Political transition has implications far beyond the polling booths and the halls of parliament.

Gender identities are not just about men and women but are used to express national and subnational identities (as the proposed regional regulations clearly indicate). Tom Boellstorf shows us in Chapter 8 how, on the one hand, heterosexual marriage is an important component of modern Indonesian identities, but also how – in the context of the outbreak of internecine regionalism in the reform era – *gay* and *lesbi* identities emerge as models of truly national identities which draw on hegemonic ideologies of the nation (*nusantara*). Boellstorff gives us one example of counter-hegemonic ideologies, arguing that *gay* and *lesbi* Indonesians show us that 'it is always possible to invent new ways of living that are still authentically Indonesian' (p. 98). Indeed, Boellstorff suggests that *gay* and *lesbi* Indonesians may have been the New Order's greatest (albeit least-intended) success story. Another example of the way in which hegemonic ideologies have been co-opted is mentioned above: the manner in which women successfully founded their activism on their identity as mothers in the period leading up to the downfall of Soeharto.

The 'uniformisation' of gender identities through state ibuism – particularly in the two main official women's organisations, the Family Welfare Movement (PKK) and Dharma Wanita – represented the apex of the homogenising strategies of the authoritarian New Order state. While regional autonomy is a response to this, so too are the emergent contested forms of gender identity, referred to by Lies Marcoes in her analysis of Islamic women's groups (Chapter 15). In Chapter 20 Ria Gondowarsito underscores the importance of recognising the distinctiveness of gender orders in achieving successful development interventions. Contrary to the enforced uniformity of gender relations under the New Order, relations between men and women differ markedly across the archipelago (Robinson 2000). Development interventions need to be sensitive to these differences. Gondowarsito also points to the benefits that civil society and non-government organsations bring to development, and to the important but often vexed issue of 'outside' input, agendas and control.

In the past, issues relating to women's rights within marriage, including polygamy and marriage age, were high on the agenda of women's organisations (Blackburn and Bessell 1997). In the current era of political transition and economic crisis, new priorities have emerged. Blackburn (2001) has noted that a key issue for women's organisations in the post-New Order period is the lack of formal political representation for women. In this volume, Oey-Gardiner (Chapter 9) and Surbakti (Chapter 17) emphasise the extent of that underrepresentation. Oey-Gardiner points out that while women are politically active, heading several of Indonesia's most prominent non-government organisations, they remain a small minority in national parliament, the judiciary and the upper echelons of the civil service. In response, women parliamentarians at the national level and in some regional parliaments have established women's caucuses. The PDI-P and National Awakening Party (PKB) have introduced quotas for women – although, as is the case in many countries, there remain serious questions of implementation. Quotas have also been proposed for the recruitment of senior officials, police and military officers. While the proportion of women parliamentarians has dropped – from 12 per cent in the final New Order parliament to 9 per cent currently – the situation in the newly empowered district assemblies is far worse.

Many have no women at all, and rarely do the numbers even approach the national figure. Oey-Gardiner notes that in April 2000 only one of the 27 provincial parliaments was chaired by a women, and of the 70 deputy chairs, only one was a woman. One Jakarta district has moved to ban anyone but household heads – who by formal definition are usually men – from sitting in village assemblies ('Perda Dewan Kelurahan Diskriminasi Perempuan', *Kompas*, 27 February 2001). Oey-Gardiner makes the important point that it is not sufficient to have a women at the top – it is also necessary to overcome the obstacles that prevent women from entering decision-making positions at all levels. Equal representation for women in decision-making and leadership roles is set to remain a dominant theme in Indonesia in the coming years.

Under the New Order efforts were made to depoliticise women's movements, while state-sponsored organisations – in particular the PKK and Dharma Wanita – were fostered. In the reform period, there have been repeated demands by women's groups for the disbanding of these organisations, seen as key players in the exercise of state hegemony. Dharma Wanita, once compulsory for all wives of civil servants, has been transformed into a voluntary organisation. Renamed Dharma Wanita Persatuan, it is now more democratic in its organisation, with purportedly better links to the community. The PKK has also undergone a change in name, from Pembinaan Kesejahteraan Keluarga (literally, Guidance for Family Welfare) to Pemberdayaan Kesejahteraan Keluarga (literally, Empowerment of Family Welfare), to stress 'empowerment' rather than 'guidance' as the key state function. Lies Marcoes reveals a fascinating development with regard to the PKK which suggests that in a large proportion of instances (contrary to the assumption of many feminist groups), local communities do feel a sense of 'ownership' of their branches and of the Posyandu (Integrated Health Posts) as organisations that provide support and services to mothers and families at the local level. Interestingly, Marcoes concludes that the women's arms of large Muslim organisations have not been able to fill the role of these organisations. Rather than benefiting from the entry of the Islamic organisations into the mainstream political arena, they have been sidelined by party politics and have not been able to effectively develop broad-based and inclusive agendas.

Representations of women are being reformulated not only through political action and policy, but also through popular culture and the media. In Chapter 11, Barbara Hatley notes that under the New Order, official gender ideology was promoted directly through government-controlled media and less directly through propaganda, imagery and the co-option of cultural forms such as film, theatre and literature. In an insightful analysis of representations of gender in women's writing, Hatley notes that a 'review of the development of dominant gender ideology in Indonesia illustrates the historical roles of mythical archetypes of male and female, their representation in cultural forms and the significance of their contemporary contestation' (p. 132). She suggests that while the stereotypes of the New Order continue, women's fiction is increasingly challenging such stereotypes. While challenging and diverse fiction is by no means new, the post-New Order political climate allows new approaches to flourish.

Like women's fiction, women's art is developing in new and exciting directions in an environment of greater freedom. In Chapter 10, Carla Bianpoen explores the ways in which a new generation of women artists is challenging stereotypes, re-creating images and contributing to the reformulation of gender relations. At the same time, she sees them continuing a long tradition of Indonesian women challenging masculinist norms.

Among the reforms that took place in 1998–99 under the Habibie government was increased press freedom after decades of tight control. This had included the closure of magazines and newspapers considered dissident by the Soeharto regime. In the post-authoritarian period media freedom is flourishing, with both positive and negative consequences. Krishna Sen explores the way in which the media has portrayed political developments and contributed to political debates, particularly those around the role of Megawati (Chapter 2). As Sen demonstrates, the perception of Megawati as a housewife rather than a political leader has in no small part been fuelled by media representations of her. On the one hand, a free media provides the space for public discussion of gender equality and inequality. The lack of women's political representation, women's limited economic opportunities and the gendered dimensions of poverty, and violence against women are but a few of the issues that have been played out in the press in recent years. On the other hand, greater media freedom has brought new forms of stereotyping that have serious implications for gender equality. As Baso and Idrus point out in Chapter 16, the positive change of greater media attention to the serious problem of violence against women is somewhat diminished by sensationalist modes of reporting, particularly noted in cases of sexual violence, where gratuitous reports victimise women further, amounting to what Baso and Idrus describe as a 'second rape'.

If political transition is impacting on gender equality in Indonesia, so too is the ongoing economic crisis. In Chapter 12, Lisa Cameron explores its impact on women's and men's labour market participation. Drawing on data from the National Labour Force Survey (Sakernas), she concludes that unemployment rose more sharply among men than among women during the crisis, in part because women tend to be concentrated in the informal sector. Cameron also notes that while men's real wages appeared to decline more than women's at the height of the crisis in 1999, they have subsequently rebounded more than women's wages. As a consequence, the gender gap in wages is now larger than it was prior to the crisis. There are also urban–rural differentials: while women in urban areas seem to have gained relative to men in terms of their share of wage employment, in rural areas they appear to have been displaced from the formal sector. This has serious consequences not only for gender equity, but also for patterns of development and poverty in Indonesia. As Mohammad Sadli argues in Chapter 5, poverty has important gender dimensions – the so-called female face of poverty – that are often overlooked, especially by male-dominated bureaucracies. Cameron concludes that increases in women's access to the formal sector will be necessary if they are to participate fully in and benefit equally from the processes of development.

Graeme Hugo notes in Chapter 13 that another apparent consequence of the crisis has been an increase in already well-established international labour migration, particularly among women. As is well documented in other countries, particularly the Philippines, labour migration results in substantial remittances to the country of origin, but holds potential dangers of exploitation and abuse abroad. The protection of migrant workers is likely to become an issue of increasing importance and sensitivity in Indonesia in coming years.

In Chapter 18, Gavin Jones notes the impact of labour migration – among both women and men – on Indonesian households. Large numbers of Indonesian workers in Malaysia and the Middle East have given rise to missing family members, including husbands/fathers and wives/mothers. As Jones points out, mothers who work overseas rely on the extended family – particularly their own mothers – to look after their children. Again, the experience of the Philippines gives rise for concern about the social consequences of overseas labour migration.

Despite dire predictions early in the economic crisis that levels of contraceptive use would diminish dramatically, Hull and Adioetomo – while warning of the difficulty of assessing contraceptive usage accurately – indicate that the levels have been maintained. While the family planning program has been an important dimension of Indonesia's national development strategy for several decades, access to family planning also has important implications for women. Indar Parawansa describes family planning in terms of both better health for women and freedom: freedom for self-advancement and self-actualisation.

While political transition and economic crisis dominate current debates about gender, equality and development in Indonesia, Jones reminds us that changes to the Indonesian household and to the lives of young Indonesian women are largely due to longer-term patterns of change. Smaller families are largely a result of declining fertility, while lower rates of widowhood (due to longer life expectancy) and of *de jure* divorce have resulted in less marital disruption. Later age at marriage is impacting on both the family and individuals, particularly young women. As Jones points out, this – combined with increasing levels of education and greater labour force participation – means that the lives of young women in particular, but also young men, are quite different from those of earlier generations. Jones also draws our attention to the increasing numbers of elderly people in Indonesian society. The majority of these are women; only a minority are literate; and very few (male or female) have access to pension schemes. Thus providing for the aging will become an increasingly pressing issue for Indonesia in coming years. Marcoes shows us that this challenge is being taken up, to some extent, by Posyandu in some areas. Generally associated with promoting child health, some Posyandu are now developing health and exercise programs for the elderly. This is a practical response to Indonesia's changing demographics, and supports Marcoes' suggestion that the Posyandu maintain their relevance to local communities in the post-Soeharto era.

The papers presented in this volume demonstrate the vital link between gender, politics, equity and development. The economic changes accompanying both the 'boom' of the New Order and the 'bust' of the *krismon* have had profound effects on men's and women's economic and social participation. In spite of the lack of increase in women's representation in the formal institutions of government, women are organising themselves for greater political participation. The symbolic importance of a woman president puts gender issues fully in the public view. The rethinking of relations between men and women is at the very heart of the changes being pursued under the democratisation agenda of *reformasi*.

NOTES

1   Hamzah Haz is the current vice-president. A Sumatran, he is head of the Islamic United Development Party (PPP).
2   Sen (1998) has noted the contradictory impulse in official policy, to 'discover' the role of working women, in concepts like the dual role (*peran ganda*), as well as the entry of many middle-class women into the workforce through the 1980s.
3   Coté (1992, 1995) provides an introduction to and English translation of these letters.
4   This 'uniformisation' operated through the 1979 village government law, and also through gender policy, with single definitions of women's roles promulgated in legislation such as the 1974 Marriage Law, but also in the ideology of official women's organisations such as the PKK and the organisation for civil servants' wives, Dharma Wanita.

2   THE MEGA FACTOR IN INDONESIAN POLITICS: A NEW PRESIDENT OR A NEW KIND OF PRESIDENCY?

*Krishna Sen**

Textbooks of politics and media studies now tend to start from the assumption that 'the conduct of democratic (or undemocratic) politics nationally and inter-nationally depends more and more' on the media (McQuail 1994: 1). Indonesia is no exception. The line between published news and unpublished information is now very fine: confidential documents with uncorroborated sources are con-stantly 'published' on the internet. In a fundamentally transformed media in post-Soeharto Indonesia, politics is increasingly better understood from what is in the press, on television or on the internet than from confidential briefings and private conversations at the presidential palace. The sources of understanding in and of Indonesia are now many, diverse and contradictory. This update is in large measure an interpretation of what has been 'news' in Indonesia in recent months.[1]

A MEGA IMAGE ISSUE

In the late afternoon of 23 July 2001, Megawati Sukarnoputri became the fifth president of Indonesia, and the third in as many years. There was little mention in the national media that only two years earlier the political elite of all colours had written her off as a possible president for Indonesia. From the end of 1998, and particularly from the time of the spectacular success of the Indonesian Democratic Party of Struggle (PDI-P) in the 1999 elections through to the instal-lation of Abdurrahman Wahid as president, conservative Islamic and liberal intellectual leaders found dozens of reasons to publicise why Megawati could not and should not become the nation's leader.

The Islamic argument, coming from sections of Nahdlatul Ulama (NU) and the United Development Party (PPP), is well known.[2] It had two main themes.

Dr AM Saefuddin, PPP office-bearer and with credentials as an Islamic intellectual, was repeatedly quoted in the media as saying that Mega (as Megawati
Sukarnoputri is popularly known in Indonesia) was not from the Islamic community (*kalangan Islam*) and, indeed, might be a Hindu. The argument that
received even more media coverage was that a woman president was not acceptable under Islam. Repeated by several senior NU figures, this view was based on
the *hadis* interpretation which translates roughly as: 'A community that makes a
woman its leader will not prosper' (cited in Ulil 1999: 156).

Such comments, apparently anchored in the Islamic faith, were variously
explained and legitimised by liberal intellectuals within and outside of Islam,
who would not themselves wish to be associated with positions that would be
embarrassingly patriarchal in a global intellectual context. Ulil, arguably one of
the NU's finest young thinkers, explained the Islamic rejection of Megawati as
follows: 'The issue of Megawati's nomination [for the presidency in 1999] arose
at exactly the same moment as the Islamic constituency felt ready to assert itself
as a competitor ... for the leadership of the nation' (Ulil 1999: 157). The anti-
Mega position and the later support for Gus Dur (as Abdurrahman Wahid is
called) need to be seen together as part of that assertion and not in relation to
Islamic ideology as such. But Ulil's analysis does not explain the large common
ground between the Islamic and the liberal intellectual rejection of Mega.

Nurcholish Madjid, an internationally respected liberal Muslim thinker, summarised Megawati's weaknesses in a long interview with *Forum Keadilan* just
before the 1999 election. First, as a woman, she was not acceptable to Muslims.
Second, her policies were not acceptable to the global media: she did not want
to condemn (*menghujat*) Soeharto; she did not want to question the dual function (*dwifungsi*) of the military; she did not want to amend the 1945 Constitution; she did not want federalism; and she saw East Timor as an integral part of
Indonesia. 'Perhaps she could change', he said, 'but this is all on record in the
international media', including CNN, which had also questioned her party's
position on aspects of economic policy (*Forum Keadilan*, 27 June 1999).

A week earlier, an interview had appeared in the same magazine with Arief
Budiman, in many ways the liberal political conscience of the nation since 1966
and now a senior academic in Australia. In the article, called 'Kalau Mega Presiden Bisa Berbahaya' (Could Be Dangerous if Mega Becomes President), Arief
noted that 'Mega's capacity for leadership is indeed limited, but her support base
is exceptionally strong'. He went on to elaborate on both these aspects of the
Mega issue. Her mass support, he said, came from the working class (*buruh*).

In 1955, this would have been the PKI's [Communist Party's] labour base. Now that
labour is not represented, [the workers] have been looking everywhere, and finally
have run to Mega, as other parties are too Islamic and the PAN is too intellectual. So
to my way of thinking the masses [which here seem to be synonymous with the work-
ers] have turned to the PDI-P, not to the SPSI [the authorised workers' union under

the New Order] because it was previously manipulated by the government. Because they had no other channels, in the end they all entered the PDI-P (*Forum Keadilan*, 20 June 1999).

The second aspect of the danger perceived by Budiman is that Megawati may be influenced by the wrong groups: 'Mega's supporters are of various kinds. There are some that are mischievous and others who are good. So if Mega becomes president the danger is that, because her capacities are limited, she will be unable to take advice judiciously. She is more likely to take an instinctive decision than a rational one'. Whatever the authorial intentions of Arief Budiman, in this interview Megawati's mass base – her appeal to the 'man in the street'[3] combined with her own 'ordinariness' – becomes ominous and constitutes the 'danger' of her prospective presidency.

At a conference held in December 2000 in Tasmania, I suggested that the views of those conservative Muslims who objected to a *woman* leader in general, and of liberal male (and some female) intellectuals who objected to *this woman* in particular, were in fact grounded in the same gendered view of politics in Indonesia (Sen 2002). That is not the position I wish to pursue here, although I will return shortly to the fear of the destructive potential of Mega and her masses to suggest a very different, and somewhat more optimistic, reading of the potential for popular democracy in 'Megawati's' Indonesia.

When Abdurrahman and Megawati took office as president and vice-president in October 1999, the Jakarta-based national media almost universally presented this as the dream team. But this was an ideal political resolution precisely because the politics of the Poros Tengah (Central Axis) had managed to contain the dangers that Mega and her masses had represented.[4] By January 2001, it had become clear that Abdurrahman would not last beyond the August session of the People's Consultative Assembly (MPR).[5] The intellectual and religious views on Megawati had not been revised, but Abdurrahman had ceased to be a credible president. The only constitutionally valid option was for the vice-president to take over.

While the national press seemed to heave a collective sigh of relief when Megawati took office on 23 July, the international media remained doubtful. A blind cleric had been replaced by a none-too-clever housewife – neither are particularly potent symbols of power in the West.

Megawati is known to be camera-shy. One need only look at television coverage of the president over the last few months to observe that she always appears in long or mid-shot. Although no one has told me this, I would be reasonably confident that palace staffers have been told not to allow close-ups. If a camera pans in close, an invisible hand immediately seems to pull it away. By contrast, Vice-President Hamzah Haz and other ministers face close encounters with the increasingly intrusive cameras and microphones on a daily basis.

Bambang Kesowo, who is quickly emerging as one of Megawati's most trusted lieutenants, has stated quite explicitly that the new president is not going to be available to the media:

> Is there a requirement that the president should be outspoken, and that she has to speak up every two hours? [What is important is that] the flow of information, the decision-making and the flow of decisions taken by the President can be channelled properly and quickly to implementing agencies, to ministers or government bodies. It's not necessary that every time the president makes a decision she must come and speak directly to the media (*Jakarta Post*, 9 August 2001).

In the international media, Megawati has always been compared unfavourably with other female political figures in Asia such as Cory Aquino, Aung San Suu Kyi and even Benazir Bhutto. She shares many of their political disadvantages – like Aquino she is a 'mere housewife', like Suu Kyi her charisma is really only 'reflected glory from her father', like Benazir she is saddled with a 'husband who is a liability'. However, Megawati does not have any of the redeeming qualities that make these women favourites with the Western media: she does not speak English fluently and she has not been 'Westernised' in her social behaviour by long years of living in England and America. Western journalists have always written sniggeringly of her personal style. Within days of her becoming president, a well-known journalist wrote in a prominent Australian newspaper that even when Mega was a leading opposition figure in Soeharto's Indonesia, she did not make the grade at diplomatic parties:

> Megawati's reputation as a conversationalist was so poor that no one seemed to feel sufficiently charitable to put up with her one-word answers and nervous giggles. Attempts in the media to portray Megawati as an Indonesian Aung San Suu Kyi ran out of puff and a consensus quickly emerged that the lights might well be on but no one seemed to be home. The fact that Megawati has now become president of the fourth most populous country is nothing less than extraordinary (*Business Age*, 2 October 2001).

Perhaps one need not draw the inference here that the capacity to make small talk at parties is an essential qualification for a president! But the point to which I want to draw attention, and to which I will return, is the constant elision between Mega's silence and her lack of leadership capacity – a common thread that runs through domestic and foreign criticism of the Indonesian president.

THE FIRST 60 DAYS

So the candidate did not impress. But what does Megawati's report card look like after the first 60 days in office?[6]

The Presidency

Megawati has inherited a severely weakened presidency – an institution battered by Soeharto's fall and then by the ineffectual, erratic, tarnished policies of the two transitional presidents. The sacking of Abdurrahman Wahid underscored both symbolically and in fact the post-New Order relationship between the MPR and the presidency – between the legislative and executive arms of government. A few days after Megawati's appointment, the prominent Indonesianist Takashi Shiraishi commented in a long interview, 'The political system in Indonesia has changed ... clearly now there is no longer a strong presidential system; you have a very weak presidential system with aspects of parliamentary system contained within it' (*Jakarta Post*, 3 August 2001).

Megawati's comments on the formation of a constitutional commission in her state of the nation address have already provided a ground for testing the parameters of power between the president and the parliament. It would appear that, for the time being, the president has stepped away from the battle, leaving the debate over the appointment of such a commission to be argued out within parliament (DPR) by the party factions, and between the DPR and large sections of the NGO movement, which generally supports the president's position on this issue. However the particular issue of the constitutional commission is resolved, we should anticipate continuing struggles between the presidency and parliament as the two centres of political power.

It is clear that Megawati intends to wield the president's rightful control over executive power. Within days of becoming president she made this explicit in her still relatively rare media interviews. She asserted that she had already had nearly a year's experience of leading the cabinet following the signing by Abdurrahman in August 2000 of Presidential Decree 121, which had transferred the day-to-day running of the government to her as vice-president. Second and more importantly, she signalled that the decree would now be amended to return the job of running the government to the president.

Equally importantly, the balance of power between the vice-president and president is now very different from the one that prevailed under Gus Dur. The PPP, led by Hamzah Haz, obtained about 11 per cent of the votes in the 1999 general elections, while all the Central Axis parties together accounted for only about 20 per cent of the votes. It was clear that Hamzah could only win the vice-presidency against his chief rival Akbar Tanjung (backed by Golkar, which had substantially more seats in the MPR) with the support of Megawati and the PDI-P. It could be argued that Megawati strategically chose the politically weakest of the three main contenders for the job: the former army general Susilo Bambang Yudhoyono, Akbar Tanjung and Hamzah Haz.

The Cabinet

Megawati's first major test was the appointment of a cabinet. On 9 August 2001, Abdurrahman's 'National Unity' cabinet was replaced by Megawati's 'Mutual Help' (Gotong Royong) cabinet – more than two weeks after the president took office. In the interim, both the international and Jakarta media had pronounced this delay a proof of her slowness and indecisiveness, speculating wildly about all the interest groups who might influence her decisions. A cover story in *Tempo Interaktif* – compulsory reading for Jakarta intellectuals and Indonesianists around the world – had declared Megawati's Indonesia to be 'life in the slow lane'. By the end of her first week as president there were reports in the international media that she had gone to see the children's film *Shrek* instead of announcing her cabinet! But when the cabinet was announced, it received widespread approval from the political elite, political commentators and, it would seem, more widely in so far as opinion polls can be taken as indicative.[7]

In the end neither her husband nor his shady business allies seem to have got what they wanted. She did have to pay off some debts to the political parties, but on the whole, apart from supporting the vice-presidential bid by Hamzah Haz and rewarding the 'Wibisana' of Abdurrahman's National Awakening Party (PKB), Matori Abdul Jalil, with the Defence Ministry, she seems to have managed to get away with giving the parties many of the less significant ministries and securing the key economic portfolios for the professionals.[8]

The army secured two key positions, the Ministry of Internal Affairs (Dalam Negeri) and the Coordinating Ministry of Political and Social Security (Polsoskam), but even they do not seem to have got all that they wanted. This is worth emphasising, as many liberal intellectual leaders of *reformasi* have had serious concerns about Megawati's natural alliance with the army over the issue of separatist movements and ethnic conflict around the archipelago, and indeed because of her general political conservatism. There was a strong belief in some sections of the political community, including the left wing of the student movement, that in large measure Gus Dur's undoing was that he had been moving too rapidly against the army. The fear was that the military would extract from the new president the price of the office they had helped deliver to her. But the hand of the army in the making of the new cabinet, hailed by many as the best in post-Soeharto Indonesia, was not that obvious.

The national political commentators found serious problems with only two appointments – those of Bambang Kesowo and Muhammad Abdur Rahman. Bambang Kesowo, Megawati's secretary as vice-president, was now in the newly combined and powerful position of Secretary of State (Sekretaris Negara) and Cabinet Secretary (Sekretaris Kabinet). It was widely known that Megawati, as vice-president, had depended on him and that he was one of the key influences in determining the shape of the new cabinet. He is a career bureaucrat and has been described as a 'disciple' (*anak-buah*) of two ex-New Order heavyweights – former Secretary of State Sudharmono and former Minister of Internal Affairs Moerdiono. He is all too easily seen as a throwback to the New Order.

The new attorney-general, Muhammad Abdur Rahman, was perhaps the most controversial of Megawati's appointments. It had taken the president five additional days to name her attorney-general. It was widely reported that senior figures in the military had effectively insisted on a veto on possible candidates for this position. In the end the man who was appointed was a poor substitute for his predecessors, Baharuddin Lopa and Marzuki Darusman, who, for different reasons, had long-established national credentials as critical intellectual political figures. Abdur Rahman, by contrast, had had an undistinguished career as a lawyer within the attorney-general's office. It seemed that Wiranto and other military figures had got what they wanted – someone who would not have the nerve to push through corruption and human rights abuse cases against the disgraced generals. But interestingly, it was not, apparently, pressure from the army that had determined Megawati's decision, but rather her conviction that the correct interpretation of the relevant laws required that the attorney-general be an insider to the department. This might be unimaginative use of the legal system but, after the erratic disregard of rules and regulations in the last days of her predecessor's rule, it is perhaps somewhat reassuring.

The Media

Two positions abolished under Gus Dur's first cabinet were restored – the Ministry of Social Affairs and the Ministry of Communication and Information – both with substantially lower status than they had had in the Soeharto era. Understandably, most of the criticism in the media has been directed at what could be seen as the re-creation of the much hated Department of Information. As most will recall, Abdurrahman had received loud support from the national and international media when he abolished this institution.

Under Soeharto, the Department of Information had become a powerful instrument for government censorship in the 1980s. But it had always, even in the heyday of the New Order, been much less effective as an instrument of propaganda. I have argued elsewhere that by the mid-1990s, for a variety of reasons, it had become largely ineffective in its censorship function as well (see Sen and Hill 2000). Beyond the symbolism of the act, Gus Dur's abolition of the department signified little in terms of the state's relationship with the media – in very large measure this body had become ineffectual anyway.

With its abolition, the huge bureaucratic staff of the Department of Information did not disappear. Most were reconstituted in a new body called the National Information and Communication Board (BIKN), which at the start of 2001 shed more staff and was renamed the Institute of National Information

(LIN). At the provincial level, the Department of Information was renamed the Office of Regional Information and Communication. In the two years or so since the abolition of the department, there have been attempts within its remaining bureaucracies to reconstitute the new organisations into effective public relations bodies on behalf of the government. Perhaps it is too early to tell how the LIN and its provincial counterparts will develop under the new Communication and Information Minister, Syamsul Mu'arif. He is a career politician who has come up through Golkar ranks, and is not well known in the media. His only experience related to communications was a stint as a student of *dakwah* (Islamic preaching) at a State Institute for Islamic Studies (IAIN) in Banjarmasin. In interviews he has indicated that he sees his task as two-fold: 'to work towards equity in distribution of information, particularly to the rural population' (www.kompas.com/data/kabinet/, 9 June 2001); and to act as a conduit of information between the central and various local levels of government. There is no indication at this stage that the government will try to reinvent any of the Department of Information's censoring tasks, and *no* possibility that it would succeed if it did.[9]

In one sense the new Communication and Information Ministry may signify a return to the media policy of the last decade of the New Order. I have argued elsewhere that in the mid-1980s senior bureaucrats in the Department of Information became aware that the censorship mechanisms were starting to break down and that, in the context of the 'mediascape'[10] of the time, there was no possibility of returning to the relatively successful mechanisms of the 1970s. The subsequent media policy of the New Order government was driven by the need to extend the reach of the Jakarta government's voice to distant peripheries (see Sen and Hill 2000, especially Ch. 4).

The revival of the Information Ministry in the current cabinet may be a continuation of this effort by the centre to talk to the nation's peripheries, a need seemingly made more urgent as the state television channel, TVRI, becomes increasingly autonomous in redefining itself in the new political and economic circumstances – no longer a government television station but a 'public broadcaster', no longer a government department but a state-owned enterprise (BUMN). These shifts were in part precipitated by the democratic commitments and economic constraints of the Abdurrahman government. TVRI's new BUMN status, under discussion in the closing years of the Soeharto regime, was confirmed in the final few days of Abdurrahman's rule. If indeed the new Communication and Information Ministry is, in part, the Megawati government's move to have its voice reach citizens in distant provinces, it may represent another trajectory of Indonesia's democratisation: a recognition of the transformed political topography of Indonesia, where the non-elite, non-metropolitan populations begin to matter.

My reading of the new ministry may sit oddly with still vivid and none-too-distant memories of the notoriously corrupt, bureaucratic and repressive Ministry of Information under Soeharto. But, as I hope will become clear in the final section of this chapter, this is a new kind of presidency whose instruments for the exercise of power are necessarily different from those of the New Order, even when the institutional structures seem, ominously, to be replicated.

The State of the Nation

The next political test for the new president was her 'state of the nation' address before the DPR on 16 August 2001. The six-point program she laid down for her government was a set of motherhood statements, which surprised no one and gave no additional indication of policy directions. She apologised to the Acehnese and Papuans – ineffectual symbolic gestures that had no apparent effect on the war in Aceh or on dissent in Papua. Her subsequent visit to Aceh and the previous signing of the Nanggroe Aceh Darussalam autonomy bill seemed to be equally fruitless gestures. There were elements in the speech, however, that seemed to be particularly marked by Megawati's personality, and which, in the aftermath of the speech, started to be reassessed positively.

The morning after the speech Jakarta newspapers were awash with positive reactions from just about everyone, from seasoned Golkar politician Akbar Tanjung to prominent human rights lawyer Mulya Lubis – not natural allies on most issues! A senior government official was quoted as saying, 'It was powerful and straight talk, using the language of housewives, which is unsophisticated but easy to understand' (www.thejakartapost.com/detailnational, 17 August 2001). This was a radical reappraisal of the political impact of a 'none-too-bright housewife'. Her intellectual shortcomings, seen so widely as a serious problem for a president, were now being reassessed as an advantage.

It was a very clever speech and addressed, without being overly explicit, two major sources of political weakness embedded in her personal life. First, she spent quite some time explaining that the process of recovery was going to be slow, that the transition from past authoritarianism to a democratic future would be even slower and, indeed, that there were dangers in rushing into dramatic changes – thus turning into a virtue the 'life in the slow lane' so much lamented by her critics.[11]

Then she went on to promise that her anti-graft campaign would start with her own family. Megawati is entirely aware of what she has called her 'Bhutto factor' – a husband with shady connections including, particularly, former Soeharto cronies. The foreign media has reported extensively on the business interests of her husband, Taufik Kiemas, and other members of her extended family. There were allegations that during her period as vice-president lucrative contracts had gone to companies associated with Taufik and other family members, not through any direct intervention by Megawati, but simply because old habits die hard and foreign investors continue to see those close to power as points of economic access to the country.

In her address she said:

> Unlike a feudalistic society which does not tend to see Corruption–Collusion–Nepotism (KKN) as a big mistake, a democratic society sees this as a tremendous problem. Regardless of how trivial they may be, KKN practices will transgress public trust and violate one's official oath. In this context, allow me to humbly report … that I have privately gathered all members of my immediate family requesting them to solemnly pledge not to open the slightest window of opportunity for the recurrence of KKN in my family. They have given me their solemn pledge, and I hope that they will be able to resist the many temptations around them.

She then asked her cabinet ministers to make the same pledge. Corruption allegations have dogged every president in Indonesia, but Megawati was the first to acknowledge that her own family would have to struggle with temptation. The uniqueness of this aspect of her address was registered in the mainstream media in a number of ways. Thus, again, she had turned a perceived weakness into a strength.[12]

My rather positive spin on the first two months of the Megawati government is not, of course, the only possible reading of the events of this period. One could equally interpret these early days as a series of unresolved problems. If Aceh and Papua were to be her two main tests, then they seem not a step closer to solution – although special autonomy bills for both these regions have now been passed by parliament. In purely electoral terms, her symbolic sway over the urban lower classes in Java, who form the mainstay of her mass support, may be waning. Throughout July and August 2001 there were running battles between street vendors and trishaw (*becak*) drivers on the one hand, and Jakarta police on the other. There were reports that as part of their action the *becak* drivers had burned their PDI-P membership cards.

FROM *REFORMASI* TO DEMOCRACY

It is much too early to answer the two questions on everyone's mind: will Megawati last until 2004, and will she be able to find solutions to the crises that plague Indonesia at the moment? In some ways these are the wrong questions to ask. There has been a fundamental shift in Indonesia's politics such that we need to get away from looking at the small leadership at the top and stop reading the political will of that leadership as central to the fate of the nation. For too long, Indonesia watchers have been watching only the political elite.

In a very interesting recent analysis of Indonesian studies, Simon Philpott (2000) has identified the ways in which the foundation texts of this discipline, starting with Kahin and Feith but even including Robison, have focused on a small group of well-educated urban Indonesians who are directly engaged in political debates in ways that are available to Western observers and seem legitimate within Western political discourses. This focus on the political elite (both in power and in opposition) became the Indonesianists' common sense for three decades under the New Order. Under its particular form of governance, politics seemed to consist of the actions of the Soeharto government on the one hand, and of a group of committed, courageous, clever, internationally connected opposition figures on the other. In many ways this kind of elite study is always of very limited use – evidenced, one might argue, by the repeated failure of Indonesia specialists to predict the direction of New Order politics. In the post-Soeharto period many observers have called for new paradigms – for new ways of keeping an eye on the many political balls in the air. It is clear even to the passing observer that in today's Indonesia politics is played out as much in parliament and in the streets as it is in the presidential palace, and that there are complex webs that connect the many political dynamics.

Some at the more radical end of Indonesian politics have seen the rise of Megawati as a serious regression from the reformist trajectories of the Abdurrahman and even Habibie governments, signifying a return to a New Order-like unholy alliance between the military, Golkar and parts of the PDI-P's upper echelons. Others emphasise the overlaps and continuities, in both policies and personnel, with the Abdurrahman era. More recently, Ed Aspinall has argued that the valorisation of the democratic credentials of the Abdurrahman government may need to be tempered by the knowledge that his rise to the presidency was secured by a coalition of ex-New Order forces, military figures and the Golkar leadership, which feared a 'Megawati-led clean sweep of senior officialdom' (Aspinall 2001: 23) Indeed, as Aspinall points out, precisely the same forces later supported Megawati for the top job.

I want to push our understanding of the nature of the Mega presidency beyond the New Order versus reformist binary that underlies such analysis. In this final section of the chapter I want to suggest that, to understand Indonesian politics a little better (acknowledging of course that this is still provisional and incomplete), we need to look at the much finer lines of dissonance between the ideals of *reformasi* and the practices of popular electoral democracy.

Let me start with Ignas Kleden's evocation of the German political philosopher Habermas in an effort to understand some of the changes underlying the transition from Gus Dur to Megawati. Ignas Kleden writes in the *Jakarta Post*:

> The basic assumption of [Habermas's notion] of 'deliberative democracy' is that citizens' participation in the democratic process [has] a rational character; that voting, for example, should not simply aggregate preferences but rather follow on a process in which citizens become informed of the better argument and the more general interest.

Kleden then lists several problems in trying to apply this to the realities of political life that are *in fact* not motivated by a 'new enlightenment' which emerges from arguments competing on the basis of their truth value. He goes on to say somewhat ruefully that the 'political changeover in Jakarta on July 23 can exemplify some of the difficulties in applying Habermas' theory to realpolitik' ('Our Democratic Tug-of-war', www.thejakartapost.com/detaileditorial.asp/, 9 August 2001).

Habermas is evoked in a similar way in a review essay by John Sidel (2001). Sidel's purpose is to point out the limits of the democratic ideals embedded in Hefner's reading of liberal Muslim intellectuals, including (particularly importantly, from my point of view) Abdurrahman Wahid:

> Muslim intellectuals are 'great democrats' not only because they spent long years of the Soeharto dictatorship engaged in Habermasian discussions and debates on the seminar circuits and newspaper editorial pages of Jakarta, but also because their association helped to restrain and domesticate the uncivil forms of political participation favoured by many other Indonesians. ... [The] elite Muslim intellectuals ... are identified with universal values – liberal democracy, civic spiritedness, tolerance – against a backdrop of dangerously illiberal, uncivil, and sectarian mass politics (Sidel 2001: 114).

This gap between mass-based democracy and the democratic ideals of the intelligentsia has a long history in Indonesia, and cuts across the Islamic–secular binary (so frequently evoked in analysis of Indonesian politics). In 1973, Liddle, writing of the urban middle-class 'secular modernising intellectuals' in the transition from Sukarno to Soeharto, noted their fear and ignorance of the masses (Liddle 1973: 200). Two elements common to intellectual political actors (cutting across a variety of differences) identified in Liddle's account are worth recalling in particular: first, their sustained critique of party politics (pp. 182–7); and second, their conviction of 'the centrality of their own role' (p. 186).

The convictions of the intellectuals could only have been reinforced during the three decades of Soeharto's Indonesia. New Order repression made any sort of mass politics impossible, and democratic ideals could only be developed and nurtured as an intellectual project in the relative security of university classrooms, small magazines and, later, internet news groups and web pages. Gus Dur, whatever his popular appeal as the leader of the NU, was equally importantly part of the intellectual community which engaged in the discourse of democracy in Soeharto's Indonesia. The pluralist and very civilised ideals of democracy contained in the *reformasi* movement of the 1990s, like the democratic ideals of the intellectuals in the 1970s, are not easily reconcilable with the practices of a mass-based electoral politics of the street, or even of parliament.

The criticism of – indeed resentment against – Megawati mentioned at the start of this paper needs to be understood against this simultaneous rejection of mass politics and valorisation of a 'deliberative' (and necessarily intellectual) model of democracy. Megawati, while part of a political elite by birth, shared nothing with the intellectual political actors who had honed their 'deliberative' ideals precisely in opposition to her father's mass mobilisation. In the last years of the Soeharto era, as the intellectuals (mostly male – though perhaps that is not important to the argument here) revived their discourse of democracy, she remained an outsider to this group – not just because she was a woman, but because of the kind of woman she was. She was silent; she did not speak; she could not hold her own in a conversation; she could never be part of the seminar circuit that was the home ground of the critics cited earlier, from Nurcholish Madjid to Arief Budiman. She was relatively uneducated, having never finished university. Her only non-domestic work experience, until she was persuaded to join the Indonesian Democratic Party (PDI) in 1985, appears to have been her co-ownership of a flower shop! She could not be part of the idealised, elitist, deliberative democracy where the best ideas win. Perhaps her victory is a signal that the intellectual politicians, as John Sidel (2001: 122) has said so nicely, 'have had their salad days in the late Suharto and early post-Suharto periods'.

Megawati Sukarnoputri, much more than her predecessor, is both the symbolic vehicle (as Sukarno's daughter) and the product (as the winner of the largest number of votes) of mass politics. For the Western observer of Indonesia, the comfortable prism of the military dictator versus the intellectual democratic hero is now once again broken. Popular electoral democracy will not produce the quickest solution to Indonesia's massive problems. It may produce inhumane, prejudiced, short-sighted governments that act in ways that are incompatible with idealised democratic principles. (One need only look at the recent actions of the major Australian political parties in relation to refugees to understand the contradictions between the moral ground of democracy and the practices of electoral politics everywhere.)

Democracy in Indonesia under Megawati is producing a new kind of politics – different from our own democracy and different too from the ideals of Indonesia's reformist intellectuals. We now need to learn to describe its new contradictions.

NOTES

*   This essay draws extensively on material in Indonesian periodicals, in particular the newspapers *Kompas* and *Jakarta Post*, the internet-based *Tempo Interaktif* and the weekly magazine *Forum Keadilan*. Most of the references in the text are to their websites: www.kompas.com/kompas-cetak, www.thejakartapost.com and www.tempointeraktif.com/majalah. The *Forum Keadilan* articles are from a compilation by Tio (2001).

1   Many thanks to Charles Coppel, whose Indonesia@unimelb list has for the last few
     years been an invaluable conduit for Indonesian media content for many Indone-
     sianists in Australia. This paper owes a great debt to Charles's email list.
2   The NU was founded as an organisation of Islamic scholars (see Cribb 1992:
     309–10 for details). The PPP was one of the three political parties under the New
     Order, and was formed through an amalgamation of Islamic parties.
3   I use this gender-specific phrase here advisedly. These 'dangerous' masses have
     largely been construed as young, male, uneducated, urban and poor. Indeed their
     characterisation as ominous rests in large measure on the fact that they are male and
     therefore have greater potential for physical violence.
4   The Central Axis is a loose parliamentary alliance of Islamic parties formed in the
     aftermath of the 1999 election, in large measure at that stage to keep Megawati from
     becoming president. Its support was crucial to both the rise and the fall of Abdur-
     rahman Wahid's presidency.
5   The MPR is Indonesia's Upper House of parliament. It consists of all members of
     the DPR plus nominees from the regions and sections of society. Its only role in the
     Soeharto era was the five-yearly appointment of the president.
6   This paper was delivered exactly two months after Megawati was sworn in as pres-
     ident and should be seen as an analysis of the politics of that moment. As I finalise
     this essay at the end of October 2001, in the midst of fairly large anti-US demon-
     strations on the streets and Megawati's measured response to these, my optimistic
     reading of the overall democratic trajectory of Indonesian politics, expressed at the
     end of this chapter, is confirmed.
7   I should add that newspaper polling in the first week of her appointment had ranked
     her as by far the favoured candidate for the presidency, compared with Abdurrah-
     man Wahid, even in polls in East Java papers such as *Jawa Pos*. Polls, undepend-
     able in most countries, are notoriously unrepresentative in Indonesia, since none
     reach beyond the urban middle class with access to telephones. Nonetheless, they
     do get us beyond the very small, vocal political elite whose views and voices dom-
     inate the news and features section of the media.
8   Wibisana is a mythical character from the Indian epic Ramayana. A brother of the
     demon king Ravana, he joined the God-king Rama's campaign against the demons.
     The analogy seems particularly apt given the support Matori Abdul Jalil gave to
     Megawati's presidential bid while remaining PKB chairman.
9   In Sen and Hill (2000), we describe in some detail the collapse, politically, techno-
     logically and culturally, of the censorship mechanisms of the New Order. The logic
     of that account suggests that post-New Order information policy is necessarily a
     'post-censorship' policy.
10   This is a neologism created by Appadurai (1990); it has since been used extensively
     in studies of global media. The notion of the mediascape needs to be explained in
     relation to a landscape, which in some fundamental sense limits the options of those
     who live and work in/with that geo-physical context. Similarly the mediascape is
     the overall media context within which any particular government or company
     deals with its individual goals, policies and so on.

11   During the last four years our whole nation has lived under constant fear,
        because we were stricken by monetary, economic, security and political crises
        coming one after the other and, worse, we experienced an institutional crisis and
        conflict. This was not only felt at the central level but also in the villages. It is
        understandable, therefore, that many were very concerned whether or not the
        Republic, painstakingly established by our founding fathers, would not be able
        to survive or would disintegrate. ... Under such conditions, it is not surprising
        that many questions arose as to whether we would be able to resolve the multi-
        faceted problems quickly and holistically. ... Like a disease, a crisis can erupt
        very suddenly; however, its recovery obviously requires time.

        The full text of the speech in English translation was on the *Jakarta Post* web-
        site and was forwarded to many academics around Australia by Charles Coppel,
        Melbourne University. All references to the speech in this essay are from the
        Jakarta Post's English translation.

12   As I finalise this paper for publication at the end of October 2001, just under 100
        days into her presidential term, Megawati has endorsed the investigation into graft
        allegations against DPR Speaker Akbar Tanjung, thus providing evidence that the
        promise of clean government in the address may well be backed up by real action.

3 THE DOWNFALL OF PRESIDENT ABDURRAHMAN WAHID: A RETURN TO AUTHORITARIANISM?

*Edward Aspinall**

In late 2000 and throughout the first half of 2001, Indonesian politics was dominated by the drawn-out crisis of the Abdurrahman Wahid presidency. Serious problems in the government began shortly after Abdurrahman's appointment to the presidency in October 1999. As Mietzner (2001: 29) noted in the last political report in this Indonesia Assessment series, 'By [the first month after his election], the first minister had been sacked, with six more to follow before the formation of a new cabinet in August 2000'. From the very first months in office, the pattern of politics was set, with Abdurrahman rapidly losing the support of the coalition of parties that had put him in power and, as a result, entering into an increasingly confrontational relationship with the legislature. An early denouement had seemed possible during the annual session of the People's Consultative Assembly (MPR) in August 2000, but the president saved his position by ceding much of the daily responsibility for government to his vice-president, Megawati Sukarnoputri (although this remained a paper concession and was not seriously implemented by the president in subsequent months).

It did not take long for the confrontation between the president and parliament to resume with renewed force. In July, before the MPR session, almost 237 of the 500 members of the People's Representative Council (DPR) had signed a letter proposing that it formally investigate allegations that the president had been involved in the improper use of Rp 35 billion from Bulog, the national food logistics agency, and had improperly received a donation of US$2 million from the Sultan of Brunei. On 23 August Abdurrahman announced a new cabinet, dashing the hopes of the political parties for greater representation. Within a week, the DPR had agreed to pursue the graft allegations; shortly thereafter it established a special committee (*pansus*) to investigate them. By October 2000 there was open press speculation that this process would result in Abdurrahman's removal from office ('Kasus Bulog, Sandungan Buat Presiden?', *Kompas,* 20 October 2000).

The first major blow to the president came on 1 February 2001, when the DPR voted 393 to 4 to accept the *pansus* report that there was circumstantial evidence of his direct involvement in the two scandals, and that he had violated his oath of office and an MPR decree on elimination of corruption. This 'memorandum' gave the president three months to respond, and represented the first formal step necessary to bring about his removal from office. A second memorandum passed on 30 April stated that the president had failed to heed the first memorandum.[1] Many party spokespersons in the DPR added new charges – that the president had failed to overcome the political problems of the country, such as ethnic riots and separatist tensions ('DPR Berikan Memorandum Kedua. Presiden Diberi Waktu Selama Satu Bulan', *Kompas*, 1 May 2001). On 30 May, the DPR met once more to evaluate the president's further response, only two days after the attorney-general's office announced that it had found no evidence to implicate the president in the scandals ('Kejakgung Umumkan Wahid tak Terlibat', *Media Indonesia*, 29 May 2001). Even so, the DPR called for the convocation of a Special Session of the MPR on 1 August to demand 'accountability' from the president and, if this was not provided to their satisfaction, to replace him.

Throughout this period there was extreme political tension. From the start, the president denied all the charges against him and insisted on the illegality of the *pansus* and the impeachment process. He refused to respond to the charges brought against him by the DPR, or did so in a dismissive and perfunctory manner. Following the first memorandum, supporters of the president from his Nahdlatul Ulama (NU) heartland in East Java attacked buildings owned by rival political parties and organisations, and it was feared that unrest would worsen in the capital itself. As the crisis escalated from about February, it became increasingly clear that the president was determined to resolve the conflict by dissolving the legislature and declaring a state of emergency (although he at first denied that this was his intention). Initially, he was dissuaded from this course only by the insistence of his senior security ministers and by the manifest disinclination of the armed forces and police to enforce such an order.[2] The president also continued to sack ministers and other senior officials at an accelerating rate, with those dismissed from their posts sometimes finding out from the media. Abdurrahman's relations with the senior leadership of the military and police force became increasingly tense, with the president attempting to secure their acquiescence in his planned move against parliament and, when this proved impossible, to replace them with more pliant officers. The looming confrontation between the military and the president even gave rise to speculation about a military coup.

The crisis deepened in June when the president announced that he had made the national police chief, General Surojo Bimantoro, 'non-active', at the same time appointing Inspector-General Chairuddin Ismail as deputy chief, with full authority to exercise his superior's powers. This move was of questionable legality, given that an MPR decree, passed in August 2000, required the appointment and dismissal of the national police chief to be approved by the DPR. A presidential decree enacted only the previous April had abolished the post of vice-chief of police altogether. The move was thus widely viewed as being preparatory to an attempt to move against the legislature.

Most senior police officers refused to acknowledge Bimantoro's removal, a position backed by the DPR. With the MPR Special Session drawing closer, on 12 July the president ordered the arrest of Bimantoro and the Jakarta police chief, accusing them of insubordination. In response, the chair of the MPR, Amien Rais, and other MPR leaders brought the session forward to 21 July. Abdurrahman still insisted that the entire process was illegal and rejected final attempts to broker a compromise that would have left him as a figurehead president without power to make cabinet appointments ('PDIP Siap Ditinggalkan Partai Golkar dan PPP', *Media Indonesia*, 19 July 2001). With Abdurrahman suggesting that the 'masses' would bring its proceedings to a halt, the MPR convened ('Lihat saja, MPR Bisa Selamat atau tidak', *Media Indonesia*, 22 July 2001). Confronting political extinction, and losing support from his ministers, at shortly after 1 a.m. on 23 July, President Abdurrahman finally issued the long-threatened decree by which he dissolved the DPR and MPR, 'froze' Golkar (the party which had been the mainstay of President Soeharto's New Order regime) and ordered fresh elections in a year's time. Despite fears that this would trigger mass violence, or a split in the security forces, the police and Indonesian National Army (TNI) ignored the decree and maintained a protective cordon around the parliament building. The MPR members, in turn, immediately set about bringing the impeachment process to a conclusion. With members of Abdurrahman's own National Awakening Party (PKB) boycotting the session, the MPR finally removed the president from office, unanimously replacing him with Megawati.

SIGNS OF RENEWED AUTHORITARIANISM?

A theme in many interpretations of the fall of Abdurrahman Wahid, at least in sections of the foreign media, was that the change represented a return to political authoritarianism. Many journalists and media commentators argued that the central political dynamic underlying the replacement of President Abdurrahman with Megawati was a resurgence of the military, of Golkar and of various 'corrupt New Order forces'.[3] In this view, the president was replaced because, by supporting democratic reform, he represented a threat to the entrenched interests of these groups. A particular theme of some media coverage was that Megawati had a special relationship with, or was even a tool of, the TNI.

This interpretation drew heavily on the views of Abdurrahman and his supporters. For example, the president's 'freezing' of Golkar in his 23 July decree was an obvious attempt to link the survival of his government to that of the reform process as a whole. The decree itself described the ban as an attempt to 'save the movement for total *reformasi* from obstruction by New Order elements' ('Presiden Berlakukan Dekrit', *Kompas*, 23 July 2001). Some longstanding advocates of democratisation in Indonesia were in agreement with this analysis. Many prominent members of human rights organisations, non-government organisations (NGOs) and other pro-democracy groups admired President Abdurrahman for his personal commitment to pluralism and human rights and, as Krishna Sen argues in Chapter 2, were suspicious of Megawati because of her apparent closeness to the army.

Even if they had doubts about Abdurrahman's personal style and behaviour and did not wish to be drawn into a dispute within the political elite, many radical and liberal activists believed they were duty-bound to defend the president against attack from his political foes, who clearly included the majority of the TNI leadership and Golkar ('Gerakan Prodemokrasi Jangan Terjebak dalam Keruwetan Politik', *Kompas*, 7 June 2001). Some of the more radical pro-democracy groups, such as the small, left-wing People's Democratic Party (PRD) – one of the more important products of the student radicalisation of the 1990s – attempted to mobilise their supporters in defence of the president, although they failed to do so in the large numbers of the old anti-Soeharto and anti-Habibie movements. During his final week in office, many NGO leaders gathered around the president, and when he finally vacated the presidential palace on 26 July, he was farewelled by a crowd of several thousand supporters, including many pro-democracy activists.

There is an element of truth in the 'return to authoritarianism' argument, although, as I shall argue below, it is important not to exaggerate it. Those who moved against Abdurrahman had many and diverse motivations, some of which related to threats made by the president against their interests. It is obvious that some elements of the military resented his attempts – especially early on in his presidency – to pursue armed forces reform, promote reformist officers and advocate conciliation with secessionists in Aceh and Papua. Throughout his presidency, numerous senior officers had gone on public record to make their complaints known. No doubt some elements in Golkar were fearful of corruption investigations, especially after Abdurrahman appointed Baharuddin Lopa as attorney-general on 1 June. Under Lopa, who had a reputation for fearlessness, there were numerous signs that, for the first time since the resignation of President Soeharto, truly rigorous investigations would be carried out into graft, a campaign cut short by the attorney-general's death only a month after his appointment.[4]

It is also true that from about late 2000, as Abdurrahman's hold on the presidency loosened, there was something akin to a return to coercive politics visible in Indonesia, primarily in two areas. The first was the handling of secessionist movements in Papua and Aceh. From late 2000, but accelerating through the first part of 2001, security forces largely abandoned the formerly permissive approach encouraged by President Abdurrahman in these two provinces. Targeted arrests of pro-independence activists, and their trial under the draconian 'spreading hatred' and sedition articles of the criminal code, were combined with 'limited' military operations, especially in Aceh. This approach was conceived in cabinet, it would appear, as a finely honed policy of targeting only diehard independence supporters, while attempting to win over others by concessions (the chief of these being special autonomy laws which, *inter alia*, contained generous provisions for the distribution of proceeds from natural resource industries). However, the Indonesian military and especially the police proved to be very blunt instruments for such a highly targeted policy, and there were many reports of abuses perpetrated against civilians. The violence was particularly bad in Aceh, with many human rights advocates saying conditions there by mid-2001 resembled the Soeharto-era 'military operations zone' period. Most estimates suggest that at least 1,000 people were killed (although not all by the military) in the first six months of 2001.[5] While in the short term these policies had some success in forcing secessionist movements into retreat (by the second half of the year military spokespersons in Aceh were boasting of a return of 'security' in the territory), they are unlikely to contribute to long-term restoration of stability in either Papua or Aceh, given that past indiscriminate use of state violence in both places largely accounts for the current alienation with Jakarta.

A second area where a return to the security approach has been apparent, although in much less pronounced form, is in the handling of protest by radical or lower-class groups, as authorities attempt to contain what they typically describe as anarchic or radical manifestations of the *reformasi* movement. For example, in the first half of 2001 many members of the left-wing PRD were arrested or otherwise harassed in Jakarta, Bandung and elsewhere. At times, peaceful protests by lower-class groups were disrupted or broken up, as in September when 10,000 farmers from the Indonesian Farmers' Alliance (API) were blocked on the outskirts of Bandung from demonstrating outside a meeting at which MPR members were discussing agrarian reform ('Ribuan Petani Gagal Masuk Bandung', *Kompas*, 15 September 2001). Attacks on labour protestors, left-wing groups and the like by civilian thugs (*preman*) or Muslim paramilitary groups – frequently, it seems, with tacit military and police backing – have also become more common.[6]

THE ABDURRAHMAN FACTOR

Although real and important, it is important not to extrapolate too widely from these trends. The central dynamic underlying the replacement of Abdurrahman by Megawati was largely separate from the apparent return to more authoritarian practices in particular sections of political and social life. This is not to deny that, at heart, President Abdurrahman had a philosophical commitment to pluralist democracy, as well as social and religious diversity. He also had some significant achievements. He appointed some prominent reformers to cabinet and other posts. Early on he took several important steps to reduce the military's political role. He encouraged legal reform, promoted dialogue with secessionist leaders in Aceh and Papua, and reconciliation with the East Timorese, and attempted to end discrimination against Indonesia's ethnic Chinese minority. Even so, many of the major reforms carried out during his presidency (such as decentralisation) were merely the implementation of legislative changes made under his predecessor, Habibie. Abdurrahman himself initiated very few institutional reforms.

It is difficult to sustain an argument that battle lines in Indonesian politics in 2001 were drawn between 'reformers' around the president and 'conservatives' around Megawati. Indeed, one of the great disappointments of the Abdurrahman period was that his political style meant that he failed to pursue systematically the reform ideas he had espoused. Most tellingly, he failed to construct a strong reformist bloc within the government, parliament or society. For example, personal loyalty rather than reform credentials became the key criterion for the rise and fall of cabinet ministers – conservatives and reformists alike. This was evidenced by the April 2000 dismissal of Minister for State Enterprises and Investment Laksamana Sukardi, widely seen as one of the cleanest ministers in cabinet, and his replacement by the poorly regarded Abdurrahman loyalist, Rozy Munir. Rozy's appointment was widely interpreted at the time as enabling the PKB and NU to access the huge funds at the disposal of the department. At times, the president indicated he was willing to cooperate with the most discredited elements of the New Order period, publicly arguing, for example, that corruption and other charges against favoured businessmen should be 'postponed' ('Untuk Sinivasan, Prajogo, dan Sjamsul Presiden Tunda Tuntutan Hukum', *Kompas*, 10 October 2001). A private meeting with Hutomo Mandala Putra ('Tommy' Soeharto) in October 2000, after the latter had been convicted under corruption charges, led to allegations of deal-making, especially because this was one of the last public sightings of the former president's son before he became a fugitive from justice. Potentially most destructive to the long-term consolidation of democracy, however, was Abdurrahman's disregard for constitutionality in his attempt to avoid dismissal, as well as his endeavour to enlist the military and police in his attempt to dissolve the legislature, dragging these institutions back into the centre of political life. As Tim Lindsey has pointed out, had his attempt to prorogue parliament been successful, 'Wahid said he would rule by decree for 12 months leading up to the elections' ('Wahid Acted Outside Law', *The Australian*, Letters to the Editor, 2 August 2001).

It is worth remembering that the election of Abdurrahman as president in October 1999, although interpreted by many sections of the foreign press as representing a victory for 'reformist forces', was in fact based on a coalition which drew heavily on the political machinery of Soeharto's New Order. Many Golkar and military leaders feared a Megawati-led clean sweep of senior officialdom, while others in the major Islamic-based parties were equally fearful that a secular-oriented Megawati presidency would reverse the advances they had made in the late Soeharto and Habibie periods. These two blocs provided Abdurrahman with the votes he needed to attain the presidency. In putting together his first coalition government, he therefore had to appease these groups. A cumbersome 'National Unity' government resulted. At the point that Indonesia's first democratically elected president assembled his government, therefore, it proved impossible to draw a clear line between the New Order past and the democratic future. This basic fact dogged all subsequent attempts to carry out substantial reform, and has not been seriously altered by the transition from Abdurrahman's to Megawati's stewardship. Indeed, the continuity between the two presidencies is underlined by the fact that the political coalition which underpins the new government is virtually identical to that which supported Abdurrahman's first cabinet in late 1999. Indeed, about two-thirds of Megawati's cabinet members had served in one of the cabinets of her predecessor.

Rather than a system-wide return to authoritarianism, the primary cause of the change in presidency was Abdurrahman's own erratic and increasingly destructive leadership style. As noted above, from the beginning of his presidency he had undermined the very coalition which had put him in power. Armed with infinite self-confidence and imperious indifference to criticism, he almost wilfully alienated his ministers, rode roughshod over the legislature, switched policy positions in the blink of an eye, made and broke promises in a cavalier style and frequently made bizarre and blatantly false public claims. Reports of large-scale graft within the presidential palace became rife and his management of staff was conspicuously bad. This kind of behaviour resulted in the alienation of all the major parties in the DPR except his own PKB, which held only 10 per cent of the seats. It was the president's alienation of almost the entire spectrum of Indonesia's new political elite that accounted for the end of his presidency, not a supposed alliance of the 'status quo'.

This dynamic had been clear during the first year of Abdurrahman's presidency, but it became far more obvious as the confrontation with the legislature deepened. Through the first six months of 2001, the president passed up many opportunities to strike compromise deals with his opponents, even when there were many opportunities to do so. There was also considerable disunity within the two major parties, Megawati's Indonesian Democratic Party of Struggle (PDI-P) and Golkar, about what attitude to take towards the president, with some groups (notably supporters within the PDI-P of Megawati's husband, Taufik Kiemas) favouring compromise. However, the president failed to take advantage of these splits. On the contrary, he frequently undermined the possibility of compromise by making personal attacks on the very individuals he was attempting to win over (telling *Newsweek* magazine in its 21 May 2001 edition, for example, that Megawati 'never said she would cling to the rule of law') or by making demonstrably false claims that they had agreed to accede to his demands.[7]

Politics through the first half of 2001 thus became increasingly bizarre. On the one hand, the president made numerous bellicose statements about his opponents, threatening to mobilise his supporters and at times making none-too-subtle threats that there would be a 'civil war' if he was replaced. At other times, the president ordered his followers to refrain from mobilising and from violence. Sometimes, Abdurrahman's threats served only to further undermine his own credibility, such as his repeated warning that six provinces would break away from Indonesia if he was ousted. With the president oscillating wildly between panicky intimidation and confident assertions that all was under control, even his closest supporters became increasingly confused and exasperated.[8]

Abdurrahman's behaviour may partly be explained by his apparently genuine belief that the impeachment process was indeed unconstitutional. His refusal to cooperate with the DPR and its investigation into the two financial scandals was always explained in these terms. In fact, although there was debate among Indonesian constitutional experts about the propriety of the process, a large majority of legal opinion agreed that the MPR had the power to remove the president (Fealy 2001: 1). It is true that the constitution does not explicitly set out the means by which a president may be impeached. However, according to most interpretations impeachment is an implicit power of the MPR, in part because the constitution states clearly that the president is accountable to it. In any case, MPR Decree No. 3 of 1978 (with MPR decrees being second only to the constitution in Indonesia's hierarchy of laws) sets out, in cases of presidential impropriety, a protracted process of memoranda by the DPR leading to the convocation of a Special Session of the MPR at which the president may be replaced. It is this procedure that was followed by the legislature.[9]

It is hard to escape the conclusion that a second major factor behind Abdurrahman's often bizarre behaviour when faced with impeachment was his deteriorating mental state. Since suffering two strokes in 1998, many observers had noted that he had lost much of his old mental acuity. His loss of eyesight, and the resultant dependence on a narrow circle of family members, friends and other advisors, had increased his isolation. Palace insiders paint a picture of an increasingly erratic and irritable president during his final months in office, prone to lashing out angrily at those who counselled caution. (*Tempo* quoted one witness who recalled him shouting, late on the evening of 22 July, 'Kalian semua banci' (one translation in this context is 'You're all faggots') at Agum Gumelar, TNI Commander Admiral Widodo and acting Police Chief Chaeruddin Ismail, when the three refused to endorse his decree dissolving parliament and his plan to appoint Brigadier-General Johny Lumintang as Vice-Commander of the TNI.)[10] A series of press interviews conducted after his removal seems to confirm the mental decline, with one journalist reporting: 'During the interview his thoughts seemed to slip from one track to another as though a switch had failed. His answers sometimes seemed to respond to some private inner thought. At times they burst forth with confident assurance before the question had quite been asked' (Mydans 2001).

UNDERLYING PROCESSES

A widespread sense in Indonesia that the impetus of reform is ebbing away, and the recurrence of authoritarian approaches in the two areas I mention above have more to do with deeper processes than the contest over the presidency. Four phenomena are particularly noteworthy.

First is the persistence of patrimonial patterns of social relations, and the pervasiveness of corruption and rent seeking through virtually the entire polity. This is partly a direct carry-over from the New Order period, with institutions like the police, judiciary and attorney-general's office still being notorious redoubts of corruption. Such practices also pervade the institutions which lie at the heart of Indonesia's new democratic system. There have been numerous reports, for instance, to indicate that corrupt deal-making is rife in the national legislature; one member of the new State Official Wealth Audit Commission (KPKPN) suggested that a 'fantastic' increase in the wealth of legislators from 1999 to 2001 (that is, precisely the period following their election to legislative seats) was cause for suspicion that such wealth had been corruptly obtained ('Harta Anggota DPR Meningkat Pesat, KPKPN Minta UU No.28/1999 Direvisi', *Media Indonesia*, 3 September 2001). At the local level, greatly encouraged by the additional political and financial powers devolved to the regions under decentralisation, new coalitions among political party leaders, local bureaucrats and business people have emerged, reminiscent of the local 'bossism' of places like Thailand and the Philippines. At the apex of the state, allegations of corruption have been common, with Megawati's immediate family (see Chapter 2) and Abdurrahman Wahid both being affected.[11]

Second is the deep and widespread unease about national identity and the challenges to it. Many in the political elite are prepared to accept repression of those groups that threaten national 'integrity' and 'unity'. Thus in late 2000, leaders of the avowedly reformist, modernist Islamic-based party, the National Mandate Party (PAN), led condemnation of President Abdurrahman's policy of conciliation towards supporters of independence in Papua.[12] While Megawati herself has made many public professions of sorrow for human rights violations in Aceh, the historical parallels she used to explain her Aceh policy to an audience in Washington shortly after becoming president left little doubt that she is willing to contemplate a military solution:

> Abraham Lincoln, one of your greatest heroes, carried out a similar policy about one and half century ago. America became great because, among others, the principle of national integrity was upheld by Lincoln and other heroes of that era. As I said, we will certainly pursue a peaceful political approach. But as did Lincoln in the United States, we will defend the integrity of Indonesia no matter how long it will take (address by Megawati Sukarnoputri at Usindo Gala Dinner, Washington DC, 19 September 2001).

A third factor is the great financial pressure on the government and the consequent difficulty of meeting all manner of demands from what is now a much more assertive society (see Chapter 4). It is widely agreed in the government that it is necessary to reduce budget expenditures to service debt and cover basic development costs. Measures to achieve this, such as the removal of fuel subsidies, have aroused considerable opposition. In June 2001, following a rise in fuel prices, there were large student demonstrations and public transport strikes, resulting in some serious clashes between protestors and security forces.

The fourth and perhaps most important factor is, ironically, the institutionalisation of the initially mass-based impetus for *reformasi*. The campus revolt which began in February–March 1998 gave birth to a large and variegated mass movement for democratic change throughout the archipelago. Immediately after Soeharto's resignation on 21 May 1998, there was an explosion of Indonesian civil society. Demonstrations forced corrupt village heads, regents and mayors from office all round the country; peasants occupied land which had been taken from them in preceding years; scores of new political parties, labour unions, anti-corruption bodies and other organisations were formed. Since May 1998, a major thrust of formal politics has been to capture the energies of this popular efflorescence, and make it an institutionalised, permanent, but also domesticated, feature of Indonesia's political landscape. It is thus important to note that, despite the sometimes debilitating conflicts in the political elite, the establishment and consolidation of democratic institutions continued through 2000–01. Among the plethora of new institutions formed over the last year or two that have now begun to make a mark on the political system are several anti-corruption watchdog bodies, such as the KPKPN and the National Ombudsman's Commission. Even more new democratic institutions are in the pipeline, or are at least possibilities, including ad hoc human rights courts, an anti-corruption commission, a constitutional court, and a truth and reconciliation commission. Major constitutional redesign remains on the cards, including the introduction of an assembly of regional representatives (DPD) as a component of the MPR, and direct presidential elections. Even the protracted confrontation between President Abdurrahman and the legislature may partly be interpreted as a shaking out of Indonesia's new institutional format, being essentially a battle over the delineation of authority between legislature and executive, resolved in favour of the former. It is thus important to recognise that the institutionalisation of democratic forms has continued, albeit not at the pace hoped for by the most radical supporters of *reformasi*, including many of those who pioneered the movement against Soeharto and now feel disillusioned with the results.

It is also important not to exaggerate the return of coercion. For example, violence in some labour disputes has taken place against a backdrop of a much liberalised labour regime. If Indonesia's formal democratic structures have gradually become more institutionalised since 1998, a similar process has been visible in civil society. By June 2001 there were something like 43 officially registered trade unions ('Idealnya Dikelola Buruh Sendiri', *Kompas*, 24 June 2001). Their new organisational strength allowed workers to mount some very large mobilisations during 2001. These included a wave of truly massive demonstrations in June 2001, when the government, citing the need to attract foreign investors, attempted to cancel a Habibie-era decree setting generous terms for workers' entitlements and severance pay. With some of these protests involving tens of thousands of workers (and resulting in a serious riot in Bandung), the government agreed to suspend implementation of the new decree and come up with a new formula that would satisfy both business and labour representatives ('Kepmennaker No 150/2000 Diberlakukan Kembali', *Kompas*, 16 June 2001).

As for Papua and Aceh, it is apparent that a political consensus is developing in Indonesia that these two provinces are 'special'. With the exception of a few courageous voices, much of elite Indonesian political opinion at least acquiesces in repressive policies in defence of national unity. This is the case even if such acquiescence is usually expressed as support for 'limited military operations', or some similar formula. While obviously a negative development for the inhabitants of these territories, it is a moot point as to how far this might lead to an erosion of democracy in the nation as a whole. Many countries in Asia and beyond (the Philippines is one example, India is another) have long practised ruthless repression of secessionist movements, while more or less adhering to the rules of formal democracy at the centre.

In summary, among the main political processes taking place in Indonesia today, three of the most prominent are: first, an incremental, but very messy, process of reform in state institutions; second, the flourishing of money politics and rent seeking within a formally democratic political framework; and third, the normalisation of more repressive practices in the periphery of the nation state and, less clearly, against lower-class groups. These three phenomena epitomise the kind of politics we have long been familiar with in the more open, competitive, semi-democratic or even liberal-democratic systems of some of Indonesia's neighbours, such as Thailand, the Philippines or even India. However, they do not signify a return to Soeharto-style New Order authoritarianism. As Krishna Sen explains in Chapter 2, the frustrating contradictions and shortcomings of Indonesia's emerging political system – personified so amply by Megawati Sukarnoputri herself – call for a new way of conceptualising Indonesian politics, one that transcends the binary opposition of New Order past and idealised democratic future.

NOTES

* Some parts of this article have appeared in my article 'Mother of the Nation' (Aspinall 2001). My thanks to the late Herb Feith, who commented on an earlier version of this article, and especially to Greg Fealy, who has contributed much invaluable insight and commentary. Any errors remain the responsibility of the author.

1 See ICG (2001a).

2 See, for example, 'Wawancara dengan Menko Polsoskam: Presiden Berencana Keluarkan Dekrit Pukul 12.00 Kemarin' (*Kompas*, 29 May 2001).

3 See, for example, Greg Sheridan, 'Suharto Forces Are Moving in' (*The Australian*, 1 June 2001) and David Van Praagh, '"Coup" in Indonesia a Blow to Democracy' (*Toronto Star*, 30 July 2001).

4 There were even reports that Lopa had been especially ordered by Abdurrahman to investigate allegations of corruption involving Megawati's husband, Taufik Kiemas ('Lopa Dapat Misi Khusus usut Taufik Kiemas', *Media Indonesia*, 5 June 2001). Lopa died of a heart attack on 3 July in Riyadh, Saudi Arabia.

5 In September, the local branch of the Indonesian Red Cross reported that it alone had dealt with 1,500 corpses in 2000 and 2001 ('Sejak Tahun 2000, PMI Evakuasi 1.860 Korban', *Serambi Indonesia*, 24 September 2001).

6 See, for example, 'Police Suspect Army Officer behind Kadera Raid', *Jakarta Post*, 7 April 2001.

7 An example of this was a claim in April that Megawati had promised to support Abdurrahman's remaining in office until 2004, a statement which Megawati's office immediately and publicly rebutted ('Tidak Pernah Mendukung Presiden hingga 2004: Megawati Meralat Wahid', *Media Indonesia*, 21 April 2001).

8 For example, after Abdurrahman informed the Central Leadership Council of the PKB in early May that the political crisis was 'over', several participants expressed their frustrations to the national press, with one telling *Kompas*: 'We don't understand why the political crisis is said to be over. What's the basis for saying that, and why does Gus Dur say so?' ('Fraksi Kebangkitan Bangsa Berperang Tanpa Senjata', *Kompas*, 4 May 2001).

9   See Fealy (2001: 1) and Lindsey (2001). The two main objections that could be
     made with regard to the DPR's and MPR's adherence to this process were the addi-
     tion of extra grounds for impeachment that had not been included in the first mem-
     orandum, and the acceleration of the timetable for impeachment after Abdurrahman
     ordered the arrest of Police Chief Bimantoro.

10   See Wens Manggut, Andari Karina Anom and Setiyardi, 'Dekrit Angin Lalu'
     (*Tempo*, 5 August 2001: 32). *Banci*, according to Dede Oetomo, is a label for a per-
     son who appears 'androgynous in dress and/or physical features or behaves androg-
     ynously'. At the same time, 'As an epithet, *banci* is used to describe men who are
     wishy-washy and cowardly. Student organisations that shy away from criticising the
     government, for example, are often sent parcels containing bras, panties, lipstick
     and a powder-case' (Oetomo 1999: 261–2).

11   A report by the International Crisis Group had the following to say on the Abdur-
     rahman presidency:

     As leader of the NU, Gus Dur had for years been raising funds for mosques and
     religious schools from political leaders and big businessmen in exchange for
     political support. On becoming president, the only difference was that the
     sources of such funds were more numerous, the amounts much larger and the
     favours requested more damaging to the nation (ICG 2001b: 3).

12   See, for example, the comments by PAN legislator A.M. Fatwa in the *Indonesian
     Observer* ('Rebels Funded by Foreign Groups', 24 October 2000).

4 THE YEAR IN REVIEW: FROM BLIND MAN'S BLUFF TO MEGA EXPECTATIONS

Mari Pangestu

The peaceful change in leadership from President Abdurrahman Wahid to President Megawati Sukarnoputri in early August 2001 has led to expectations of a rapid return of political stability and to a more positive mood in the country. The immediate rebound in confidence was clear, with the rupiah strengthening from Rp 11,000 to Rp 9,000 against the US dollar. Despite initial low expectations about the new president's leadership capability and intellectual capacity, she passed the first test by not compromising on professionalism and experience in forming her cabinet. The economic cabinet is made up of professionals or experienced bureaucrats known to be market-friendly and outward-looking. The cabinet certainly worked hard to clear the important hurdles that had eluded the Abdurrahman government since the end of 2000, namely rebuilding trust with the International Monetary Fund (IMF) and the international creditor community through successful approval of the IMF Letter of Intent, thus clearing the way for disbursement of the long-overdue US$400 million loan tranche, phase two of Paris Club II negotiations and preparations for the next Consultative Group on Indonesia (CGI) meeting. President Megawati has also sent out clear messages on eliminating corruption, openness of the economy and reforms. One could say that she has initially surpassed 'Mega expectations'.

Unfortunately the events following the September 11 terrorist attacks on New York will have a wider and longer impact than earlier thought. The slowdown of the US and world economy has become a certainty, with projections for recovery now being longer than previously anticipated. Business and consumer confidence has been affected, while protests and increased anti-West sentiment have once more affected confidence and perceptions of law and order and security. The rupiah weakened to Rp 11,000/US$ and has stubbornly remained at around the Rp 10,500/US$ level.

This chapter reviews economic developments since the last update in October 2000 (Bird 2001) and attempts to make some short-term predictions for the coming year. It is important to bear in mind that even the best of governments would have an uphill task to achieve significant results given the changed context of policy-making in Indonesia's new-found democracy and the weakness and lack of capacity of the country's institutions. Nevertheless, there is scope for progress to be made on reform and institutional change over the coming year if the leadership and government are committed to act, and deliver, in a number of priority areas.

REBOUND – AND DECLINE – OF CONFIDENCE

The first eight months of 2001 were marked by growing political instability and a decline in confidence. President Abdurrahman Wahid became increasingly unpredictable, sacking ministers who did not agree with him and defying the parliament as well as the international community of creditors, especially the IMF. The situation up to the end of July was still very fluid and confidence had reached rock bottom. The level of mistrust in the external creditor community was high, with the Coordinating Minister for Economic Affairs and then Finance Minister, Rizal Ramli, openly at odds with the IMF. As a result the signing of the IMF Letter of Intent was delayed until August, the World Bank reduced the amount of loans to Indonesia and investor ratings for the country hit their lowest level ever. Consumer and business sentiment indices were all declining (Danareksa Research Institute 2001), and as a result macroeconomic indicators worsened. The exchange rate weakened from around Rp 8,500/US$ in August 2000 to below Rp 11,500/US$ at the end of May 2001. The stock market index declined from 500 in August 2000 to a low of around 350 in April 2001, before rising slightly to 400 in July 2001 (Figure 4.1).

The smooth transition of power from President Abdurrahman Wahid to President Megawati Sukarnoputri ushered in a more positive mood marked by cautious optimism rather than exuberance. The rupiah strengthened from Rp 11,000/US$ to Rp 8,500/US$, stabilising at Rp 9,000/US$ just before the September 11 terrorist attacks on the United States. However, in the wake of the attacks, perceptions of security concerns and the downturn in the world economy once more eroded confidence in Indonesia. The honeymoon period for President Megawati and her Gotong Royong (Mutual Assistance) cabinet is over. As the recent CGI meetings attest, Indonesia's progress on structural, institutional and legal reforms and on the battle against corruption is still deemed insufficient. The rupiah has continued to weaken since mid-September and was hovering at around Rp 10,500–11,000/US$ in the first week of November 2001 (Figure 4.1).

Other indices of confidence, such as the consumer confidence index and index of business confidence in government put out by Danareksa Research

Figure 4.1 Rupiah and Stock Market Performance, 2 June 2000 – 6 November 2001

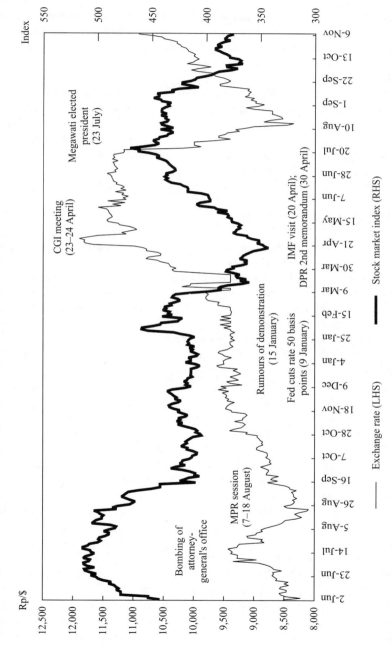

Institute, have also been falling. These indices showed a steady improvement in confidence after President Megawati took office, followed by a decline since the beginning of October (Danareksa Research Institute 2001). The main areas of concern are weak economic fundamentals and the lack of progress in effecting reform, reflecting increased ambivalence about the present government's achievements.

The high risk premium placed on Indonesia is evident from the risk premium of Yankee bonds over US Treasury Bills of 585–867 basis points, compared with 67–121 basis points for Singapore. Indonesia's ratings have also been sliding: after an upgrade to CCC+ when Megawati became president (that is, still below investment grade), the latest Standard and Poor's rating downgrades Indonesia to CCC, with a negative outlook.

SLOWDOWN IN GROWTH

The rebound in growth experienced in 2000 of 4.8 per cent will not be repeated in 2001. The main reasons are the adverse external environment as well as the deterioration in confidence and economic and political stability experienced for most of the year. As a result, growth projections have continually been revised downwards, from 4–5 per cent predicted at the beginning of the year to 3–3.5 per cent in the revised 2001 budget and IMF Letter of Intent. The real GDP growth rate at the end of the second quarter of 2001 was 3.5 per cent per annum on an annualised basis, compared with 3.2 per cent in the previous quarter. Growth should be higher in the third quarter due to seasonal factors, but is expected to plummet in the fourth quarter as the effects of the world economic slowdown and deteriorating confidence begin to have an impact. The Asian Development Bank (ADB) and ten analysts recently polled by Reuters have forecast growth of 3.2 per cent in 2001; the World Bank projects 3.3 per cent growth.

The main source of growth remains the manufacturing sector, due to exports rather than domestic demand. The trade, hotels and restaurants sector and the transport and communications sector are the next biggest contributors. These three sectors together accounted for around 50 per cent of GDP in 2001 but close to three-quarters of growth. They have experienced greater or more stable growth than the agricultural and most service sectors, which have experienced a decline in growth rates (Table 4.1).

A large portion of the recovery in 2000 was attributable to high export growth and some resumption of investment. Given the adverse developments in external demand this year – the US economy is expected to grow at less than 2 per cent and the Japanese economy is already in recession – export growth is expected to be less than half that experienced last year. Nevertheless, with domestic demand sluggish and a sustained recovery in investment yet to materi-

Table 4.1 Real GDP Growth by Sector, 2001–01 (%)

Sector	Year-on-year Growth			Contribution to Growth		
	2000	2001 (Q1)	2001 (Q2)	2000	2001 (Q1)	2001 (Q2)
Agriculture	1.7	1.6	1.3	6	9	6
Mining & quarrying	2.3	1.1	2.3	5	3	6
Manufacturing	6.2	3.6	4.8	34	29	36
Electricity, gas & water	8.8	7.3	9.9	3	4	5
Construction	6.7	0.1	1.0	8	0	2
Trade, hotels & restaurants	5.7	5.8	5.3	19	28	24
Transport & communications	9.4	7.2	6.1	14	16	13
Financial, ownership, business	4.7	2.9	2.4	7	6	5
Services	2.2	1.3	1.6	5	4	4
GDP	**4.8**	**3.2**	**3.5**	**100**	**100**	**100**

Source: BPS, *Berita Resmi Statistik* [Official Statistical News], taken from CSIS (2001a).

alise, exports will still be the main contributor to growth. Like exports, investment and consumption demand have been affected by the crisis in confidence and deteriorating economic conditions in Indonesia in 2001. The brief respite after 1 August proved short-lived, so growth for the year is likely to end up at around 3.2 per cent.

It was only in 2001 that real GDP finally regained its 1996 level. The recovery in Indonesia has been slower than in the other crisis-affected economies, with most of them returning to their pre-crisis levels of real GDP in 1999 or 2000. The loss due to this slow recovery is even more evident when we consider the potential level of output if there had been no crisis. Before the crisis the average rate of real growth stood at around 7 per cent. The estimated level of real GDP in 2001 is only three-quarters of the level that would have been achieved if the economy had continued to grow at an average rate of, say, 6 per cent since 1996 (Figure 4.2).

With only weak demand for exports and no sharp rebound expected in domestic consumption and investment, the prospects for renewed growth in 2002 are poor (Table 4.2). The world economy slowed considerably in 2001 and

Figure 4.2 Actual and Potential Real GDP, 1996–2001

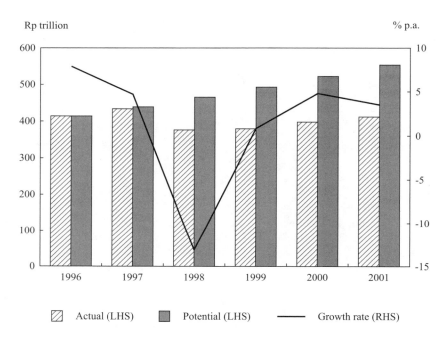

Rp trillion   % p.a.

Actual (LHS)   Potential (LHS)   ——— Growth rate (RHS)

Source: BPS, *Neraca Pendapatan Nasional* and *Berita Resmi Statistik* [Official Statistical News].

a recovery is not expected until the end of 2002. Other countries in the region have resorted to domestic stimulus packages to offset the adverse external environment, but given budget constraints, the scope for Indonesia to conduct a major domestic stimulus package is limited (see below). Therefore, the government's projected growth for 2002 of 5 per cent, set at the time the budget was presented in September 2001, will not be achievable (Table 4.3). The government has already revised the growth rate down to 4 per cent, with the ADB forecasting growth of 3.9 per cent assuming improvements in political conditions and confidence. The World Bank is less optimistic: it predicts a lower growth rate of 3.5 per cent as the government 'muddles through' difficult reforms. The World Bank has also issued a warning that Indonesia has only a six-month window of opportunity to vastly improve confidence and thus attract back the capital inflows needed to spur growth.

The cost of a lower growth rate is evident in the time it will take Indonesia to reach its potential level of real GDP. Using optimistic growth assumptions of

Table 4.2 Real GDP Growth by Expenditure, 2001 (%)[a]

Item	Year-on-year Growth		Contribution to Growth	
	(Q1)	(Q2)	(Q1)	(Q2)
Domestic consumption	0.9	1.1	16	18
Government consumption	1.0	1.1	2	2
Gross fixed capital formation	5.2	5.9	21	19
Exports	8.6	8.8	61	61
GDP	**3.2**	**3.5**	**100**	**100**

a   Import components are subtracted from each type of expenditure to give a better measure of the sources of growth.

Source: BPS, *Berita Resmi Statistik* [Official Statistical News], taken from CSIS (2001a).

5 per cent for the next two years and 6–7 per cent thereafter, this would take five years, or until 2006. Slow progress on reforms and restructuring, as well as continued weak confidence, would mean lower growth rates and a longer time period – anything from eight to ten years – for Indonesia to reach the potential real level of income. Low growth rates also imply lower employment creation, including reduced capacity to absorb new entrants into the labour force.

INFLATION AND MONETARY POLICY

After a period of low inflation and even deflation, on a year-on-year basis inflation has been rising steadily since July 2000. It reached double digits in March 2001 and rose to 13 per cent in July. By the end of October it had dropped back slightly to 12.5 per cent, due to deflation in August (Table 4.3). The causes of inflation are supply shocks following an increase in administered prices, depreciation of the rupiah and excessive monetary expansion. The government raised fuel prices by 30 per cent in July 2001 and this had a significant impact on prices: transportation prices subsequently increased by 7 per cent and inflation by 2.1 per cent. The weakening of the rupiah throughout the latter part of 2000 and first half of 2001 also contributed to imported inflation. At the same time

Table 4.3 Macroeconomic Indicators: Actual and Targeted, 2000–02

Indicator	2000	2001 (first budget)	2001 (revised budget)	2001 (realised)	2002 (draft budget)
Real GDP growth (% p.a.)	4.8	5.0	3–3.5	3.3 (Q3)	5.0
Inflation (year-on-year, %)	9.3	7.2	9–11	12.5 (October)	8.0
SBI 3-month interest rate (% p.a.)	13.1	11.5	15.0	17.6 (September, week 1)	14.0
Exchange rate (average, Rp/US$)	8,534	7,800	9,600	10,194 (5 November)	8,500
Oil price (US$ per barrel)		24.0	24.0	17.9 (November, week 2)	22.0
Oil production (million barrels per day)		1.5	1.46	1.30 (semester 1)	1.23

Source: Ministry of Finance (various years), Budget; BPS (various years), *Economic Indicators*, www.bps.go.id; Bank Indonesia (various years), *Economic and Financial Statistics*, www.bi.go.id/data.

money supply growth has been excessive, with base money growth still far above the target.

The central bank has not been effective in reducing liquidity in the economy or in dampening money supply growth. Despite evident inflationary pressures, it did not conduct a sufficiently tight monetary policy in 2000, resulting in high growth rates of base money that far exceeded the IMF target. The central bank has attempted to tighten monetary policy since the end of 2000 and interest rates have increased measurably since then. Three-month Bank Indonesia Certificate (SBI) interest rates rose from 12 per cent towards the end of last year to nearly 18 per cent at the end of October 2001 (Table 4.3). The growth rate of base money at the end of October was still high at 20 per cent (Rp 117 trillion), well above the indicative target of 12–14.5 per cent (Rp 112 trillion) given GDP growth and inflation assumptions. Deposit interest rates, at 14–15 per cent, have not kept up with increases in SBI rates. Faced with double-digit inflation and a 20 per cent tax on interest income, people are spending their money, largely on consumer durables, rather than depositing it in the bank (CSIS 2001a: 10).

Inflation is likely to be 2–3 per cent higher in 2001 than even the revised target of 9 per cent, since price increases are likely to persist through November and December – that is, through the fasting month of Ramadan and the feast of Idul Fitri, which falls on 17 December 2001. Rather than the target of 8 per cent for 2002, inflation is likely to be 9–10 per cent, given that the rupiah could weaken still further and another 30 per cent increase in fuel prices will take effect in the early part of the year.

FISCAL SUSTAINABILITY

The 2001 Budget

In view of the deterioration in economic conditions and the size of the government's domestic and foreign debt, fiscal sustainability has become an urgent and high-priority issue for Indonesia.[1] Changing macro conditions and disagreements with the government on how to finance the deficit led the IMF to make its review mission conditional upon revisions to the 2001 budget announced at the beginning of the year. The most contentious issue was the proposal by the former Coordinating Minister for Economic Affairs, Rizal Ramli, to issue US$500 million (Rp 5 trillion) in bonds backed by revenue from gas exports to Singapore. The multilateral agencies and bilateral creditors under the Paris Club objected strongly to this plan, which they saw as violating the terms of Indonesia's external borrowing, whereby they were senior lenders and had first right to any government revenues.

After much debate, the cabinet finally approved a revised budget and backed down from the asset securitisation proposal at the end of May 2001. The then vice-president, Megawati Sukarnoputri, in her capacity as chair of the economic cabinet meeting, was already demonstrating that she had the capability to lead the country out of its economic decision-making paralysis. She invited two New Order technocrats, Professor Widjojo Nitisastro and Professor Emil Salim, to advise on the budget and in particular to stress the importance of approving it so that the process to sign a new Letter of Intent could begin. At the time her move was considered in a positive light – as taking action at once rather than waiting until she might be able to form her own government in August.

The revised 2001 budget incorporated new assumptions: a lower growth rate of 3.5 per cent, higher three-month SBI rates of 15 per cent, higher inflation of 9.3 per cent and a weaker exchange rate of Rp 9,600/US$ (Table 4.3). Without any changes to the current budget, this would have resulted in a deficit amounting to 6 per cent of GDP, particularly as some programs were either not realised or, like the fuel price increases planned for April 2000, only partially implemented. By introducing a package of measures to reduce expenditures and increase revenues, the government managed to reduce the size of the deficit to 3.7 per cent of GDP.

The most concrete measure taken in the revised budget to reduce expenditures was to cut fuel and electricity subsidies. Fuel prices for non-industrial users were raised by 30 per cent, completing the price increase originally scheduled for April 2001; electricity prices were increased by an average of 17.5 per cent for large consumers. To offset the impact of these price increases on the poor, Rp 2.2 trillion has been allocated to programs such as a subsidised rice scheme and health and education programs, to be financed from project funds. Some of these programs have been delayed, and the effectiveness of those that have been implemented is not yet clear (World Bank 2001a).

Another measure taken to reduce expenditure was to reschedule debt payments under the Paris Club mechanism. After a six-month delay, the new government was able to conclude negotiations for the rescheduling of payment on principal amounting to US$2.8 billion for the period ending April 2002. Debt servicing accounts for 6 per cent of GDP and 41 per cent of routine expenditures (compared with 3.4 per cent of GDP and 35 per cent of routine expenditures in 1996/97, the fiscal year prior to the crisis) (Table 4.4). Domestic debt servicing of government bonds related to bank restructuring is double that of foreign debt servicing. In the revised budget, foreign debt servicing increased by Rp 5.3 trillion due to exchange rate changes, while domestic debt servicing rose by Rp 7.7 trillion due to higher interest rates. Planned development expenditures have also been reduced, mainly by slowing down the implementation of development projects because of limited capacity to absorb such expenditures.

Despite the revisions, changes in assumptions and unmet targets could mean that the financing of the deficit could become problematic. Since the budget was revised in May, oil prices have fallen, the rupiah has weakened to around Rp 10,200/US$ compared with the target of Rp 9,600/US$, and interest rates have risen to around 16 per cent compared with the assumption of 15 per cent (Table 4.3).

Furthermore, the government has received no revenue at all from privatisation despite a target of Rp 6.5 trillion carried over from last year (Table 4.4). The recent delay to the sale of PT Gresik Cement, which would have yielded most of this revenue, indicates how political pressures can override the national interest. It is estimated that the plan of the Mexican company, Cemex, to exercise its option to increase its share in Semen Gresik from 25 to 51 per cent would generate US$356 million, or close to 80 per cent of the targeted revenue from privatisation. However, this plan has met with strong resistance from residents living near Semen Padang, Semen Gresik's West Sumatran subsidiary. The provincial government wanted the subsidiary to be spun off and recently voted to take it over. The outcome has been an impasse: the government has neither approved Cemex's put option nor come to a decision about the spin-off requested by the provincial government. In the meantime, the deadline for the put option has been extended to 14 December 2001. The uncertainties thus created have worsened an already fragile investment climate. In addition, following the precedent set with Semen Padang, South Sulawesi has initiated similar moves with regard to Semen Tonasa, Semen Gresik's other subsidiary.

The sale of assets held by IBRA, the bank restructuring agency, is not too far from the target, with the exception of Bank Central Asia. IBRA has raised around Rp 21 trillion through the divestment of liquidated and restructured banks and the sale of non-performing loans. The asset sales have experienced delays, as the case of Bank Central Asia illustrates. IBRA owns 60.3 per cent of the bank, with the remainder owned by the public since Bank Central Asia listed in 1999. Under the August 2001 Letter of Intent, the sale of IBRA's share was to be completed by the end of the year, but based on statements made by government officials this target is unlikely to be met. After a heated debate, parliament finally approved the sale of up to 51 per cent of the bank's shares to an outside investor, but in two stages. Although a number of investors have expressed interest, it is still not clear whether the deal will attract the right kind of strategic investor, or at the appropriate value. It is reported that to date there have been 23 indications of interest, of which ten were from foreign investors, including Standard Chartered and ABN Amro.

The government has little room to manoeuvre to finance the deficit, but two possibilities have been suggested. One is to disburse as quickly as possible the undisbursed US$9.3 billion of CGI loans, which would mean meeting various conditions, improving project proposals and assessing rupiah financing needs. The conditions which have not been met are the passage of three laws on electricity, investment and money laundering. This will be difficult to achieve in the very short time left before the end of the year. The second proposal is for the government to draw down its deposits in the government account, reported to stand at around Rp 18 trillion. However, such a draw-down would add to the money supply in the economy and lead to higher inflation, especially if the central bank did not sterilise the increased liquidity.

The 2002 Budget

As a prerequisite for IMF negotiations to continue, the government had to prepare a draft budget for 2002 and obtain approval for it from parliament. The budget, which was approved in the first week of September, assumes growth of 5 per cent, annual inflation of 8 per cent and an exchange rate of Rp 8,500/US$ (see Table 4.4). A large part of the deficit is related to bonds issued in the process

Table 4.4 Budgets for 2001 and 2002

Item	2001 Budget		Revised 2001 Budget			2002 Budget		
	(Rp trillion)	(% of GDP)	(Rp trillion)	(% of GDP	(% of total expen-- diture)	(Rp trillion	(% of GDP	(% of total expen- diture)
Total revenue & grants	**263.2**	**18.4**	**286.0**	**19.5**	**84.0**	**289.4**	**17.1**	**87.1**
Domestic revenue	263.2	18.4	286.0	19.5	84.0	289.4	17.1	87.1
Tax	179.9	12.6	185.3	12.6	54.4	216.8	12.8	65.2
Non-tax	83.3	5.8	100.7	6.9	29.6	72.6	4.3	21.9
Total expenditure	**315.8**	**22.2**	**340.3**	**23.2**	**100.0**	**332.5**	**19.6**	**100.0**
Central government expenditure	234.1	16.6	258.8	17.6	76.1	242.1	14.3	72.8
Routine expenditure	190.1	13.4	213.4	14.5	62.7	195.0	11.5	58.6
Personnel & material expenditure	49.7	3.5	48.1	3.3	14.1	52.2	3.1	15.7
Interest payments	76.5	5.4	89.6	6.1	26.3	87.0	5.1	26.2
Domestic	53.5	3.8	61.2	4.2	18.0	59.6	3.5	17.9
Foreign	23.1	1.6	28.4	1.9	8.3	27.4	1.6	8.2
Subsidies	54.0	3.8	66.3	4.5	19.5	46.2	2.7	13.9
Other	9.9	0.7	9.4	0.6	2.8	9.5	0.6	2.9
Development & net lending	44.0	3.1	45.5	3.1	13.4	47.1	2.8	14.2
Balancing funds (to regions)	81.7	5.7	81.5	5.5	23.9	90.3	5.3	27.2
Deficit	**−52.5**	**−3.7**	**−54.3**	**−3.7**		**−43.0**	**−2.5**	
Financing	**52.5**	**3.7**	**54.3**	**3.7**		**43.0**	**2.5**	
Domestic financing	33.5	2.4	34.4	2.3		25.4	1.5	
Bank	0.0	0.0	0.0	0.0		0.0	0.0	
Non-bank	33.5	2.4	34.4	2.3		25.4	1.5	
Privatisation proceeds	6.5	0.5	6.5	0.4		4.0	0.2	
Asset recoveries	27.0	1.9	27.0	1.8		21.5	1.3	
Government bond issuance (net)	0.0	0.0	0.9	0.1		0.0	0.0	
Bond issuance	0.0	0.0	0.9	0.1		3.9	0.2	
Bond repayments	0.0	0.0	0.0	0.0		−3.9	−0.2	
Foreign financing (net)	19.0	1.3	19.9	1.4		17.6	1.0	
Program loans & debt rescheduling	13.7	0.9	16.3	1.1		34.7	2.1	
Project loans	22.3	1.6	23.7	1.6		24.4	1.4	
Amortisation of foreign debt	−17.0	−1.2	−20.2	−1.4		−41.5	−2.5	
GDP	**1,425.0**		**1,468.0**			**1,693.0**		

Source: Ministry of Finance (September 2001).

of bank recapitalisation and cannot act as a stimulus to the domestic economy as has been the case in the last few years. In the face of a world economic slow-down, the room to conduct fiscal stimulus, as is being done in other countries, is limited.

One of the main features of the budget is an increase in tax revenues of as much as 1.3 per cent of GDP. This implies a substantial improvement in tax administration and collection procedures, which will require political will and commitment to achieve. The targets of Rp 6.5 trillion for privatisation and Rp 27 trillion for asset recoveries are unlikely to be met given progress to the end of October 2001. The government has not earned any revenue from privatisation, and the sale of Semen Gresik, although under consideration for a long time, has not proceeded.

On the expenditure side, allowance has been made for a modest increase in civil servants' salaries. The allocation for development expenditures is 2.8 per cent of GDP, down from 3.1 per cent in 2001. The debt overhang on the one hand and the lack of progress in increasing revenues on the other, is affecting the amount that can be allocated to development spending, with consequences for infrastructure development and the provision of social services. Other adjust-ments on the expenditure side include a further reduction in fuel subsidies and changes in the formula for allocating central grants to districts to bring them more in line with previous funding levels.

On external financing, the assumption that Indonesia will be able to resched-ule its foreign debt has already been incorporated in the draft budget. This pre-sumes a successful conclusion of the Paris Club negotiations for the period April 2002 to April 2003, to start early next year. Given budgetary constraints and goodwill from donors, the government is planning to ask for better terms to be applied not only to payment of principal but also to payment of interest.

The budget deficit has been lowered to 2.5 per cent of GDP, from 3.7 per cent in 2001 (Table 4.4). However, with slower growth, higher interest rates and lack of progress on privatisation and asset recoveries, there are already concerns that the deficit could be larger. Adjustments in expenditure and revenue assumptions will need to be made. In addition, efforts must be accelerated to negotiate better terms on debt rescheduling, obtain new soft loans and access the undisbursed amounts held by the IMF. Japan has already expressed its commitment to rescheduling debt under Paris Club III, and has offered a further US$400 million in new loans under very favourable terms.

FINANCING THE DEFICIT

The deficit is to be financed from external (25 per cent) and domestic (75 per cent) sources. The sources of external financing are further debt rescheduling, new loans and undisbursed funds. Barring a serious breakdown in relations with multilateral and donor agencies, which would delay disbursements or lead to further cancellations of loans, the amount of foreign financing should be secure.

The World Bank has, however, predicted yet another difficult year for Indonesia and indicated that without significant progress US$1.3 billion of CGI loans will not be disbursed because conditions will not have been met. The major conditions relate to privatisation of state-owned enterprises and asset recoveries under IBRA. The World Bank's sobering conclusion is based on what it terms a realistic assessment given 'strong vested interests, weak institutions, ambitious decentralisation, and the turbulent transition to democracy' (www.worldbank. or.id).

It is the question of domestic financing and domestic debt that remains problematic. All three sources of domestic financing – privatisation, asset sales and bond issues – are subject to great uncertainty. The amount to be raised by privatisation (Rp 6.5 trillion) will not be met this year, and the target for 2002 has been lowered to Rp 3.9 trillion. The target for IBRA asset sales has also been lowered, from Rp 27 trillion to Rp 21.5 trillion. The amount of recapitalisation bonds remains large and 25 per cent of revenue is used to make interest payments on domestic bonds alone. For every 1 percentage point rise in interest rates, the deficit expands by 0.15 per cent of GDP, increasing the contingent liabilities for the government as banks face greater risk and a greater need for recapitalisation (World Bank 2001a: 7).

SERIOUSNESS OF THE DEBT OVERHANG[2]

The size of government and private debt has reached alarming proportions since the financial crisis. Total government debt has almost tripled from US$55 billion (27 per cent of GDP) in 1996 to around US$141 billion (95 per cent of GDP) currently, the bulk of it the massive domestic debt incurred through the issuance of US$70–80 billion in government bonds to recapitalise the banking system (Figure 4.3). There is in fact a danger that there will be a further need for bank recapitalisation, given that meaningful restructuring did not precede recapitalisation, the privatisation of banks taken over by the state has been slow and banks that should have been closed have remained open. At present the impact of domestic debt is felt through interest payments, which already account for 25 per cent of domestic revenues. But beginning in 2002, the government will face repayments of principal. These will reach more than Rp 52 trillion (18 per cent of current government revenues) in 2004 and peak at Rp 74 trillion (26 per cent of current revenues) in 2007. For 2002, the government is planning to replace bonds as they mature with ones of longer maturity.

Rescheduling of external debt through Paris Club I and II negotiations has

Figure 4.3 Explosion of Government Debt, 1997–2000 (US$ billion)

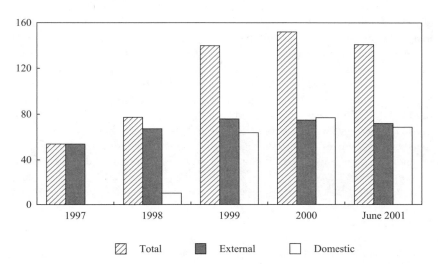

brought payments down from 37 per cent of domestic revenue in 1999 to around 16 per cent at present. However, from next year external debt service payments will be higher, at US$10 billion in 2002, US$9 billion in 2003 and US$8 billion in 2004. Without continued rescheduling of debt, such payments could amount to more than 30 per cent of domestic revenue every year for the next five years. This implies that, without any change in domestic debt servicing, total debt servicing by the government would absorb all of current government revenues. Debt service payments have already crowded out development expenditures and constrained the scope for domestic stimulus, a situation that is only likely to worsen. The government therefore needs to put a comprehensive strategy in place to manage debt, including obtaining the best possible terms for external debt rescheduling (for example, the rescheduling of interest payments, not just principal) and new external loans – with all that this implies for commitment to reform and undertaking the measures required by donor nations and agencies. Such a strategy would also involve specific measures to increase domestic revenues through privatisation, asset sales and tax reforms; to deal with domestic debt by ensuring the creation of a secondary bond market; and to prevent a further expansion of domestic debt due to the failure of bank restructuring or the reform program more generally. The government must also do all it can to ensure high economic growth so that Indonesia can 'grow' out of its debt through increased incomes and tax revenues.

The debt overhang also involves the private sector. Private debt currently amounts to US$130 billion, consisting of US$63 billion in domestic debt and US$67 billion in external debt. The private debt service ratio (to exports) dropped from 50 per cent in 1998 to 29 per cent in June 2001, but remains high and will continue to put pressure on the balance of payments. Progress has been made on debt restructuring since mid-2000 under various schemes, although ultimately it was perhaps their high growth and stellar export performance in that year that gave companies the incentive to restructure their debts in order to be able to expand. Despite the progress made, the amounts to be restructured remain large. Total loans restructured comprise only 7 per cent of non-performing loans, and half of the cases under IBRA or the Jakarta Initiative are still at the memorandum of understanding (MOU) stage. Therefore, there is still an urgent need for aggressive restructuring of private sector debt so that the domestic economy can grow.

FRAGILE EXTERNAL BALANCE

Indonesia is facing an increasingly unfavourable balance of payments situation, especially after the record trade performance of last year. Following a sharp decline, export growth climbed to unprecedented highs in 2000, peaking at 27 per cent by year end. Annualised growth rates began to decline in the first half of 2001, and had fallen to just 10 per cent by June (Figure 4.4). The value of monthly exports continued to decline, and by September 2001 the annualised growth rate was close to zero.

Growth of oil exports declined dramatically from 45 per cent at the end of 2000 to just 3 per cent by September 2001. Compared with the same period in the previous year, oil exports actually contracted by 3 per cent in the January–September period, mainly due to declines in volume resulting from lower OPEC quotas. Non-oil exports have also declined sharply, whether measured as the January–September 2001 period compared with the same period in the previous year (a decline of close to 6 per cent) or as annualised growth to September (a contraction of nearly 1 per cent). Indonesia has less exposure to electronic products – the sector worst hit by the US and global economic downturn – than the other East Asian economies, softening the impact of the contraction in non-oil exports. Nevertheless, all major non-oil product groups experienced a decline in growth compared with the same period in 2000. With the oil price dropping precipitously from US$24 per barrel in September to US$17 per barrel in November, figures for the last quarter of 2001 are expected to show a further deterioration in exports.

The decline in demand will be felt more sharply in the last quarter of 2001 due to the September terrorist attacks on the United States, despite what is usually higher seasonal demand. Overall, exports are projected to contract in value

Figure 4.4 Export and Import Growth, December 1997 – September 2001 (%)

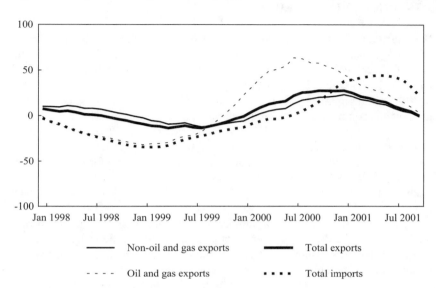

this year compared with last year. The situation is likely to worsen in 2002, especially in the first half of the year, since any recovery in the US economy will only begin to be felt – at the earliest – in the third or fourth quarter. With Japan already in recession, the impact of the world economic downturn is being felt by all the East Asian economies.

Import growth has also fallen back from the high rates experienced in 2000, but remains relatively high. Imports grew by 38 per cent last year and continued to increase into mid-2001, peaking in June at 43 per cent before dropping back sharply to 22 per cent as of September (Figure 4.4). As can be expected there is a lag between the slowdown in exports and the downturn in demand for imports used in intermediate products. Imports of capital goods remain robust.

With exports diminishing in volume and value, and continued positive growth rates for imports, the trade balance is likely to be much lower in 2001 than in 2000. Meanwhile, the need to service debt will mean a greater deficit in the services account, as well as continued net capital outflows. Net capital outflows for the first quarter of 2001 were close to US$3 billion; for the year as a whole they are projected to be around US$9.5 billion, the same as in 2000 (World Bank 2001b). Bearing in mind the current tenuous external balance situation and the prospect that it may worsen next year, it is crucial that the government acts to restore confidence and revive both foreign and domestic investment.

BANK RESTRUCTURING: FURTHER CONSOLIDATION AND RESTRUCTURING NEEDED

Bank restructuring to date has involved closure of unviable institutions, mergers of banks owned or taken over by the government, removal of non-performing loans from the balance sheets of banks, and recapitalisation of state banks and banks under IBRA by the end of 2000. The number of banks has fallen from 238 to 149, and the number of branches from 7,781 to 6,628. The post-crisis banking system is dominated by the four state-owned banks (one of which is a merger of four state-owned banks) and the banks directly under IBRA (four that have been nationalised and seven that have been jointly recapitalised by the government and the original owners), so that the state now accounts for close to three-quarters of the assets in the banking system. In recent times there have been further mergers, with Bank Mandiri taking over the troubled Bank Internasional Indonesia.

The banking system faces a number of problems. First, the growth of new credit remains slow, as banks can earn a good margin on deposits by placing them in SBIs bearing higher interest, without affecting their capital adequacy requirements. The slow recovery and cumbersome debt-restructuring process has also affected new lending. Second, although many banks have been recapitalised, the lack of a bond market means that there is little cash for them to channel out as loans. The situation is worse for banks with a higher proportion of fixed interest rate bonds: the very low interest rates on the bonds is eroding their profit margins and affecting their capital base. Third, there are a number of banks that will not meet the 8 per cent capital adequacy requirement set by the central bank, making further closures or mergers likely. It is not inconceivable that another round of recapitalisation may be needed. To avoid this, there must be further consolidations among banks, complete management restructuring and a strengthening of the central bank's capacity to enforce prudential requirements. Fourth, while there has been a fall in the number of non-performing loans, not much is known about the underlying quality of many loans. Given deteriorating economic conditions, the number of non-performing loans could rise once again. Fifth, despite the merger and recapitalisation of the original state banks, the process of organisational and operational restructuring – and of changing the incentive system – is still at an early stage. The state banks will only become sound when this process has been successfully completed.

CONCLUSION

Indonesia has come a long way since the total crisis it experienced in 1998. The new government of President Megawati offered some hope after many months of uncertainty and unpredictability under President Aburrahman Wahid, the blind president who called many bluffs. However, three months later the honeymoon is over and it is clear that the same overwhelming economic and institutional challenges remain, with little prospect of any decisive action being taken to begin to resolve them. At the same time the government must manage social problems and the massive task of decentralisation.

Indonesia's social and labour problems are by no means minor, and place a political constraint on policy-making. Based on the BPS national poverty line, the proportion of people living in poverty declined slightly over the 1999–2000 period, from 23.5 to 22 per cent. However, this still amounts to some 30 million people, and the numbers of near-poor, living just above the poverty line, are great. While open unemployment rates are low, there is a high degree of underemployment and increased concerns about labour issues, with implications for future labour absorption. The answer lies in instituting credible poverty and employment creation programs, and tackling labour issues by bringing all stakeholders together to find a solution.

The transition towards decentralisation is still continuing. The major issue remains implementation, and how to balance the demand for regional autonomy against the capacity of the regions to carry out new functions and deliver basic public services. The regions have not been granted new revenue-raising powers and remain dependent on central government transfers. They have, nevertheless, been enthusiastic in raising the level of local taxes and levies, but this has not been matched by commensurate improvements in the provision of services. Another major issue is the lack of clear guidelines setting out the relationship between the different layers of government – central, provincial and district (SMERU 2001).

The major challenge for the government is to come up with a short-term action plan to respond to the issues at hand. There are no magic formulas or shortcuts. The immediate task is to restore confidence and change perceptions and expectations, in order to attract badly needed capital back into the country. This will be crucial to alleviate pressure on the balance of payments, bring down interest rates and encourage investment as a source of growth. The government will need to give credible signals – in both the short and the longer term – that it is accelerating the implementation of the reform agenda and that it is committed to good governance and open economic policies.

Megawati and her cabinet must act decisively to coordinate the cabinet and the various parts of government, and to garner the support of parliament and other stakeholders to agree on priorities. At the general level, this must be followed by systemic improvements in decision-making and organisation of economic policies – especially with regard to privatisation, asset sales and debt management – and action to address political, legal and security issues. In addition, the government needs to take specific action to implement tax reform, alleviate poverty and address the difficulties faced by the private sector, for instance with regard to labour issues (CSIS 2001b).

NOTES

1   See Pangestu and Goeltom (2001) for more details.
2   See Pangestu, Feridhanusetyawan and Roesad (2001) for more details.

5   FURTHER COMMENTS ON THE
    ECONOMY, WITH A GENDER
    PERSPECTIVE

Mohammad Sadli

Mari Pangestu's chapter on the Indonesian economy in 2000 needs very little comment. It is an excellent account of economic developments since the last volume in this series was published (Bird 2001). Perhaps I can offer some slightly different perspectives on some of the major issues. Let me give some comments on the issues raised by Mari and then turn briefly to the question of gender, equity and development.

GENERAL COMMENTS ON THE ECONOMY

Economic Growth

There is no reason to revise the 3–3.5 per cent growth forecast for the year (writing at the start of December 2001). Apart from the numerical figure, there is a common perception that 2001 has not been a better year for the economy than 2000 (following the prospect much earlier of a steady recovery from 1999). Hopefully this is just a temporary setback, caused mainly by external circumstances such as the weakening of the global economy and the impact of the September 11 tragedy.

If Indonesia achieves 3.5 per cent growth in 2001, it will be the strongest large economy in Southeast Asia outside Vietnam – stronger, that is, than Singapore, Malaysia, Thailand and the Philippines. This is because of the size of the domestic economy and Indonesia's lesser dependence on export products such as electronics, which have become the Achilles' heel of our neighbours. Export growth in Indonesia has, however, slowed down, aggravated by the collapse of international oil and gas prices.

Domestic investments are still forthcoming but there has been little response from the major foreign investment players, who have been scared off by confused central government policies, by perceived lack of physical security at the plant or project site, and also by the prevailing weakness in the judicial system. Foreign investment approvals have skydived, and also the degree of implementation.

But there have been many small and medium-scale domestic investments to restore capacity and take advantage of new opportunities. Many of the investors do not take the trouble to go to the Investment Board (BKPM) – one can see the results in developments in Jakarta and other large cities. This is partly domestic Chinese capital parked in Singapore or Hong Kong whose owners have ongoing businesses in Indonesia. Encouraged by buoyant domestic demand they import new machines or start building new shops, shopping centres or even malls. Some of the building cranes that virtually disappeared during the crisis are back. That is an encouraging sight as one drives around Jakarta. During the current recession owners of capital can get interest of only around 2 per cent per annum if they deposit their money in banks abroad, but far greater returns if they plough it back into Indonesia. For companies regarded as sufficiently bona fide under the new circumstances, I have been told that a 7 per cent rate of return on US dollars is available.

The import figures have been weakening lately (to somewhat over US$2 billion a month, whereas US$3 billion and over would have been normal pre-crisis). However, it is uncertain whether this signals lower capital goods imports or reduced imports of raw materials for exports. Another question is whether domestic demand remains robust, as in the past two years, or whether consumer confidence has started to weaken. Demand may remain high until the end of the year, thanks to two peak demand seasons in succession, Idul Fitri marking the end of Ramadan on 17 December, followed by Christmas. Domestic demand could then fall.

Inflation and Monetary Policies

In general I agree with Mari Pangestu that inflation is too high. The inflation figure for November 2001 was 1.7 per cent, with year-on-year inflation running at close to 13 per cent. Inflation may be higher in December, with its dual celebration of the end of Ramadan and Christmas, and hence the rate for 2001 could well end up being of the order of 13–14 per cent. This is significantly higher that the target of 9–11 per cent.

There has been a running battle between the IMF and Bank Indonesia about how to manage inflation, with the IMF stressing that the central bank's control of base money has been too lax. Bank Indonesia governors, for their part, have insisted that the culprit was the continuing decline in the value of the rupiah, fuelled by political factors. They felt that the economy needed greater liquidity to cope with imported inflation. Lately, however, Bank Indonesia has given in to IMF pressure and promised to tighten up the money supply.

An inflation rate of 13–14 per cent for 2001 represents a serious slippage, but it is not a calamity if it helps to buoy consumer spending and if monetary policies are tightened as the IMF insists. The real sector has constantly been complaining about being pinched by the high rates of interest set by Bank Indonesia – SBI rates are about 17.5 per cent per annum. With inflation running at 13–14 per cent, these SBI rates are actually not too high. The lack of lending to the real sector has been caused more by the lingering trauma felt by banks due to the pile-up of bad debts during the crisis, and by the current insistence that banks meet prudential requirements.

Fiscal Sustainability and the Debt Overhang

Mari Pangestu is right about the huge challenge posed by domestic debt. A strong government is needed to prevail in face of opposing parliamentary and public opinion. Mari stresses that 'tremendous political will' is required. Another view is more pragmatic. The government should deploy greater skill in communicating with the general public, including the parliament and the political elite, about its policies, intentions and programs. In other words, it should develop greater persuasive powers. In the end, President Megawati cannot remain silent or aloof on important economic matters. The effectiveness of the government, or cabinet, need not be based on political (that is, party) strength, because the composition and nature of a presidential system do not make this a realistic proposition. But better coordination between the chief ministers (the so-called Menko), and between them and the whole cabinet and top bureaucracy, must be forthcoming and is achievable.

The US presidency, for example, has its own strong support system (consisting of councils, staff members and so on). Unfortunately, the Indonesian system is probably a bad combination of a parliamentary and a presidential system. Members of the DPR, when accused of too much meddling in executive affairs, often assert that it is their job to control and supervise the executive. However, if the government were more vocal, clear and positive in its stance, then members of parliament might respect it more.

As Mari notes, short and medium-term fiscal sustainability now looks difficult to achieve, especially against the backdrop of a huge debt overhang. External debt relief depends very much on the goodwill of the international creditors. At the moment Indonesia is being helped out by Paris Club debt rescheduling, but on a yearly basis.

On the other hand, Indonesia is not entirely devoid of trump cards. It is the biggest country in Asia after China, and historically the lynch pin of ASEAN. These things count. It is not a less developed country existing without much hope, like so many African nations. During the 32-year reign of President Soe-harto Indonesia had the capacity to manage its economy reasonably well, pro-ducing better than 6 per cent growth on average. Professional capabilities are still there. As a matter of fact, human resources in aggregate are now numerically greater than 30 years ago.

The big difference is that the governance system has to find a new equilib-rium in a much more democratic environment. There may be more years of 'muddling through' in the process of learning by doing, but pressures from the donor community, and especially the IMF with its Letters of Intent, may do the trick in the end.

Indonesia deserves more credit for what has been achieved so far on the road to fiscal sustainability. First, since the Habibie period there has been a law to guarantee the independence of Bank Indonesia. The sole mission of the central bank is to control inflation, and it cannot advance money to the government to finance the budget deficit. Second, there is political consensus, embedded in laws, that the large subsidies on domestic fuels and electricity (still running at some 4 per cent of GDP) should be phased out by the end of 2003. The ratio of domestic taxes to GDP should be raised from 11 per cent of GDP to the ASEAN standard of 16 per cent.

The remaining stumbling block is the privatisation of state enterprises. So far the results have been nil. As Mari shows, the sale of assets under IBRA, the bank restructuring agency, has seen some progress, but this is a less ideologically and politically sensitive area. Privatisation became bogged down because too many authorities had a say in the process. Besides this there were two dilemmas: would the price be right at the time of disposal, and what should be done about the original owners of the assets, the much despised conglomerates? The latter have not paid their huge debts to IBRA. Should they be permitted, directly or by proxy, to buy back their old assets and enjoy them after the balance sheets have been cleaned up? I leave this dilemma for you to ponder on.

THE GENDER DIMENSION

Mari Pangestu does not touch on the gender dimension of economic policies in her chapter. In reviewing the economic situation of Indonesia over the last year, where might gender have played a role? Perhaps in two aspects: first, in the rise of Megawati Sukarnoputri as president; and second, in the main economic poli-cies of her government.

The Gender Aspect in Megawati's Presidency and Government

Was the ascendancy of Megawati Sukarnoputri as president due to gender? No, it was because of her role as the leader of her party, the Indonesian Democratic

Party of Struggle (PDI-P). And how did she become the leader of the party? This clearly had much more to do with her surname (Sukarnoputri), and her being the oldest child of former President Sukarno, than with her sex. The PDI-P is an amalgam of nationalist parties, and the first president of the country was of course a strong charismatic unifying force, especially with the crowd and the masses – that is, the electorate.

But why, one may wonder, didn't any of the sons of 'Bung Karno' or Megawati's younger sister Rachmawati – who is much more politically vocal, and ideologically closer to her father – become the leader of the PDI-P? After all, Megawati was better known as a sheltered palace girl at the time her father occupied the Merdeka Palace. She was a first year drop-out of the Psychology Department of the University of Indonesia; and as a married woman she had the tastes and habits of a regular middle-class housewife, enjoying social life and frequenting national day receptions held by the Jakarta diplomatic community. Her political career is said to have been influenced by her husband, Taufik Kiemas, who had always been a party stalwart and at some point encouraged her to accept the leadership of the party. Sukarno's sons have never had any political ambitions and would prefer that the family stayed out of politics altogether. Why Rachmawati did not make the grade is more difficult to explain, but her health is fragile, and she probably did not have the right sponsors.

As party leader Megawati passed several tests of perseverance, starting from when she had to survive the machinations of the Soeharto regime to prevent her from assuming the leadership at all. The New Order government intervened to promote Suryadi over Megawati as the winning candidate in the election for leadership of the (earlier) Indonesian Democratic Party (PDI). The Megawati faction then split from the PDI to form the PDI-P – aptly, the final 'P' stands for *perjuangan* (struggle). In the 1999 general elections the original PDI lost out completely while the PDI-P gained one-third of the votes to become the largest party. This must have had something to do with the charisma and power of Megawati's name.

Megawati in her own way has proven leadership qualities and has passed three survival and leadership tests – the first at the Medan PDI convention, the second during the storming of the PDI-P headquarters in Jakarta in 1996, and the third at the Bali convention two years later when she consolidated her leadership.

Her knowledge of economics was practically nil. But, she once retorted, why should a housewife not understand economics when she has to make ends meet every month using just ordinary common sense? President Abdurrahman Wahid entrusted her to chair the weekly cabinet sessions on economic affairs. In that capacity she became concerned about the stand-off between the government and the IMF dating from December 2000. She observed the impact this was having on Indonesia in a constantly declining rupiah exchange rate.

However, rather than turn to her ministers for an explanation (at the time the

Coordinating Minister for Economic Affairs was Rizal Ramli), she spoke to 'Uncle Frans Seda', whom she knew as somebody close to her father. Frans Seda had held several ministerial positions, including the post of Finance Minister during the last year of Sukarno and first year of Soeharto. He advised her to call in Professors Widjojo Nitisastro and Emil Salim, who had a great deal of experience in working with the IMF. Widjojo would be able to explain to her in simple terms (as he had done with Soeharto) what the problem was about. Megawati asked them for help in contacting the IMF to inquire about a return to normal relations. The IMF presented a few preconditions, which she was able to arrange through her Finance Minister and her cadre in parliament. In June IMF officials made a visit to Jakarta. This eventually led to the restoration of normal relations and the signing of a new Letter of Intent with the IMF in August 2001, soon after Megawati became president.

The complaint of the women's movement is that Megawati is not sufficiently gender conscious. She has never tried to politicise gender issues, or asked women for their electoral support. Her predecessor, Abdurrahman Wahid, was probably more gender conscious than she is. He certainly had greater awareness of the gender perspective, probably due to the influence of his wife, Sinta Nuriyah, who has been active in the women's movement.

It took Megawati more than two weeks to choose her cabinet after being elected president. The women's movement tried to raise public – and also Megawati's – interest in increasing the number of women ministers from the two in Abdurrahman's cabinet (Erna Witoelar, the Minister for Housing and Regional Development, and Khofifah Indar Parawansa, the State Minister for Women's Empowerment). In the end, Megawati's cabinet also contained two women ministers, Rini Suwandi as Minister for Trade and Industry and Sri Rejeki Sumaryoto as State Minister for Women's Empowerment. Rini Suwandi was a last-minute compromise candidate put up by the National Mandate Party (PAN), while Sri Rejeki Sumaryoto was probably more of a gesture to Golkar and is completely unknown as a women's activist. The two women in Abdurrahman's cabinet were regarded as effective and the women's movement had hoped that they would be retained. After all, Megawati had got to know them while serving as vice-president in Gus Dur's administration. But politics and political considerations came to the fore when the composition of the cabinet was decided.

Megawati probably would not know what she is missing by not having a stronger female voice in her government, but in the end it may not be very relevant. Two strands of policy are very important for her government. First, she must make a firm stand against corruption – in the Indonesian terminology, KKN (*korupsi, kolusi, nepotisme*). Second, poverty alleviation is a very important cornerstone of overall policy, also heavily favoured by the donor countries.

The new president would conceivably have more moral support in her fight against corruption if she turned more to her women supporters. Under any circumstances, this struggle will be fierce and unrewarding in present-day Indonesia because of the influential vested interests that remain from the Soeharto period. The champions of the anti-corruption commitment are the media, the NGOs, the younger generation outside the government, and the international donor community. For Megawati to make strong attempts to eliminate corruption will require great moral courage and conviction. Perhaps her female colleagues in government could provide such support.

Of course, the support of women for anti-corruption measures cannot be taken for granted. It was not demonstrated by other women presidents or prime ministers in Asia. In Megawati's case, it depends on what personalities she includes in her inner circle. Male leaders of political parties and technocrats have not distinguished themselves as uncompromising crusaders against corruption, with the exception of Kwik Kian Gie, the Minister for Planning from the PDI-P. But his outbursts are like the cries of a lonely wolf in the desert.

Gender Mainstreaming

With respect to poverty alleviation, some (including my wife, Professor Saparinah Sadli, who is an activist in the gender movement) have said that 'poverty has a female face', at least in many developing countries. Megawati might exploit this orientation.

Many poverty alleviation programs have an important gender dimension, including social safety nets, health care projects, programs to reduce the dropout rate among primary school children or to provide milk to babies, small and rural credit programs, and activities aimed at the informal sectors of the economy.

The World Bank, influenced by the women's movement in donor countries, has procedures to take the gender dimension into account. There is an officer in its Jakarta office, for instance, who must screen proposals and programs for their gender focus. In the Indonesian bureaucracy, the National Development Planning Board, Bappenas, has a unit responsible for gender mainstreaming (*pengarusutamaan jender*), and for coordinating similar units in other ministries. Women's groups and NGOs could be asked to participate in the delivery of poverty alleviation programs, and this may also help to reduce the risk of corruption down the line. Megawati should consider such a strategy. It could work to her advantage.

6   INSTITUTION BUILDING: AN EFFORT TO IMPROVE INDONESIAN WOMEN'S ROLE AND STATUS

Khofifah Indar Parawansa

Efforts to improve women's role and status in Indonesia began long ago. In each period of history – colonial, post-independence, New Order and post-New Order – the women's movement has revealed its own dynamism, whether the initiative has come from the people or from the government. The movement started from a spirit of struggle – against polygamy, and for the education of women. Since 1999, when the era of transition to democracy began, the motivation has changed to empowering women to achieve gender equity and equality. This goal reflects the emphasis in today's Indonesia on strengthening civil society by enabling people to manage their own affairs.

THE SITUATION BEFORE INDEPENDENCE

Throughout its history Indonesia has had women leaders who were famous for their wisdom and tough queens who ruled over their kingdoms for extended periods, including Tri Buana Tungga Dewi. In the 19th century a few well-known women participated actively in the fight against colonialism, among them Cut Nyak Dien, Cut Mutiah, Marta Christina Tiyahahu and Nyi Ageng Serang.

During the colonial era, the struggle to improve the condition of women focused on the provision of education for women, which was felt to be a prerequisite for national liberation. The other main issues uniting women activists of the time were their opposition to polygamy, and to restrictions on women's activities in the public domain.

As the number of women supporting the endeavour to improve women's role and status grew, their efforts were institutionalised in the first women's organisation, Poetri Mardika. Established in 1912, Poetri Mardika was supported by the first independence organisation for men, Budi Oetomo. The fight by the early

feminist, Kartini, against feudalism and colonialism (the source of much suffering for Indonesian women) inspired the creation of more women's organisations,
many of them based on religion, ethnicity or region.

In the spirit of national integration, a more broad-based umbrella organisation of 20 women's groups was established at the first National Women's Congress, which was held on 22–26 December 1928. The congress attracted the
participation of 31 women's organisations from all regions of Indonesia, and
passed an important resolution calling for improvements to women's access to
education and the provision of better information at the time of marriage on
women's divorce rights.

During this era, the ideal of the 'good wife and mother' was firmly
entrenched in Indonesia; a good woman should be able to manage her family and
home well. Thus any effort to improve the condition of women necessarily
involved improving their capacity to manage their responsibilities in the domestic domain. 'Woman' was synonomous with 'wife', as implicitly understood in
the name change of the principal women's federation in 1929 from Perikatan
Perempuan Indonesia (Indonesian Women's Association) to Persatuan
Perkumpulan Isteri Indonesia, or PPII (Union of Indonesian Wives' Associations). This organisation for wives openly published its support for nationalism,
something the 1928 congress had not done.

In 1941, the National Women's Congress announced its support for the
demand by Indonesian political groups that a parliament be established as a
means to improve political representation. Universal education was supported by
both sexes, as it was recognised that women would be an important element in
liberating the country from colonial rule, and that educated women would be
more likely to support the freedom struggle. Since the two issues of women's
emancipation and national emancipation were closely related, and the women's
movement was supported by the independence movement, at this time women's
organisations received little if any support from the colonial regime.

It was not until the period of Japanese colonisation (1942–46) that an
'Indonesian' women's organisation was first supported by the ruling regime.
Fujinkai, established by the Japanese, was the only such organisation permitted
under the regime. Its purpose was to disseminate colonial propaganda on Japan's
concept of a 'Greater East Asia Co-prosperity Sphere'. Although all other
women's organisations were banned from carrying out public activities, many
continued to operate clandestinely.

THE SITUATION AFTER INDEPENDENCE

In 1945, the overwhelming national interest to defend Indonesia's newly proclaimed independence deflected attention from women's issues. Nevertheless, the National Women's Congress continued to develop relationships with women's organisations abroad. In time, the Indonesian government gained international recognition. The newly independent government accommodated women's interests by, for example, training a few women to do police work such as body searches of women crossing into areas controlled by the republic. Women's political organisations were established, and wives' organisations, including those associated with national defence institutions, flourished.

When the Republic of Indonesia gained recognition as an integrated country in 1949, the women's movement was considered an important part of the nationalist movement. But it was not long before women's issues became marginalised: in 1952, for example, the government promulgated Regulation No. 19 permitting polygamy, despite the vigorous campaign women had conducted against this practice for so many years. After the 1955 election, issues raised by the women's movement were largely disregarded.

Nonetheless the acceptance in 1957 of ILO Equal Remuneration Convention No. 100 (1951) under Law No. 80/1957, to adopt the principle of 'equal wages for women and men for equal work', could be interpreted as government concern for women's work conditions. Furthermore, the government allowed the development of women's organisations as part of political parties. One example was Gerwani, a communist-led mass organisation whose goals of countering colonialism, feudalism, imperialism and capitalism were supported by a membership of educated women with high political aspirations. Five members of Gerwani were elected to parliament as Communist Party (PKI) representatives in the 1955 elections, as were five members of Muslimat, the women's wing of the mass Islamic organisation, Nahdlatul Ulama (NU).

WOMEN'S ISSUES UNDER THE NEW ORDER GOVERNMENT

Following the fall of President Sukarno in 1965, Indonesia experienced a period of very high inflation of the order of 600 per cent. As a result, women's issues were once again pushed out of the public arena. The focus of Sukarno's successor, President Soeharto, was on improving economic conditions. The new government succeeded in its economic stabilisation policies, bringing inflation down to single-digit levels by 1969 and setting the preconditions for continued economic growth. Such success gave the government the power to be the most important agent of development.

During the New Order era, the central government was so powerful that it was able to intervene in the activities of all other political agents. The largest and most powerful women's organisations were those established and supported by the central government – the Family Welfare Movement (PKK), Dharma Wanita and Dharma Pertiwi (see Oey Gardiner, Chapter 9, and Marcoes, Chapter 15).

These organisations were designed to allow wives to further their husbands' careers, and were an important vehicle for government propaganda on development.

It is implicit that the government vision was similar to that of the colonial regime: women's issues predominantly concerned their position as wives and mothers. Government policies on women did not address their advancement as such but rather improvement of their status within the family. Nevertheless, it was in this era that a regulation was first implemented requiring government officials to obtain the permission of both their first wife (in accord with the 1974 Marriage Law) and their work supervisor to take a second wife, or face sanctions at work.

In 1978, in response to the United Nations' declaration of the Decade for Women (1975–85), the government established the Ministry for the Role of Women. Its mission was to increase women's capacity to manage their dual role (*peran ganda*) in the domestic and public spheres. The word 'women' was first used in the 1978 Broad Guidelines on State Policy (GBHN) – the term 'gender' was not introduced until 1999. In 1995, the effort to improve women's capacity was strengthened further through Decree No. 17/1995 issued by the Minister of Home Affairs. This instructed district (*kabupaten*) and provincial governments to establish the Women in Development Management Teams (Tim P2W). Tim P2W were set up to coordinate the women's programs of the various government departments and act as an extension of the Ministry for the Role of Women in the regions (as a state ministry it had no formal representation in the regions). This was followed in 1996 by Presidential Instruction No. 5/1996, which appointed the vice-governor of each province and the secretary of each district to chair the Tim P2W.

The New Order government's support for women was reflected in its ratification of several international conventions and agreements on women, including the UN Convention on Political Rights of Women (under Law No. 68/1968) and the Convention on the Elimination of All Forms of Discrimination against Women (Law No. 7/1984). It endorsed the resolutions of the International Conference on Social Development in Copenhagen in 1994, International Conference on Population and Development in Cairo in 1994 and Fourth World Conference on Women in Beijing in 1995.

Nevertheless, women remained firmly subordinate to men. Even though organising the domestic domain was held to be the task of women, they were not fully empowered to act even in household decision-making. Men were the beneficiaries of most government development programs. While in the latter part of the New Order women were given access to some of these programs, the budgets allocated to them were very small compared with the overall budgets for programs accessed mainly by men. The productive activities of women were regarded as 'side jobs' to supplement the husband's income, and the time spent on non-household activities was secondary to household tasks. In the domain of politics, female representation in the legislature did not reflect women's actual advancement because most women politicians were appointed on the basis of their connections with prominent men.

Development did bring progress for women. For example, the success of family planning programs freed women to enter the public domain, in retail and labour markets, while improvements to transport infrastructure increased their mobility. Government programs to reduce poverty led to a fall in the number of poor, and the maternal mortality ratio dropped from 549 per 100,000 mothers in 1986 to 308 in 1998. Life expectancy for women rose from 63 years in 1990 to 67 years in 1998, compared with an increase from 60 to 63 years for men. Women's participation in education began to catch up with that of men, particularly during the first nine years of schooling, which were compulsory for both girls and boys.

The National Family Planning Coordination Agency (BKKBN), under the motto 'small and prosperous family', had a direct influence on family lifestyles. As the average number of children per family fell, women experienced better health and had more time for their own self-advancement and self-actualisation. When the first family planning programs were introduced in the early 1970s, the total fertility rate was 5.61; by 1997 this had fallen to 2.78.

WOMEN'S ISSUES IN THE TRANSITION TO DEMOCRACY

The democratic values introduced under Soeharto's successor, B.J. Habibie, were continued by Abdurrahman Wahid in 1999–2000. A democrat, he disseminated the need to empower civil society by letting people manage their own affairs.

The monetary crisis and general economic crisis that followed led to the collapse of many the conglomerates that had dominated Indonesia's economic activities since the mid-New Order era. Micro, small and medium-scale economic units, whose endurance had been tested by hardship, now received greater government attention. The number of women entrepreneurs – who tend to be engaged mainly in micro and small enterprises – increased.

The opening of the transition period gave Indonesians the opportunity to reposition themselves. This has certainly been true of the relationship between women and men. Freedom of speech encouraged people to express their opinions and aspirations, especially in urban areas. Consequently, the number of non-government organisations (NGOs) representing women's interests and demands has greatly increased.

A new approach based on gender analysis was introduced in the 1999 GBHN. This stated that 'empowering women is achieved by improving women's role and status in national life through national policy implemented by institutions that struggle for the actualisation of gender equality and justice', and sets the goal to 'improve the quality and the role and self-reliance of women's organisations by maintaining the value of integration and the historical value of women's struggle in continuing to empower women and society'.

The machinery to achieve these aims has not yet been developed, and to date the implementation of laws to protect women has been gender-biased. Penalties for rape, for example, tend to be minimal, and there is no law on witness protection in rape cases. The Women's Ministry has compiled a book of jurisprudence on violence against women, to be used as a reference work in court verdicts on this matter.

The change of name in 1999 from State Ministry for the Role of Women to State Ministry for Women's Empowerment heralded a renewed determination to achieve more equitable treatment for women in the family, society and nation. Among the challenges facing the ministry are patriarchal social values embedded in such legislation as the Marriage Law, Law on Citizenship and Law on Population, particularly in the context of the national family planning program (see Hull and Adioetomo, Chapter 19). About 19 laws are acknowledged to be gender-biased.

Such patriarchal values are also evident in the bureaucratic structure, both civil and military. Women hold only 7 per cent of executive positions in the civil service (that is, echelons I and II) – and there are very few high-ranking women in the military. In politics, women's representation stands at about 9.2 per cent in the legislature (DPR) and 9 per cent in the general assembly (MPR) (see Oey-Gardiner, Chapter 9).

Religious teachings have strongly influenced society's mind-set and the way of life in Indonesia. Unfortunately, many *ulama* (Muslim religious scholars), preachers and religious leaders do not have enlightened views on gender. Even though the new president of Indonesia is a woman, gender mainstreaming will still be required to effect a change in attitude.

It is not clear whether regional autonomy, implemented from 1 January 2001, will restrain women's advancement or open up new channels for them to communicate their aspirations to a closer, local level of government. One of the unexpected consequences of decentralisation has been the proposal in a few regions – such as West Sumatra and East Java (see Noerdin, Chapter 14) – to introduce regulations to prevent women going out at night, supposedly for reasons of safety.

The reinvigorated Women's Ministry has been collaborating actively with women's organisations, religious organisations, NGOs, professional associations, political parties and other institutions with an interest in women's affairs. A major outcome has been the National Plan of Action to empower women, running from 2000 to 2004. The plan covers five key areas: (1) improving women's quality of life, (2) raising awareness of justice and equity issues nationwide, (3) eliminating violence against women, (4) protecting the human rights of women and (5) strengthening women's institutions.

Improving Women's Quality of Life

During the Abdurrahman presidency, the State Minister for Women's Empowerment was also the chair of BKKBN; at this time its motto was changed from 'small and prosperous family' to 'quality family'. Under the National Plan of Action, the BKKBN has sought to increase male participation in family planning programs, with the pleasing result that this increased from 1.1 per cent in 1999 to 1.8 per cent in 2000. It is expected to increase further to 2.6 per cent in 2001 and 8 per cent in 2005 (see Hull and Adioetomo, Chapter 19).

The Ministry for Women's Empowerment also has responsibility for child protection and welfare. In cooperation with NGOs, over the past two years it has conducted a program to reduce the maternal and infant mortality rates; an initiative to increase women's bargaining position in household decision-making by expanding the income-generating opportunities available to them; and – in the context of increased regional autonomy – a capacity-building program to improve women's skills and knowledge, and develop networks (including business networks) to facilitate their access to regional decision-making.

In the area of women's economic empowerment, the BKKBN has instituted a program to increase family incomes through micro-credit initiatives and other activities aimed at small women-entrepreneurs; the Ministry of Resettlement and Regional Infrastructure has developed a rescue program for women who lost their jobs during the crisis; and the Ministry of Fisheries and Maritime Affairs is helping women in the relatively poorer and less developed coastal areas through its Coastal Women's Empowerment program.

Raising Awareness of Justice and Equity Issues

The State Ministry for Women's Empowerment is supported in its efforts to raise the profile of gender issues by Presidential Instruction No. 9/2000, which states that all government departments, including regional bureaucracies, are to conduct gender mainstreaming. This has been followed by capacity-building programs for departments and regions, including within the ministry itself. These have the primary goal of changing the underlying culture of the civil service by creating widespread awareness of gender issues, particularly among those responsible for making and implementing policy.

Eleven focal points (that is, bureaucratic positions with responsibility for the dissemination of gender-mainstreaming programs and for facilitating communication) have been established in the line ministries. These are located in the National Development Planning Board (Bappenas), the Ministry of Health, the Ministry of Justice and Human Rights, the Ministry of Home Affairs, the Ministry of National Education, the Ministry of Religious Affairs, the Ministry of Agriculture, the Ministry of Manpower and Transmigration, the State Ministry for Cooperatives and Small and Medium-scale Enterprises, the State Ministry for the Environment and the Coordinating Ministry for Political and Security Affairs.

The Women's Ministry is collaborating with the Central Bureau of Statistics (BPS) to produce a series of statistical books and indicators on gender so that progress can be monitored. The provision of disaggregated data is expected to help decision-makers develop policy that takes account of the needs of women. Two national-level statistical volumes were published in December 2000 to coincide with Hari Ibu (Mothers' Day), followed by four provincial-level volumes in 2001. Sixteen provincial officials and representatives of women's studies centres are currently being trained in statistical techniques, with more to follow. It is expected that within two years all the provinces will be equipped to publish disaggregated data based on the national model (see Surbakti, Chapter 17).

Eliminating Violence against Women

The State Ministry for Women's Empowerment has built a close relationship with other government departments and NGOs to develop machinery for the elimination of violence against women and children. The most important of the line of services now being offered are Special Investigation Rooms served by women police, which have been established in police stations in 19 provinces and 163 districts and cities; facilities in health centres and some hospitals to provide medical help for the victims of violence; and women's crisis centres provided by *pesantren* (Islamic boarding schools) and NGOs (see Marcoes, Chapter 15, and Baso and Idrus, Chapter 16).

Protecting Women's Human Rights

The protection of human rights needs to be extended to internally displaced persons. Their numbers have risen to over one million, more than half of them women and children. The women are potential targets of violence and harassment and at high risk of reproductive health problems. Moreover, the sanitation in the refugee camps is very poor. Many NGOs have developed trauma-counselling centres to serve the women and children in the camps, and help them manage under these difficult circumstances.

Strengthening Women's Institutions

Women's institutions are an important vehicle for increasing community participation in gender equity programs. A network of religious women has been
formed to raise awareness of issues related to gender equity and justice, and of
the peril of drugs. The State Ministry for Women's Empowerment has strengthened its collaboration with women's studies centres. There are now 84 such centres in state and private universities throughout the country. It has also welcomed
NGO involvement in its working groups – in training, research and other activities such as Hari Ibu celebrations.

The ministry has supported the development of women's networking in politics, leading to the establishment of caucuses for women politicians at the
national and, to a lesser extent, provincial level. The ministry has proposed a
quota of 30 per cent for women in the top two echelons of the bureaucracy and
in the legislature. This is now being considered by many government organisations, including the Ministry of Home Affairs, which is responsible for local
government. The same quota has been proposed for the recruitment of civil and
military leaders, including the top management of training institutions in the
civil service, police and military.

At the regional level, there has been an increase in the number of women's
units in the bureaucracy. Before the implementation of regional autonomy, 16
provinces had a high-level civil servant at the head of their bureau for women.
With the reorganisation and mergers of institutions that have taken place since
then, there are now only eight provinces with an executive-level head of bureau.
Other provinces have appointed lower-level officials to manage their women's
units. The New Order government's Tim P2W (see above), now revitalised as
Women's Empowerment Teams, are active at the regional, provincial, district
and city government levels.

Organisations for 'wives' have changed their names and aspirations in line
with the new dynamic of reform. The PKK, for example, has changed its name
from Pembinaan Kesejahteraan Keluarga (Family Welfare Movement) to Pemberdayaan Kesejahteraan Keluarga (Family Welfare Empowerment Movement)
(see Marcoes, Chapter 15).

Post-New Order governments have introduced new measures directed at
women, and revived old ones submerged by the previous regime. On 28 February 1999, Indonesia ratified the optional protocol of the Convention on the Elimination of All Forms of Discrimination against Women. It has also accepted ILO
Convention No. 111/1985 concerning Discrimination in Respect of Employment
and Occupation (Law No. 21/1999), which outlaws discrimination in the workplace on the basis of sex as well as other characteristics such as race, religion or
political beliefs. The State Ministry for Women's Empowerment has raised the
issue of amending the Marriage Law (Law No. 1/1974), which constrains

women's role to the domestic sphere. It has proposed that a working group of experts from the relevant departments be formed to consider how to amend the law so as to improve the lives of women. One strategy that has been suggested is to raise the minimum age at which women can marry from 16 to 18 years, the high school graduation age (the legal minimum age for men to marry is 19). This initiative has been supported by the Ministry of Home Affairs and the BKKBN, which favours an age of 21 years for women and 24 years for men.

The State Ministry for Women's Empowerment has openly raised the question of young women who have been forced to discontinue their studies after becoming pregnant. This issue has created much public debate, with some people feeling that allowing these young women to return to school would undermine moral values. However, the Ministry of Education has responded positively to the argument that these young mothers would be better equipped to provide for themselves and their babies if they could finish their education. As well as the economic benefits, this would help boost their self-confidence and let them get on with their lives.

Another group in need of targeted government assistance is women migrant workers in the informal sector. The government and NGOs have cooperated in establishing an information service centre at Jakarta airport in March 2001 to assist newly returned migrant workers (see Hugo, Chapter 13).

CONCLUSION

The initiatives described in this chapter are designed to improve the quality of Indonesian women's lives and open up new opportunities for them in the public domain. However, it is still the case that women bear primary responsibility for the family and household. In order that the end result is not simply to increase the burden on women, men must be persuaded to take on a greater share of unpaid household work.

NGOs have an important role to play in the advancement of women. Their numbers have expanded greatly in the post-New Order era; they now reach many more women than before; and they have built up capacity over a far broader spectrum of issues. Most concentrate on a particular area, such as protection of women's rights, elimination of violence against women, provision of crisis and trauma centres, assisting women migrant workers or lobbying for political and legislative change. The government and civil society must continue to work together on behalf of Indonesian women.

COMMENTARY

Sue Blackburn

It is a pleasure to comment on the speech by Ibu Khofifah. Having listened to her words, I don't think anyone can be in any doubt that a new era has dawned in Indonesia as far as gender issues are concerned. So many things she has said would never have been expressed by anyone who held an official position under the New Order regime. When we recognise her awareness of gender issues and her outspoken defence of women's rights in Indonesia, we must pay tribute not only to her as an individual but to the presidency of Abdurrahman Wahid which appointed her as a minister in 1999 and supported her in her work.

Ibu Khofifah made her mark on her ministry as soon as she took office. Its name was changed from the staid 'Ministry for the Role of Women' to 'State Ministry for Women's Empowerment'. This was in line with the philosophy of the ministry, and reflected the new age of democracy in Indonesia. It marked the end of women's affairs being seen as issues restricted to wives and mothers; the approach is now to tackle the construction of gender in Indonesian society that limits women's rights to equity and equality.

Another notable change was the transfer of the National Family Planning Coordinating Agency (BKKBN) to her ministry, so that she became the chief of that agency – the first time it had been headed by a woman. The move clearly signalled that family planning was taking a new turn: instead of having birth control as its overriding aim, it was now predominantly concerned with reproductive health. True to the ministry's commitment to gender equity, men are required to bear more of the burden of family planning.

The tenor of Ibu Khofifah's speech today reflects how close she is to the new style of women's organisations in Indonesia. As she said, under the New Order the women's movement was dominated by the wives' organisations which were clearly subordinate to men. But since the fall of Soeharto, women's organisations that saw themselves as defenders of women's rights have surged to the fore, and Ibu Khofifah, like her president and his wife, were open and accessible to those organisations. They worked together on a number of important issues, such as violence against women. Under her ministry, the whole agenda for gender issues changed radically, in rhetoric and in action. What a far-reaching list of demands she has outlined for us today. A quota of 30 per cent women at the top levels of the bureaucracy and in parliament is a revolutionary request in the context of most societies in the world today. Raising the marriage age for girls in Indonesia to 18 years, protecting female workers, reforming religious and legal practices to prevent the domestication of women – these too are initiatives that would have immense repercussions in Indonesian society.

Unfortunately democratic government came to Indonesia at a most difficult time. The country faces enormous problems. As you could see from her talk, Ibu Khofifah is aware that it is a struggle to keep gender issues high on the agenda when pressing matters of economic recovery, communal violence, corruption and regional revolt preoccupy the government. The strategy she was pursuing is that of gender mainstreaming, making sure that people are aware of the gender dimensions of every issue and that women are not neglected in the day-to-day business of government. It is a massive task to make officials throughout the state system – in government, the bureaucracy, the judiciary and the military – aware of gender inequity in their sphere and prepared to deal with it.

Moreover, this is a time when the power of central government is declining in Indonesia. Partly this is a result of a voluntary move by the government to decentralise control, embodied in the regional autonomy legislation that took effect at the start of 2001. Ibu Khofifah recognises that the challenge is to ensure that regional governments also are committed to gender equity and equality. One attempt to move them in this direction is to require them to produce gender-disaggregated statistics, so that progress towards greater equality can be monitored. This was an initiative of the Abdurrahman government.

Ibu Khofifah's achievements are immensely impressive. The future of the ministry under the current Megawati government is not yet clear, but it seems likely that the momentum that she set in train will carry policy forward for some time. At least now there is a strong and growing independent women's movement in Indonesia which will keep up the pressure on the government. As leader of one of the main Islamic women's organisations, Muslimat NU, Ibu Khofifah will be part of that movement and continue to play an important role in Indonesian women's affairs.

Ibu Khofifah is a symbol to us of what is most encouraging in Indonesian society today. She appears to be unhampered by the constricting baggage of the New Order era. Here is an Indonesian woman, a devout Muslim, who is prepared to speak and act in a forthright way in the name of the rights of women. We thank you for your presence here and for sharing your vision with us.

7 FEMINISM IN INDONESIA IN AN INTERNATIONAL CONTEXT

Saparinah Sadli

I was originally asked to write a paper on 'Indonesian feminism in an international context'. I changed the title to 'feminism in Indonesia' because I am not sure that we in Indonesia have developed an Indonesian theory of feminism. From my experience as the past chair of the Graduate Women's Studies Program (Kajian Wanita) at the University of Indonesia, which is now ten years old, I know that we have accumulated much empirical data about women and women's issues, particularly in the theses written by graduate students. Based on these studies we have developed new insights about Indonesian women and women's issues in our country's varied cultural settings; but this does not yet constitute a body of knowledge which can be used to develop a distinctively Indonesian feminism. Hence I am reluctant to use the term 'Indonesian feminism'.

Since 1998, when Indonesia began its transition towards a more democratic society, many women's groups have been working actively on women's rights issues within the context of feminism. Consequently the application of feminist ideas has become more visible, although I should add that in Indonesia feminism and women's rights are still the concern of a relatively small group of women and some men. At the start of the 21st century, feminism remains problematic for many Indonesians, especially those who are not directly concerned with women's issues or who are not familiar with the development of feminism in the north or in Asian countries such as India, the Philippines or Malaysia. The terms 'feminism', 'feminist' and even 'gender' are still questioned by the majority of Indonesians. They are considered by many to be non-indigenous concepts that are irrelevant to Indonesian values. Certain assumptions remain common: feminism is a Western or northern concept; it is anti-men; it perceives men to be the source of all gender inequity; it promotes the acceptance of lesbianism and so forth. This is despite the fact that the principle of gender equality is embodied in article 27 of the 1945 Constitution, and in other basic laws of the Republic of Indonesia.

In this chapter, I share my personal experiences as a women's studies scholar. I will discuss briefly the establishment of Kajian Wanita at the University of Indonesia. I will also share my experience of two feminist activities: the Convention Watch Working Group, established in 1994, and the Stepping Stones project, established in 1995.

THE ESTABLISHMENT OF KAJIAN WANITA

Kajian Wanita cannot be dissociated from feminist scholarship, or from the role of northern feminist scholars in developing the academic discipline called women's studies. It is perhaps for this reason that for almost ten years Kajian Wanita was the only graduate women's studies program in a country of more than 200 million people.

For several years, women lecturers at established universities such as Gadjah Mada University in Yogyakarta, Erlangga University in Surabaya and Hasanuddin University in Makassar had proposed introducing graduate women's studies programs at their universities. These proposals were met with scepticism or criticism by the leaders of the universities, who were mainly men. Many of the professors questioned the academic validity of such a program, saying that there was no clear academic discipline called women's studies. In 2000, however, after long debate, a graduate program in women's studies was finally established at Hasanuddin University. This was Indonesia's second such program.

I was lucky compared to my female friends at other universities around the country. Kajian Wanita was established not by women academics already active in women's and feminist issues, but by a man – the rector of the University of Indonesia. Although I was not the only lecturer at the university interested in feminist scholarship, the rector appointed me to establish the new graduate program in women's studies. This was a real challenge for several reasons.

- There were no undergraduate courses in women's studies as an academic preparation to enter the graduate program.
- There were no scholars – female or male – at the university with experience in teaching a graduate course in women's studies.
- Within the university's existing structure every master's program was four semesters in duration. This meant that we had to transform a sufficient number of lecturers from diverse professional backgrounds into women's studies scholars.

FEMINISM AND FEMINISTS AT KAJIAN WANITA

Feminism recognises women's different personal experiences, which cannot be separated from their cultural backgrounds. Allow me, then, to tell you briefly about my personal background.

I am a Javanese Muslim woman and I am 74 years old. I was brought up during the colonial period in a feudalistic family. I went to a Dutch elementary school, reserved mainly for Dutch children and the Dutch-speaking children of Indonesian civil servants. After I finished elementary school, I wanted to go to a regular junior high school. Against my will, my parents enrolled me in the Van Deventer school, a special girls' school inspired by Kartini's aspirations for the education of *Inheemsche* (native Indonesian) girls. This was a school with very strict rules; all the girls (again, mainly the Indonesian children of Dutch civil servants) had to wear Javanese dress. Luckily for me, I spent only a year at the school before the Japanese invaded and all the Dutch schools were closed down. I then went to a regular Indonesian high school and my parents reluctantly allowed me to pursue post-secondary studies. I became an assistant pharmacist before beginning my career as a psychologist.

I married when I was 27 years old and accompanied my husband to America where he obtained a degree in economics. Because of his meagre stipend, I was not able to study while we were in the United States, but I continued my studies in psychology when we returned to Indonesia. It was as a psychologist that I became interested in the psychology of women, which became a division of the American Psychological Association in the 1980s. This interest acquainted me with feminist scholarship as practised by women psychologists in the north.

My view of feminism in Indonesia is, therefore, that of an elderly married woman, from a middle-class Javanese family, with a Dutch and Indonesian educational background, influenced by Javanese values. My personal experiences and academic background as a psychologist have directly and indirectly influenced my perception of feminism at Kajian Wanita.

The first task facing us was to develop a curriculum for the program. In the early 1990s both women and men scholars still had a negative attitude towards the terms 'feminism', 'feminist' and even 'gender'. For instance, at the formal opening of the graduate women's studies program, a woman lawyer who was also a senior lecturer in the law faculty advised me that, as chair of the new program, I should make sure I was not overly influenced by Western feminism or feminist ideas. She did not provide any justification for her views, and I listened diplomatically to her advice without answering her at the time. But such advice did influence our actions at the newly established graduate women's studies program.

In the beginning, we were very careful not to use terms like 'gender perspective' or 'feminist perspective'. Instead, we adopted the term 'women's perspective', even though we were in fact discussing the methodologies usually known as feminist or gender perspectives. This decision was taken to avoid unnecessary irritation within the academic community at the university.

Our approach drew sharp criticism from a group of young women proudly calling themselves Indonesian feminists. This group included the activists who had established one of the early feminist organisations in Indonesia, Kalyanamitra. These young women professionals had been exposed to feminist ideas through their personal contacts with feminist friends and their reading of feminist texts. They were very active in advocating feminist issues during the Soeharto era. It shows their determination that, despite the social and political restrictions of the New Order state and the efforts to domesticate women based on *kodrat* (biological determination or nature), they were able to find a space to develop their feminist ideas. They criticised government programs such as the national family planning program, and the co-opting into the ideology of the state of women's organisations such as the PKK (an organisation to increase family welfare), Dharma Wanita (an organisation for civil servants' wives) and Kowani (a federation of 79 women's organisations). So even during this most repressive of periods, there were subversive forces within the women's movement. Women's NGOs like Kalyanamitra empowered women by giving them the skills necessary to advocate alternative perspectives. The main criticism of these young feminists towards our graduate women's studies program was that those managing the program were not feminists, and were not well informed about feminist scholarship.

We were fortunate early on in our program to develop a three-year linkage program with the Memorial University of St Johns in Newfoundland. From 1992 to 1995, lecturers at Kajian Wanita interacted closely with Canadian feminists through reciprocal visits. Through the linkage program, we were able to develop the women's studies curriculum, based on the specific needs of Indonesians as conceived by the Indonesian lecturers. Slowly, professional development and capacity building strengthened Kajian Wanita. The exchange of lecturers included the Indonesian librarian, because the main university library did not have any of the resources needed for a graduate women's studies program. Two young lecturers obtained their master's degrees in women's studies at Memorial University and are now teaching the concepts of feminism and feminist methodology.

Introducing feminism, both as a body of thought and as a movement which focuses on the oppression of women, to the Kajian Wanita students was not a simple task. The program challenged stereotypical thinking that saw feminine traits as the product of nature, biology and God's will, rather than as socially constructed. Once students had grasped some initial understanding of feminism and its various schools of thought, they often wanted to attach a fixed meaning to feminist concepts or find an immediate solution to overcome women's

oppression and gender inequality in real life. It was not always easy to explain
to them that feminism is not a fixed body of thought but a constant evolution of
thoughts and actions related to various women's issues. This difficulty reflects
the fact that the Indonesian educational system does not actively stimulate students to develop critical thinking or teach them that while differences of opinion
should be respected, a point of view can be rejected on the basis of clear argument. Our lecturers had to make a special effort to help students understand that
these differences of opinion were not a reflection on their commitment to 'feminism' or their struggle to achieve gender equality in our patriarchal society. We
also emphasised that awareness of gender differences or gender inequality in the
Indonesian context is an asset because it provides insight into how to accommodate the varied experiences of women of different social status, and of differing
educational, religious and ethnic backgrounds.

Two activities of Kajian Wanita provide additional insights into the still-
developing concept of feminism in Indonesia in an international context.

THE STEPPING STONES PROJECT

The Stepping Stones Project uses oral history, case studies and discussions to
elicit the views and opinions of scholars at Kajian Wanita. The study aims to
understand the developing identity of the academic staff and students who are
working with feminism. It is an attempt to follow the intellectual development
of a group of women's studies scholars and activists in order to develop a more
theorised understanding of their situation.

From the project we learned, first, that students of Kajian Wanita experience
the process of becoming a 'feminist' both through their own exposure to
women's issues and the range of women's experiences as well as through the
usual academic activities such as research and reading texts related to their studies. Our scholars are diverse in age and cultural background, but their life stories
do not reflect the full range of Indonesian women's experience. On the whole
they tend to be middle class and have stable family situations. Nevertheless they
describe experiences of direct and indirect discrimination, inequality, frustration
and conflicts. More powerfully, they share a common culture and values that
have shaped their lives and enable them to understand other Indonesian women
in different circumstances.

A core group of scholars chose to begin their exploration of the women's
movement and 'feminism' in Indonesia by discussing an article on Hari Kartini
(Kartini Day), which commemorates the birth of the national heroine Kartini.
The way that Hari Kartini was manipulated by Soeharto during the New Order
period has attracted criticism from women's groups and the media.

Kartini was born into an aristocratic family in Java in 1879. She was forced into a polygamous marriage and died in childbirth at the age of just 25. During her lifetime, Kartini struggled to liberate her countrywomen from the chains of tradition and patriarchal values, including polygamy and the practice of secluding girls after the onset of puberty. Kartini herself was not allowed to finish her elementary school education because she had to go into seclusion.

The article was selected because Kartini is the only activist in the Indonesian women's movement to have put her thoughts, feelings and aspirations down on paper. The discussion was an attempt to take constructive steps towards mapping the forms of feminist thinking among Indonesian women and outlining an 'Indonesian feminism'.

The discussion divided younger and older participants, and women of Javanese and non-Javanese backgrounds. The non-Javanese students pointed to the dominance of a Javanese heroine over other women whose contributions to women's improvement had been of no less importance – and perhaps of even greater importance – than Kartini's. The students questioned whether she could be called a feminist at all or was a suitable role model for contemporary activists and scholars. The debate touched on the use and misuse of Hari Kartini and posed such questions as: 'Are we brave enough to say that Kartini was the first Indonesian feminist?' and 'Was Kartini a feminist?'

Those who considered Kartini to be a feminist stressed the importance of her profound understanding of Javanese culture during her lifetime and the implications of this for women. As one participant said: 'For me she is a Javanese feminist because she was questioning all relationships ... That is why I call her a feminist, ... a Javanese feminist because her feminism was born of women's condition in Javanese society'. Another participant observed that Kartini was faced with structural barriers but added that it was 'obvious that feminists are always facing structural barriers'. Struggle, together with an awareness of the purpose and nature of the struggle, emerges as Kartini's key legacy.

The discussion of feminism, and Kartini's brand of feminism in particular, reached two essentially different conclusions, both of which have informed Kajian Wanita's development. One was that there was a need to identify some common characteristics of a feminist or 'Indonesian feminist', such as sensitivity to women's issues, a commitment to transform cultural norms that have a negative impact on gender relationships, sensitivity to the impact of religious and cultural values on women's condition, and pluralism and openness to differences. The other was the recognition that exposure to a range of ideas challenging the status quo and derived from a women's perspective (drawn from Western ideas, but also from forerunners such as Kartini) had helped the women to see and analyse many of the problems experienced by other Indonesian women. As Dr Marilyn Porter, a Canadian feminist sociologist actively involved in the study, concluded, women's direct personal experience is enhanced and enlarged through being connected to more general experiences – a process of empathy vital to the creation of a theory and activism appropriate to all Indonesian women.

The main conclusions of the Stepping Stones Project could be synthesised as follows.

- With all the differences and similarities among the participants in defining their own form of feminism, it seems that at this stage it is too early to formulate a clear and precise definition of 'feminism' that will capture all of the experiences of women inside and outside Kajian Wanita.
- The ongoing debate about the usefulness of the term 'feminism' seems to discourage attempts to achieve social justice for both men and women. Therefore, the participants in the study placed more emphasis on the spirit of feminism than on feminist labels.
- The women in the study had a common cultural context and values that had shaped their lives and enabled them to understand the different circumstances under which other Indonesian women's lives are shaped.

THE CONVENTION WATCH WORKING GROUP

Lecturers at Kajian Wanita are constantly looking for ways to bring feminist ideas into the mainstream. One approach has been to set up the Convention Watch Working Group, which aims to evaluate Indonesia's implementation of the UN Convention on the Elimination of All Forms of Discrimination against Women (the Women's Convention). The Women's Convention was adopted by the United Nations in 1979 and opened for ratification by UN member countries in 1981. An international group of women with feminist ideas were the main force behind the adoption of the convention by the General Assembly of the United Nations.

Indonesia ratified the UN Convention on Political Rights of Women in 1958 and the Women's Convention in 1984 (by Law No. 7/84). The principle of gender equality was already embodied in the 1945 Constitution and in other basic laws. This provided the basis for Indonesia's ratification of the Women's Convention without the need to place reservations on any of the substantive articles.

Indonesian women taking part in the Indonesian National Commission on the Advancement of Women (KNKWI) – such as as Dr Yetty Rizali Noor, Ms Soewarni Salyo and Ms Nani Soewondo – were reportedly actively involved in the drafting of some of the articles of the Women's Convention at UN headquarters, and through their involvement in the first UN Women's Conference in Mexico in 1975. Although Indonesian women have long fought for feminist ideals in an international context, this older generation of women did not call themselves feminists. Rather, they saw themselves simply as concerned to increase the status of Indonesian women, working hard within the country and through international women's groups for the advancement of their fellow countrywomen. The long and impressive history of the Indonesian women's movement in enhancing women's role and status is well known but is seldom associated with feminism or feminists, either by the women themselves or by the public in general. Soewarni Salyo, for example, who is now around 80 years old, still claims that she never thought of herself as a feminist, although she was very active in fighting for what is now called women's rights.

The Convention Watch Working Group was established in 1994 as an outcome of a roundtable discussion initiated by a young lecturer in political science, Dra Smita Nugroho Notosoesanto MA, in the lead-up to an international conference on women and politics to be held in Bangkok. A core group of lecturers from Kajian Wanita attended, among them Professor Tapiomas Ihromi (a well-known lawyer and sociologist who has been active in promoting women's and development issues since her participation in the first International Women's Conference in Mexico); Ms Achie Luhulima and Ms Syamsiah Ahmad (both lecturers and, at the time, deputy ministers in the Ministry for Women's Affairs); and a number of women and men academics interested in women's advancement.

The first report to the Committee of the Women's Convention, prepared by Ms Luhulima, became the basis for discussion of the government's commitment to the convention. Since we all agreed that it was a strategic tool for the advancement of women's rights, we at Kajian Wanita decided to assess its implementation in 1994, ten years after it had been ratified. We felt that monitoring the implementation of the convention was important because this was the only gendered treaty to provide clear guidelines on women's rights as human rights. Monitoring was also seen as important because we acknowledged that ratification of an international convention would not automatically change existing cultural views, attitudes or patterns of behaviour that discriminated against women.

The activities of the Convention Watch Working Group started with a small survey of respondents (42 per cent male and 58 per cent female) assumed to have some exposure to the Women's Convention. They included men and women of various professional backgrounds, such as judges, educators, a member of parliament, activists, artists, a journalist, a military officer and architects. The objective of the survey was to obtain a general picture of existing public knowledge about the Women's Convention and create an effective strategy to strengthen its implementation. Based on the observation that increasing numbers of Indonesian women were entering the formal workforce, particular emphasis was placed on article 11 of the convention, which pertains to the rights of women workers. These include the right to equal employment opportunities and remuneration; the right to promotion, job security and all benefits and conditions of service; prohibition of dismissal on grounds of pregnancy or childbirth; the right to protection of health and safety, including the safeguarding of reproductive functions; prohibition of discrimination on the basis of marital status; and the right to social security.

The findings showed that the majority of respondents understood the concept of discrimination against women. This was demonstrated by their own definitions of discrimination, which were close to the one set out in the Women's Convention. The respondents said, for example, that discrimination meant not being excluded, treated differently or faced with special limitations because of one's gender. The majority of the respondents identified biological differences between men and women as the source of discrimination against women. Most chose the home and family as the place where discrimination against women most frequently occurred.

Our survey was conducted about eight years ago. It is safe to say that the general public and state officials still view biological differences between men and women as a justification for discrimination on grounds of gender. Since discrimination against women is often accompanied by violence, it is important to note that current data on domestic violence collected by Rifka Annisa (a crisis centre for victims of domestic violence) show that its incidence is increasing. The centre reported 18 cases of domestic violence in 1994, 82 in 1995, 184 in 1996, 188 in 1997 and 206 in 1998, and it can be assumed that the actual number of cases was far higher. Incidental data from other sources, including data from conflict areas, show that violence against women in Indonesia – both domestic and state-sponsored – is a widespread phenomenon, in times of peace as well as during times of social conflict, despite the ratification of the Women's Convention 16 years ago.

We found that, ten years after ratification, most survey respondents had minimal knowledge of the Women's Convention and only a handful had read it. Many more were not aware that it had been ratified by Indonesia. Some respondents agreed that the convention was a useful instrument to achieve equality between men and women, and that action needed to be taken to monitor and strengthen its implementation. They also saw a need to increase awareness of the convention and enforce existing laws prohibiting discrimination against women.

The survey results were used to design the Convention Watch Working Group's first program of activities, with the following objectives:

- to raise public awareness and knowledge of the Women's Convention;
- to conduct research activities to support the formulation of policies and legislation that would have a positive effect on women's lives;
- to empower women by increasing their participation in policy-making at all levels.

These objectives are still relevant today, because discrimination against women, including violence directed at women, is still occurring in the home, in the workplace and in the community.

Our program to raise awareness of the Women's Convention began in 1995 with gender sensitivity training for women from several political, social and religious women's organisations. These included Fatayat NU (a Muslim organisation), state-sponsored organisations such as the PKK, Dharma Wanita and Kowani, and a number of grassroots organisations. We selected these organisations as our first target group because we considered them strategically placed to empower their members through the dissemination of feminist ideas on women's rights as embodied in the convention. Increased awareness of the convention was perceived as a mechanism to promote and enhance women's rights, in the home and in society.

The training activities of the Convention Watch Working Group provided a concrete opportunity for academics from Kajian Wanita to work on women's rights issues together with the young activists who had been so critical of us. It also marked the introduction of now-popular gender sensitivity training, jointly organised by Kajian Wanita lecturers and the feminist organisations. International networking with feminists and gender trainers from the Philippines was another joint activity which familiarised us with feminist ideas. Today, gender sensitivity training, adapted to Indonesian needs and sensitivities, has become an integral part of many activities aiming to create awareness of women's rights and gender equality. However, such activities are still limited to programs related to women, and are received reluctantly by those people who do not support the promotion of the human rights of women. Including a gender perspective in Indonesian development programs is a continuing struggle. Most decision-makers are ignorant of the issues, or reject the inclusion of a gender perspective on the grounds that all policies and programs will benefit women and men equally.

The Convention Watch Working Group also conducted a study to assess the implementation of article 11 of the Women's Convention, mentioned earlier. Our findings were as follows:

- The principles contained in article 11 are already stipulated in existing labour laws and government regulations. Violation of these laws and regulations is punishable by imprisonment or fines.
- Traditional perceptions had prevailed in the drafting of the Collective Labour Laws, particularly as they pertained to women's rights to family allowances. However, since 1989 women workers have been eligible for these allowances provided they could prove they were the family breadwinner.
- Women workers are generally not aware of their rights, or of the existence of

protective regulations. Even when they are, they are reluctant to stand up for their rights for fear of dismissal.
• Companies are often not in a position to meet all the requirements of the principles contained in article 11.
• Even in companies with a socially 'good reputation', discrimination against women prevails.
• The ratification of the international convention has had a positive impact, evident in better legislation and policies.

Since working for women's rights requires the involvement of the legal community, the Convention Watch Working Group embarked on a program directed at law lecturers in several universities in Java and the Outer Islands, and at law enforcers such as the police, practising lawyers, prosecutors and judges, including those from the religious court. The main objectives were to assist law lecturers to design a curriculum on gender and law, and to raise awareness among law enforcers of women's rights as set out in Law No. 7/84. The legal community has been receptive to these activities, as long as they are not explicitly linked to feminism, or considered part of a feminist agenda.

The Convention Watch Working Group has to instill awareness of and commitment to feminist ideas in a cultural environment which generally is not ready for this. We do not let this discourage us, because we recognise that achieving gender equality and respect for women's rights is an important pillar in Indonesia's transition to democracy.

CONCLUSION

The ongoing debate about the usefulness of terms like 'feminism' and 'feminist' has not dampened the enthusiasm of a growing number of Indonesian women working towards women's rights as human rights. The spirit of feminism has always informed the Indonesian women's movement. Women's patriotic role both before and immediately after independence included the struggle to liberate women from cultural, traditional and religious barriers and achieve full social participation. The effectiveness of the women's movement during the Soeharto era was curtailed when women's organisations became a vehicle to celebrate women as mothers whose rightful place was in the home rather than in the public sphere. This contributed to a public debate – which continues today – about feminism, the liberation of women and unequal power relationships between men and women. Essentially the debate is polarised between two camps: those who claim to be defenders of women's rights, without necessarily calling themselves feminists, and those who claim to be defenders of religious values and so-called traditional practices.

Amidst all this, especially over the last three years, an increasing number of women of different backgrounds and experience, residing in various parts of the country, have been working tirelessly to defend women's rights and provide services to victims of violence in both conflict and non-conflict areas. Women artists are producing works that celebrate women's rights and that portray women as victims of discrimination and violence (see Chapter 10). Women lawyers are working towards the reform of laws to provide better protection for women in the public sphere as well as in the home. The issue of gender-based violence is now more widely recognised because of women's activism. Younger and older women are working together to promote women's rights through, for example, the National Commission on Violence against Women. In Indonesia's transition towards democracy, the voice of women has become a part of civil society which can no longer be ignored, or dismissed using the label of 'feminism'. Indonesians are promoting women's rights, as part of their human rights.

8 GAY AND LESBI SUBJECTIVITIES, NATIONAL BELONGING AND THE NEW INDONESIA

Tom Boellstorff

SEXUAL AND GENDERED SUBJECT-POSITIONS IN INDONESIA

At a seminar held at the Australian National University in September 2001, Amien Rais stated that for democracy to work in Indonesia's *era reformasi* (era of reform), it must include all groups in society, even those that are ignored or hated. The underlying question of this chapter responds to this train of thought, asking: 'What will the place of *gay* and *lesbi* Indonesians be in the present *era reformasi*?'[1]

For the last ten years I have been studying *lesbi* and *gay* subject-positions in contemporary Indonesia, primarily but not solely in Java, Sulawesi and Bali. I define 'subject-positions' as the historically and culturally specific categories of selfhood through which persons come to know themselves as individuals and as members of communities and societies. 'Subjectivities' are the ways in which persons occupy one or more subject-positions in a variety of ways (for example, partially or completely, antagonistically or amicably). This theoretical language offers a more nuanced framework than the somewhat problematic term 'identity', which for many implies a kind of conscious alignment that does not square with the incompletely intentional ways that people understand their place in the world.

We find in contemporary Indonesia many other 'genres' of sexual/gendered subject-position in addition to *lesbi* and *gay*. For instance, there is *waria* (known popularly by a wide variety of terms, most notably *banci*); this is a nationwide, male-to-female, transvestite subject-position whose history is still poorly understood, but is most likely about 250 years old. There are what I call 'ethnolocalised homosexual and transgendered professional subject-positions' (ETPs), which include such things as *warok–gemblak* relations in eastern Java – that is, sexual relations between male actors (*warok*) and their younger male understudies (*gemblak*) (see Wilson 1999) – or, to some extent, *bissu* (ritual Bugis priests, many of whom have historically been male transvestites; see Pelras 1996: 82) practitioners in southern Sulawesi. Many of these ETPs have histories going back several centuries. There are also female-to-male transgendered persons, known most often as *tomboi* or *hunter*, whose subjectivities are complexly linked to those of *lesbi* women. Finally, and perhaps most importantly, there are those people called *normal*, that is, 'heterosexual' men and women. While the sexual subject-positions of these persons are often assumed to be natural or biological, they are in fact historically and culturally specific as well. For instance, what it means to be a *normal* man or woman in contemporary Indonesia is quite different from dominant notions of proper manhood or womanhood 300 years ago.

I do not have space in this article to discuss these other sexual/gendered subject-positions, but there are several general points to be made. Subject-positions, from 'gay' to 'banker' to 'wife' and so on, are always culturally constructed and as a result have a history. They come into being during a certain period of time, that period of formation shapes them, and then they continue to change. Subject-positions are also always linked to some idea of social scale – local, national, regional, global and so on. This raises important questions of methodology for the anthropological study of gender – since women are usually assumed to be more linked to locality and tradition than men, and at the same time the methods of anthropology are designed to look at locality, to the extent that you often find anthropologists talking about a very different 'Indonesia' to that of political scientists or psychologists.

SEXUALITY AND NATIONAL CULTURE

One reason why *gay* and *lesbi* subject-positions are so interesting is that they are quite new: Indonesians do not appear to have started thinking of themselves as *lesbi* or *gay* until the 1970s, and the subject-positions really took shape in the 1980s and 1990s. These Indonesians are still largely ignored by the state. Nonetheless, I want to claim that *gay* and *lesbi* subject-positions have always been linked to national culture – not as the result of intentional state policy, but because national ideology has constituted an 'at-hand' way of thinking about selfhood not linked to locality or tradition.

Many *lesbi* and *gay* Indonesians still remember the 'wedding' of Jossie and Bonnie in Jakarta in 1981 as the first time that they thought of themselves as sharing a kind of selfhood with other people in Indonesia. This event was important not just because it appeared in the mass media, but because of the way these women were staking a claim to national belonging. Indeed, one reporter who covered the event in the 6 July 1981 issue of *Liberty* magazine said:

This event is indeed unique, not least because it is the first time something like this has occurred in Jakarta, maybe in Indonesia, or even the whole world – that the marriage of two people of the same sex is formalized openly, without anything to cover it … If the relationship between Jossie and Bonnie had been tied together … with an ordinary reception in the presence of their peers, anyone could have done it. It would have been no different to a birthday party. What is unique … is that this is a *lesbi* wedding formalized with a joyous ceremony, and thus constitutes a new 'dilemma' in Indonesia. Viewing the life of these two young lesbians, it is apparent that they have a different way of thinking about how to solve the problem of lesbianism in our Republic. In our estimation, both of them want to become pioneers for their people, who are not small in number. And with them both standing in front, their hopes openly revealed, who knows what will happen …

Turning to the present, we find that while *gay* and *lesbi* Indonesians are more visible in everyday life and in the mass media than they were in 1981, many ordinary Indonesians still do not know what *gay* and *lesbi* mean. They think they are English words for *waria*, or that they refer only to foreigners. Indonesians who do know what *lesbi* and *gay* mean often think of these people as 'deviants' (*orang yang menyimpang*), people who go outside the norms of society (*di luar norma-norma masyarakat*). Often it is incorrectly assumed that *gay* and *lesbi* Indonesians are part of the *kelas eksekutif* or the rich, even though most of them make under Rp 500,000 per month, do not speak English and have never travelled outside Indonesia.

In fact, these Indonesians are not deviants; their ways of thinking actually reflect many central assumptions in contemporary Indonesian society. *Lesbi* and *gay* Indonesians inhabit *national* subject-positions borne from the time of the New Order but that now continue on without the New Order. If we look at the style of thinking of *lesbi* and *gay* people, we find it to be surprisingly compatible with an Indonesia in which civil society is rejuvenated and tolerance more valued.

I am reminded of something a *gay* man in Makassar once said to me:

Culture is something that is created by humans and then believed. There are people in Indonesia who have created [*menciptakan*] '*gay*' here in Indonesia and believe in what they have created [*dipercayai*]. Thus, gayness [*kegayan*] is part of Indonesian culture.

Note how my friend refers not to Bugis or Makassar culture but to *Indonesian culture*. One of the most significant things about *gay* and *lesbi* subject-positions is that they are irreducible to ethnolocality.

I coin the term 'ethnolocality' to underscore how, in both scholarly work on Indonesia and many everyday Indonesian understandings, 'ethnicity' and 'locality' assume each other to the extent that they are, in essence, a single concept (see Boellstorff 2002). There are *lesbi* and *gay* Indonesians from every ethnolocality and religion. However, while *gay* and *lesbi* persons sometimes think of their lives in ethnolocal terms with regard to, say, kinship, in terms of sexuality they think of themselves as *Indonesians*. To date there has never been a specifically ethnolocal *gay* and *lesbi* subject-position or network. This does not mean that *gay* and *lesbi* subjectivities are the same everywhere in Indonesia – far from it! But *lesbi* and *gay* Indonesians say these differences are subsequent to a sense of belonging to the nation.

These subject-positions raise a number of important theoretical, methodological and political issues. A crucial question is how *gay* and *lesbi* subject-positions are irreducible to ethnolocality when they have never enjoyed institutional support. One factor is that they do not come from 'tradition'. The national character of *lesbi* and *gay* subject-positions is thus linked to modernity and mass media. However, this still does not tell us how *gay* and *lesbi* Indonesians understand their own subjectivities. Subject-positions are never 'imported' into Indonesia; they are always transformed to fit new circumstances. In the case of *gay* and *lesbi* subject-positions, one important aspect of this transformation is the use of 'archipelago' metaphors.

Sometimes this is explicit. For instance, the national network of *gay* and *lesbi* organisations is called GAYa Nusantara. *Gaya* means 'style', but when the first three letters are capitalised it can also mean *gay*. *Nusantara* means 'archipelago', but it can also mean 'Indonesia'. Unlike English, in Indonesian nouns come before adjectives – since 'GAYa' is both English and Indonesian, 'GAYa Nusantara' can have four meanings: 'archipelago style', 'Indonesia style', '*gay* Indonesia', and '*gay* archipelago'. The idea of a *gay* archipelago is also found in the fact that 'local' groups often retain the first word and then add a term with a local flavour, to give GAYa Dewata in Bali, GAYa Celebes in Makassar, GAYa Semarang in Semarang, GAYa Betawi in Jakarta, GAYa Priangan in Bandung, GAYa Siak in Pekanbaru and GAYa Khatulistiwa in Pontianak. (Note that not all members of these groups are *gay* or *lesbi*, and many of the groups undertake activities focused on public health or other goals.)

These names would not have much meaning if the thinking behind them was not also reflected *implicitly* in the daily lives of *lesbi* and *gay* Indonesians. This appears in the way they often think of their homosexual lives as one 'island' in a self that is like an archipelago. It also appears in the way they believe their diversity is enclosed within a unity – that *gay* and *lesbi* are fundamentally Indonesian subject-positions, only secondarily linked to ethnolocality.

This reflects a larger issue: it is problematic to explain gender and sexuality in terms of tradition (*adat*) without taking into account the fact that most Indonesians have grown up with 'local' and 'national' cultures at the same time. In the life-worlds of Indonesians, those things learned from an ostensibly local tradition are not necessarily more culturally immediate than those things learned from school, a family planning brochure or a TV show. The 'everyday life' through which one becomes enculturated is, in contemporary Indonesia, always simultaneously ethnolocal and national; one does not start out as a 'local' person and then only later come to think of oneself as part of a national culture. This is the case even if one's stance towards the national culture (or an ethnolocal culture or cultures for that matter) is antagonistic; it is perfectly possible to reject a cultural logic in whole or in part and still be profoundly influenced by that logic through the very act of resistance to it.

Finally, the impact of the archipelago concept appears in how these Indonesians see their national community as one 'island' in a *global* archipelago that includes other 'islands' such as Holland, Thailand and the United States. What is clear is that this metaphor is not part of a timeless tradition, but is derived from a key structuring principle of the nation-building project. The archipelago concept dates from the early period of nationalism at the beginning of the 20th century but gained new force in December 1957 in the context of an international dispute over maritime boundaries. In 1973 a government resolution decreed that the archipelago concept 'gives life to national development in all its aspects' – political, educational and sociocultural. It continues to be used in *era reformasi*, as we saw last year when Megawati emphasised that Indonesia is an archipelagic state, not a continental one.

HEGEMONY, NATIONAL SELFHOOD AND VIOLENCE

This transformation of the archipelago concept by *lesbi* and *gay* Indonesians is an example of *hegemony*, a concept associated with the work of the Italian social theorist Antonio Gramsci (1971) and developed by Hall (1988), Laclau and Mouffe (1985) and many Indonesian intellectuals. Gramsci recognised that groups in modern societies hold power through the force of the state only in the last instance; they primarily use culture and mass media to convince most citizens to accept their way of thinking. This hegemonic way of thinking must constantly be renewed in civil society. It must always adapt itself, and for this reason is at risk of being transformed in unexpected ways. This is exactly what we see in the case of *gay* and *lesbi* subject-positions.

These Indonesians have taken a core element of state ideology, the archipelago concept, and transformed it so as to understand their own subjectivities. Most of the time this process is not conscious, but this is what they are doing, at the same time that they transform the concepts 'gay' and 'lesbian' from outside Indonesia. It is not hard to imagine that if *gay* and *lesbi* subject-positions had arisen in Sukarno's Old Order, in the context of the Non-Aligned Movement and a strongly antagonistic stance towards the West, their character would not have been what it is now. They would also differ if they were arising now in the era of regional autonomy (*otonomi daerah*).

It is with this concept of hegemony in mind that I can make the following statement: *lesbi* and *gay* Indonesians are the New Order's greatest success story – the greatest example of a truly national culture irreducible to ethnolocality – but a success the New Order never intended! They show us that we can take concepts, even if they come from forces we don't agree with, and transform them. (This is also a point made by the early nationalists, who noted that the greatest gift of the Dutch to Indonesia was the idea of 'Indonesia' itself.) *Gay* and *lesbi* people have created something new from old ways of thinking. They show that it is possible to create a new archipelago concept based on greater tolerance and social justice. We saw this as far back as 1981, when that *lesbi* wedding was seen as staking a claim to national belonging.

However, in the last three years we have seen a new kind of violent rejection of *lesbi* and *gay* Indonesians that is also focused on staking a claim to national belonging. While most Indonesians think that *gay* or *lesbi* Indonesians are sick, sinful or deserving of pity, until recently this has rarely translated into a desire to hurt them.

In September 1999, a number of *gay* and *lesbi* groups decided to hold a national meeting to follow up on earlier meetings held in 1993, 1995 and 1997. Members from 21 organisations from Java and Bali arrived at the Dana Hotel in Solo to participate in a national working meeting (*rakernas*). By at least 7 September, several fundamentalist Muslim organisations in Solo had learned of the *rakernas* and, in sharp contrast to all previous public reactions to such meetings, declared that it was immoral and should not take place. They threatened to organise their followers to burn down the Dana Hotel and kill any *gay* men and *lesbi* women they found.

When these threats became known, the *lesbi* women and *gay* men who had gathered at the Dana Hotel cancelled the meeting and moved to other hotels for safety. However, the Muslim organisations soon learned of a back-up plan to hold a press conference at the local office of the Democratic People's Party (PRD), which includes *gay* and *lesbi* rights in its political platform. On 10 September a large group of youths went to the office. Some made death threats and threatened to burn down the office. An even more violent event took place on 11 November 2000 in the resort town of Kaliurang near Yogyakarta, when a group of 350 *lesbi* and *gay* persons holding an entertainment event were attacked and in some cases stabbed by about 150 Muslim youths; fortunately there were no deaths (Boellstorff 2002).

I do not want simply to blame these attacks on Islam: many Muslim groups are tolerant of *gay* and *lesbi* Indonesians, most of whom are Muslim themselves. While the recent breakdown of law and order and rise of militant Islam are perhaps necessary conditions for the violence, they cannot explain why the violence took the form that it did – instead of, say, a *fatwa* or finding of religious law. Hooliganism and fundamentalism do not explain why the reaction took the *form* that it did. What is particularly significant about these attacks is that they are not targeting *gay* and *lesbi* Indonesians in salons, parks or other places where they meet, which would be very easy to do. It is not simply a matter of public versus private, since parks and salons are public spaces too. Crucially, these attacks were linked to times when *gay* and *lesbi* Indonesians *claimed national belonging* – the same issue we saw talked about after the *lesbi* wedding in 1981.

In this regard it bears noting that *heterosexuality* is also linked to national belonging. For instance, nationalist literature going back to the 1920s describes the shift to an idea of the modern Indonesian citizen in terms of a shift from arranged to chosen marriage (Rodgers 1995; Siegel 1998). While there are of course still many arranged marriages today, and many that fall between arrangement and choice, what is interesting here is the ideal of chosen marriage that we find in contemporary Indonesia. When marriage is arranged, sexual orientation is secondary – desire is not the motivating factor. However, when marriage hinges on a 'choosing' self animated by love, that self fails if not heterosexual. Choice, to be national and modern, must be heterosexual choice. It is through heterosexuality that gendered self and nation are articulated.

In recounting recent events of violence I am not trying to be alarmist; there have not been any major incidents of violence against *lesbi* and *gay* people to my knowledge since November of last year, and they may not be repeated. I bring them up to point out how not only *gay* and *lesbi* Indonesians, but other Indonesians as well, are increasingly aware that *lesbi* and *gay* subject-positions are irreducible to ethnolocality and thus embody many key promises and contradictions of national belonging. The existence of *lesbi* and *gay* subject-positions holds the promise (and, in the eyes of some, danger) of redefining hegemonic notions of the proper national man or woman. Might we have something to learn from the life-worlds of *gay* and *lesbi* Indonesians? These men and women say that they did not choose to be this way. Many are very religious and believe that God intended them to be *lesbi* or *gay*. They try to live lives that are positive and good, and to contribute to society. Must they be rejected? If they are accepted, might that not be a sign that we can tolerate other kinds of difference as well?

Gay and *lesbi* Indonesians show us that it is always possible to invent new ways of living that are still *authentically Indonesian*. They show us that while hegemonies are powerful, there are ways to resist them that do not depend on the near-impossible task of total change. Hegemonies can be tweaked, twisted, reworked into new forms that offer greater possibilities for social justice. *Lesbi* and *gay* subject-positions illustrate the transformative processes by which 'national culture' has become not just state propaganda, but a deeply felt, imagined community for millions of Indonesians (Anderson 1983).

We can learn from *lesbi* and *gay* Indonesians that authenticity is not a matter of who has the longest history or the most members, but a political struggle over belonging, and that it is possible to imagine new ways of determining authenticity and belonging that include more inhabitants of the archipelago than the colonial or New Order post-colonial states ever did. In this time of uncertainty and new hope, looking at *gay* and *lesbi* Indonesians in terms of belonging rather than 'deviance' offers clues about a new national culture that respects local variation and social change, where all persons have a voice, where all can say with confidence, 'this is my home'.

NOTE

1   In this essay, as elsewhere in my work, I use the terms *gay* and *lesbi* in an insider or 'emic' sense. I define *lesbi* women as 'Indonesian women who think of themselves as *lesbi* in at least some contexts of their lives' and *gay* men as 'Indonesian men who think of themselves as *gay* in at least some contexts of their lives'. It may seem odd that I consistently italicise *gay* and *lesbi*. However, through this seemingly simple act of italicisation I mean to remind myself and the reader that these are Indonesian terms. Like better-known terms such as *adat* (customary law), the concepts *gay* and *lesbi* are part of contemporary Indonesian culture. They are not Western imports but concepts that have been reworked within Indonesia itself.

9 AND THE WINNER IS ... INDONESIAN WOMEN IN PUBLIC LIFE

*Mayling Oey-Gardiner**

This chapter examines women's political participation in Indonesia in the three years leading up to Megawati Sukarnoputri's presidency. In spite of the 'wife and mother' role assigned to them during the New Order period, women have become politically active in increasing numbers since the end of Soeharto's 32-year reign. The current period of political reform has seen the downfall of two further male presidents, B.J. Habibie and Abdurrahman Wahid.

INDONESIA'S FIRST WOMAN PRESIDENT

On 23 July 2001, Megawati Sukarnoputri became Indonesia's first woman president. This was just over two years after her party, the Indonesian Democratic Party of Struggle (PDI-P), won the first democratically held elections in more than four decades. Megawati's appointment came some 21 months after the 'election' of Abdurrahman Wahid, Indonesia's fourth president.

As Krishna Sen discusses in Chapter 2, at the time of Abdurrahman's election to the presidency in October 1999, Megawati's sex was used as an argument against her assuming the reins of government. Citing Islamic restrictions against a woman leader, powers in the People's Consultative Assembly (MPR) supported Abdurrahman – who had the advantage of being a man and the leader of an Islamic, if less popular, party (his National Awakening Party, the PKB, had gained 11 per cent of the vote at the 1999 general election). As Megawati was concerned to contain the violence that threatened to erupt at any minute, she graciously accepted the role of vice-president and requested that her supporters go home in peace.

Abdurrahman was heralded by the educated middle class, and especially by the international community, as a leader capable of bringing Indonesia into the fold of world democracies. But as the country was to learn, much to its disappointment, his expressed commitment to democracy would not be matched by his deeds. While one must recognise Abdurrahman's achievements in moving the nation towards greater freedom and democracy for the people (especially for minority ethnic groups), his erratic leadership, controversial statements and policy decisions, and personal drive to remain in power became increasingly hard to tolerate and threatened the overall political, economic and social stability of the country.

Megawati, on the other hand, rarely made public statements. This was particularly the case during the term of the Abdurrahman presidency, when her silence was often interpreted as a sign of weakness or a lack of capability. Yet, in contrast to Abdurrahman's often offensive and contradictory comments and policies, over time Megawati's silence became her strength. In some quarters she was even regarded as the nation's saviour in the struggle to overcome the imported financial crisis, then *kristal* (total crisis), that threatened to engulf the country. While Abdurrahman was busy surviving, it was Megawati who took the difficult economic decisions agreed on with the International Monetary Fund (IMF), such as a reduction in fuel subsidies. In the strongly patriarchal political environment, her sex was played down. Upon her rise to the presidency, one of the most bitter opponents of a female presidency – Hamzah Haz – accepted her offer of the vice-presidency.

Given the prevailing political anxiety and the concerns raised by her silence, Megawati's extended search for the 'right' people to occupy the 'right' positions in cabinet was again regarded as a weakness. Yet, when she finally announced her cabinet on 9 August 2001, most domestic and international reaction was extremely positive, especially with regard to her economic team (Wanandi 2001). Sri Mulyani, an economic critic of the previous government, even referred to it as the 'best team' possible (*Suara Pembaruan*, 9 August 2001). Megawati seems to have listened to demands that the cabinet represent various segments of society. In contrast to her predecessor, she assigned positions to representatives of the various political parties, albeit in largely peripheral posts. And although Megawati has few followers among women activists, she went some way towards addressing their concerns by appointing two women to her cabinet. Rini Suwandi, a professional businesswoman, holds the usually male post of Minister of Trade and Industry,[1] and Sri Rejeki Sumaryoto is the new State Minister for Women's Empowerment.

At her first cabinet meeting, held on 13 August, Megawati issued a tough policy agenda with authority. Her policy initiatives were welcomed as bold, and even the strongly patriarchal media responded by saying that she had been underrated (see, for instance, Schuman 2001). Following her first state of the nation address on 16 August, a *Kompas* editorial reiterated that earlier widespread comment about the president's low intellectual capability appeared to have been incorrect (18 August 2001). It is noticeable that when Mega does something right, her sex is not mentioned; at such times the media and commentators appear to consider the presidency to be gender-neutral. But when her statements are considered weak or when problems arise, her sex is underscored.

For all the euphoria felt by women following Megawati's rise to the presidency, experience elsewhere suggests that having a woman at the top – especially one not known for being particularly sensitive to gender issues – is no guarantee that women's issues will become a mainstream concern in public and civic life. For this to happen, women will need to occupy more decision-making positions at all levels of government and the bureaucracy, with the authority to implement their decisions. As long as women decision-makers remain in a minority, they will have to continue to meet the demands and conform to the interests of men.

THE ROLE OF WOMEN DURING THE SOEHARTO ERA

At the World Conference on Women held in Beijing in 1995, Indonesia participated actively and pledged commitment to the Conference Declaration. Soeharto, with his authoritarian political machinery, was still in full control of the country and dictating what was good for the Indonesian people – including what was good for women. Today, six years later, more women are entering the public domain. However, they continue to face serious obstacles in gaining access to formal power and their numbers are still very low.

From the beginning, Soeharto's New Order political machinery determined a role for women in the context of national development. This was not a role set in the context of power in the outside world, but a more traditional one centred on the family. Soeharto used propaganda on the atrocities allegedly committed by Gerwani, the mass women's movement associated with the Communist Party (PKI), to justify this traditional role for women. Within the state ideology, there was no room for women as individuals. Instead, they were continually reminded of their *kodrat* (inherent nature), and particularly of their household and reproductive responsibilities – to clean, cook and bear children. Their assigned role was to nurture the next generation of leaders, usually men, rather than stand forward in their own right. Women were expected to be happy in the role of *pendamping suami*, 'standing at the side of their husbands' (Wageman 2000).

It could be said that assigning the role of wife and mother to women, and continually reinforcing this stereotype, was one of the strategies the Soeharto regime used to maintain its power over the people. Women were told they had a duty to support their husbands. For those married to civil servants, this meant joining Dharma Wanita, the official organisation for civil servants' wives, which was almost 4 million strong in September 2000.[2] Women were also told they were responsible for the well-being of their families. At the grassroots level, this meant involvement in the Family Welfare Movement (PKK), a mass organisation for wives at all levels of the government apparatus (Bianpoen 2000).[3] To make sure that women cooperated in the government's plans for them in the development process, one of the criteria for evaluating civil servants' performance was their wives' participation in Dharma Wanita and/or the PKK (Buchori and Soenarto 2000).

As early as the second term of the Soeharto regime, the 1973 Broad Guidelines on State Policy (GBHN) emphasised women's contribution to the nation within the family context of guiding the younger generation. As rapid population growth was regarded as a major hurdle to economic development, women were made the target of a national family planning program. The 1978 GBHN took a broader view of women's responsibilities, recognising the need for them to participate in all fields while still emphasising their paramount role within the family. As economic and social development progressed, the GBHN of 1983 and 1988 incorporated an expanded view of women's rights, obligations and opportunities, acknowledging that women had a *peran ganda* (dual role) to fulfil. One role remained firmly anchored within the family environment, while the other acknowledged and built on women's potential in the economic and sociopolitical arenas – while still couched in terms of benefiting the family (Wageman 2000). The negative consequences for women of this 'dual role' were realised only at a later date when women became increasingly burdened with implementing government programs, usually with no or limited financial resources to support them. Rising levels of education and broadening horizons led some women activists to resist the role assigned to them by the state. This resulted in further accommodation being made in the 1993 GBHN: women were declared *mitra sejajar* (equal partners) in development, but remained constrained by male-imposed concepts of women's *kodrat* (nature), *harkat* (dignity) and *martabat* (status).

THE FALL OF SOEHARTO AND THE RISE OF MEGAWATI

Then came the 1997 financial-turned-economic crisis, which led to social and political upheaval. Demonstrations, led by students of both sexes and soon joined by activists, brought hopes of *reformasi* and an end to corruption, collusion and nepotism (KKN). After more than three decades in power, President Soeharto was forced to relinquish power to B.J. Habibie, who became Indonesia's third president on 21 May 1998.

The results of the 1999 general election were unexpected, and undesired in many quarters. Unlike the elections of the Soeharto period, which were contested by only three parties, in 1999 Indonesian voters could choose from among

48 political parties. The PDI-P won 34 per cent of the vote, displacing the government party, Golkar, which had gained landslide victories in previous elections. The PDI-P was born out of the New Order government's interference in the internal affairs of the Indonesian Democratic Party (PDI) when that party showed signs of developing into an effective opposition in the mid-1990s. Initially a party figurehead, Megawati Sukarnoputri, daughter of the charismatic first president, soon captured the popular imagination. She represented the country's political and socioeconomic 'outcasts', of which there were a few among the elite, but many more among the less advantaged.

As the leader of the party that had obtained the most votes and the largest number of seats in the MPR, Megawati should have had a good claim on the presidency. However, many of the country's politicians and religious leaders were strongly opposed to the idea of a woman as president, and used gender-based religious arguments to support their views. During this period, Megawati maintained a policy of 'no comment'. This position was taken as weakness on her part and rumours flourished about her alleged lack of intellectual capacity, leadership capability and understanding of sociopolitical affairs. Curiously, these arguments also reflected stereotypes of women as portrayed in New Order ideology.

Her party's dominant position in the MPR – the body that elects the president – failed to bring Megawati to power. Instead, intense backroom lobbying and female-unfriendly, media-fuelled resentment worked in favour of KH Abdurrahman Wahid, who became Indonesia's fourth president on 21 October 1999. Megawati, a woman, leader of the party that had won the election, had to accept the second highest position in the government, that of vice-president. Through a system of closed elections that allowed for vote buying and money politics, the male-dominated system of Indonesian politics was maintained.

Interesting developments have followed since then. The longer Abdurrahman stayed in power, the more disenchanted and irritated people became with his behaviour, inconsistency and outspokenness. Public policies could change within a few hours, and this led to tensions within the political elite, especially between the president and parliament. In particular, parliament took issue with Abdurrahman's supposed involvement in the corruption cases popularly known as Buloggate and Bruneigate, leading to his impeachment. Amien Rais, chair of the MPR and the person who had done most to engineer Abdurrahman's rise to the presidency, emerged as the loudest voice calling for him to step down. The final blow came when the president issued a decree (*dekrit*) dissolving the People's Representative Council (DPR) and the MPR, shortly after 1 a.m. on 23 July.[4]

Throughout this period of public conflict between the president and parliament, Megawati remained as silent as ever. Despite this, there was an astonishing turnaround in public opinion on her qualifications for leadership. By the time

Abdurrahman was forced to step down and Megawati, in compliance with the constitution, took over as president, she was no longer considered unfit to be president because of her sex. Instead, the nation, including many male religious leaders, regarded her as its saviour.

WOMEN MINISTERS IN ABDURRAHMAN'S CABINET

Despite her apparent lack of interest in women's issues, in the division of responsibilities between Abdurrahman and his vice-president, Megawati was given responsibility for empowering women. On 25 October 1999, she announced the appointment of two vocal women activists to the cabinet, Erna Witoelar as Minister for Housing and Regional Development and Khofifah Indar Parawansa in the traditional women's post of State Minister for the Role of Women. At the time of their appointment, both women were members of the MPR. While Abdurrahman replaced a number of ministers during his term of office, these women remained in cabinet throughout, and their portfolios even expanded. Erna's portfolio broadened when she became Minister for Human Settlements and Regional Infrastructure, while Khofifah's expanded when she renamed her office the State Ministry for Women's Empowerment.

At the time she joined the cabinet, Erna represented the widely respected Indonesian Consumers' Association Foundation (YLKI) in the MPR. Her appointment as Minister for Housing and Regional Development represented a significant step, as this was the first time a woman had been appointed to this traditionally male post. Given her background in the YLKI, Erna was well aware of the spectrum of problems faced by Indonesian women – from violence to lack of political participation – and the need for gender-sensitive public policies. She believed that her fellow women activists focused too much on violence against women and too little on women's lack of political and decision-making power. She was conscious of the need to involve women in decisions on human settlements and physical infrastructure, as well as to provide assistance to refugees, whose numbers were increasing rapidly in various parts of the archipelago.[5] Erna bore the double burden of being a woman and a minister; on top of the responsibilities associated with her ministry, she was under pressure to support various 'women's' activities, such as opening events. She has observed that other ministers do not have to cope with such a double burden on their limited time.[6]

Khofifah Indar Parawansa was a member of parliament and therefore automatically a member of the MPR as well. At 34, she was the youngest member of cabinet. A long-time politician and close confidante of Abdurrahman, she entered parliament as a member of the PKB, in which she held the position of deputy chair. Most of the PKB's supporters are members of Nahdlatul Ulama (NU), an Islamic religious group which claims some 34 million followers.[7]

Interestingly, before her appointment to cabinet, Khofifah had been a strong proponent of the abolition of the Ministry for the Role of Women, but she found herself unable to refuse this post when it was offered to her by Abdurrahman. It is no surprise that the outspoken Khofifah changed the name of the office soon after becoming minister.

WOMEN IN OTHER HIGH-LEVEL PUBLIC OFFICES

Although there have been women in parliament since independence, and although the government established a separate Ministry for Women's Affairs as early as 1978, even today relatively few women participate in policy formulation and development planning or are able to influence the course of development programs and projects. Too many women remain ignorant of their rights, while men remain unaware of the importance of women's equal participation in power and decision-making, and of the extent of their exclusion. The sociocultural environment is not conducive to women's full participation in the politics of national decision-making, and institutional obstacles continue to restrict their access to power.

Despite their increased participation in politics, women have not gained greater formal power and women's concerns remain peripheral. In 1999, large numbers of women from all walks of life participated in the general election campaign along with students and activists. Women voted in larger numbers than men, making up 57 per cent of the country's 100 million voters (*Swara*, Supplement of *Kompas*, 7 October 1999: 4). Nevertheless, women's representation in key political decision-making bodies has declined slightly over the last decade, although it has been claimed in some quarters that the current group of women holding political office 'are of better quality' (Soekanto 1999). In the past many women obtained their seats in the DPR and MPR through their nepotistic relations with officialdom. Today, they are more likely to have become members in their own right, because of their own personal achievements in party politics or in civil society.

The MPR consists of all 500 DPR members as well as a number of appointees representing regional and functional groups in society. During the New Order, the MPR had 1,000 members. The Habibie government reduced this to 700, namely the 500 DPR parliamentarians and 200 appointees. Under Soeharto the MPR's main function was to 'elect' the president. It therefore met only once every five years, the duration of the government's term. This rule has been changed and the MPR now holds annual sessions. The number of women in the DPR declined during the 1990s, from 60 in the 1992–97 session to 56 in the 1997–99 session and only 44 in the parliament elected in 1999. In the MPR the proportion of female representation has also declined, from 12 per cent in 1997–99 to 9 per cent at present (Oey-Gardiner and Sulastri 2000).

The same scarcity of women is found in other high-ranking offices. Women make up just 12 per cent of level IV members of the Supreme Court and 1 per cent of the State Audit Board;[8] only one of the 37 members of the Supreme Advisory Council is a woman (BPS 1994). At the local government level, there are no women governors, and only six of the country's 336 regents are women.[9] Women were heads of a mere 927 (14 per cent) of the 66,000 villages in Indonesia in 1991 (BPS 1992).

The local legislature is not woman-friendly either. In April 2000 (when not all local legislatures had selected their chairs), at the provincial (DPRD Tingkat I) level, only one of 27 parliaments was chaired by a woman. Of the 70 posts for deputy chair, again only one was held by a woman (Table 9.1). At the *kabupaten* or regency (DPRD Tingkat II) level, just six of 245 chairs, and ten of 657 deputy chairs, were women.

As increasing numbers of women become aware of the disadvantages they face in party politics, advances are being made to meet their demands for access to party positions. Though not yet formally spelled out in party rules, both the PDI-P and PKB have adopted the idea of quotas for women. In the PKB about 30 per cent of positions are to be reserved for women, while in the PDI-P, two

Table 9.1 Distribution of Position of Chair and Deputy Chair in Local Legislatures by Sex, April 2000[a]

Position	Males	Females	Total
Dati I (province)			
Chair	26	1	27
Deputy chair 1	24	0	24
Deputy chair 2	23	1	24
Deputy chair 3	22	0	22
Dati II (regency)			
Chair	239	6	245
Deputy chair 1	241	5	246
Deputy chair 2	233	5	238
Deputy chair 3	173	0	173

a The picture was still somewhat confused at the time the data were collected as not all positions had been filled and the number of regions was continuing to expand. In April 2000 there were 30 provinces. West Nusa Tenggara and Maluku, as well as 90 *kabupaten*, had not submitted any names. In addition, not all parliaments appoint deputy chairs.

*Table 9.2 Structural Positions in the Civil Service by Echelon and Sex,
September 2000* [a]

Structural Level	Men		Women		Total		Women at Each Echelon (%)
	(no.)	(% of all men)	(no.)	(% of all women)	(no.)	(%)	
Echelon I	235	0.1	31	0.1	266	0.1	12
Echelon II	1,359	0.8	72	0.2	1,431	0.7	5
Echelon III	14,379	8.2	1,374	4.2	15,753	7.5	9
Echelon IV	64,814	36.8	10,637	32.2	75,451	36.0	14
Echelon V	95,532	54.2	20,901	63.3	116,433	55.6	18
Total	**176,319**	**100.0**	**33,015**	**100.0**	**209,334**	**100.0**	**16**

a   The highest level of structural position is echelon I.

Source: BKN.

of every five seats must be occupied by women (CETRO, personal communication).

The 'glass ceiling' is well preserved in the civil service, too. There are five echelons of structural posts with decision-making power in the government bureaucracy. Echelon I is reserved for director generals and their deputies; directors and bureau chiefs are in echelon II, section chiefs in echelon III, subsection chiefs in echelon IV and unit chiefs in echelon V. Of the top-level decision-makers in echelons I and II, only 12 and 5 per cent respectively are female (Table 9.2). Women are much more numerous at the bottom of the pecking order, in echelon V, where 18 per cent of posts are held by women, and where 63 per cent of all women working at any echelon (compared with 54 per cent of men) are found.

Women still have a long way to go in the civil service. Even though 38 per cent of the overall civil service is female (Table 9.3), only 16 per cent of decision-making positions are held by women (Table 9.2). It is of interest to note that women are relatively overrepresented among level III civil servants (41 per cent at level III as opposed to 38 per cent overall) (Table 9.3). Given that the highest entrance point into the civil service is level III, it is probably only a matter of

Table 9.3 Composition of Civil Service by Sex and Level, September 2000 [a]

Structural Level	Men		Women		Total		Women at Each Level (%)
	(no.)	(%)	(no.)	(%)	(no.)	(%)	
Central government							
Ministry/ institute	1,131,468	46.0	579,327	39.0	1,710,795	43.4	34
Seconded to autonomous regions or other agencies	900,794	36.6	749,177	50.5	1,649,971	41.8	45
Assigned to autonomous regions or other agencies	57,808	2.3	48,565	3.3	106,373	2.7	46
Subtotal	2,090,070	84.9	1,377,069	92.7	3,467,139	87.9	40
Regional government							
Subtotal	370,949	15.1	107,695	7.3	478,644	12.1	23
Total (central + regional)	**2,461,019**	**100.0**	**1,484,764**	**100.0**	**3,945,783**	**100.0**	**38**
Civil service level (individual civil servants)							
IV	91,677	3.7	36,444	2.5	128,121	3.2	28
III	1,167,710	47.4	821,734	55.3	1,989,444	50.4	41
II	972,193	39.5	600,310	40.4	1,572,503	39.9	38
I	229,434	9.3	26,276	1.8	255,710	6.5	10
Total	**2,461,014**	**100.0**	**1,484,764**	**100.0**	**3,945,778**	**100.0**	**38**

a   The highest civil service level is level IV.

Source: BKN.

time before at least some of these women move up to level IV, ready to occupy structural posts now filled by men.

TOWARDS A NATIONAL POLITICAL AGENDA FOR WOMEN

Because of the hurdles they face in the public sector and in formal politics, women have increasingly tended to bypass formal participation and channel their efforts into civil society and non-government organisations (NGOs). Towards the end of the Soeharto regime, as the political climate became increasingly repressive, one group of women prepared to challenge the prevailing powers within the context of mainstream politics was the Indonesian Women's Coalition (KPI).

Another organisation to confront government repression was Voice of Concerned Mothers (SIP), which exploited the maternal role assigned to them by the state to campaign against the government's masculine paradigm of power and violence (Heraty 2000). In February 1998, this group of 'simple housewives', under the leadership of Karlina Leksono and Gadis Arivia, held a *demo susu* (milk demonstration) at a roundabout in front of Hotel Indonesia. As mothers, they were concerned that rapidly rising milk prices had left them unable to feed this increasingly expensive commodity to their children and elderly parents. The SIP mothers smiled, chanted, prayed and distributed flowers to passers-by and the police. Their banners reflected their genuine concern for the well-being of the nation's children. The subsequent arrest of the SIP's leaders attracted widespread local and international media attention.

It is interesting to note that the student demonstrations that culminated in the ousting of Soeharto started only two days later, on 25 February 1998. By the time these demonstrations reached their height in May, the SIP – while continuing to distribute milk to families with young children and the elderly – had become the focal point for donations of food packages to students occupying the grounds of parliament. Today, the roundabout at Hotel Indonesia has symbolic significance – it is where protesters can be guaranteed attention.

Violence against women, an important issue in the Beijing Declaration, has become a rallying point for women. The impetus for this came from the May 1998 riots, in which Indonesian women of Chinese descent were the targets of widespread sexual abuse and gang rape. This led to the establishment of the National Commission on Violence against Women, headed by Prof. Dr Saparinah Sadli, also a senior member of the National Human Rights Commission. As regional conflicts continue to exacerbate the sufferings of women, and as domestic violence has become increasingly acknowledged, the more widespread establishment of women's crisis centres has opened up greater opportunities for women to express their civic responsibilities. However, as noted earlier, there is a fear that this focus on the single issue of violence may leave too few women to continue the struggle at the political front.

At centre stage in Jakarta, increasing numbers of women are joining hands to gain political recognition. On 21 April 2001, to commemorate Kartini Day, a number of NGOs organised a rally to focus attention on the need for greater consultation with and representation of women in the political process. Attended by over 400 people (including some men), the meeting attracted so many new faces that seasoned women activists constituted a minority.

The few women in parliament have also expressed their solidarity by establishing a women's caucus. Their relatively small number means, however, that they remain dispersed as members of different committees. As women politicians in a male-dominated parliament, these women are continually having to prove that they are as good as their male counterparts. The parliamentary agenda, determined mainly by men, rarely allows discussion of issues of particular concern to women. It seems that for women's issues to enter the patriarchal public domain of politics, numbers do count.

IN CLOSING

Women have joined with men in the struggle to make Indonesian society a more humane and democratic place to live. Denied a role in political and bureaucratic decision-making, women activists have responded by joining general civic organisations. In these difficult times, it is interesting to note that a number of nationwide, gender-neutral NGOs, such as the Centre for Electoral Reform (CETRO), the International NGO Forum on Indonesian Development (INFID), the Urban Poor Consortium (UPC), the Environmental Forum (Walhi) and the consumer organisation YLKI, are headed by women. Indonesian women have heard the call and have responded.

NOTES

* An earlier version of this paper was presented as a keynote address at the International Women's Day celebration held on 8 March 2001, organised by the International Community Activity Centre in Jakarta.
1 Women activists were worried that Megawati might reduce the number of posts occupied by women, or that she would give them only traditional women's portfolios such as Women's Empowerment and Social Welfare.
2 Figure courtesy of Direktorat Pengendalian Mutu dan Tabel Referensi, BKN.
3 Research by Lies Marcoes (see Chapter 15) and anecdotal evidence suggest that at the grassroots level in several villages in Central and East Java, and even at the Rukun Tetangga (Neighbourhood Association) level in Jakarta, the PKK is still

active. This suggests that it is still owned by local communities, and providing a valuable service to them.

4 Only once before in Indonesia's history had a president resorted to issuing a *dekrit*. This was in 1959, when Sukarno dissolved the Constituent Assembly (*Konstituante*) in response to continuing disagreement among political parties and frequent changes in the cabinet.

5 These refugees were internally displaced persons who had been forced from their homes as a result of natural disasters or social and political disturbances.

6 Mentioned during a meeting with Gerakan Pemberdayaan Swara Perempuan, a women's NGO active in promoting increased political participation by women.

7 But not all NU members join the PKB – some are members of other political parties.

8 These figures were obtained from the BKN, and describe the situation in September 2000.

9 Based on preliminary data to 19 February 2001. These figures were provided by the Direktorat Aparatur Daerah, Departemen Dalam Negeri, and were processed by Insan Hitawasana Sejahtera using names to determine the sex of the person.

10 INDONESIAN WOMEN ARTISTS: TRANSCENDING COMPLIANCE

*Carla Bianpoen**

The rise of Megawati Sukarnoputri to the presidency is an inspiring story of a woman's transcendence from compliance to non-compliance, from invisibility to determined exposure. Enduring public scorn, defamation and even victimisation, Megawati has never retaliated. Instead she persisted in silence, while nurturing an inner strength that conquered the fiercest arguments against a woman becoming leader. Turning the tide, she became Indonesia's first woman president.

The rise of Indonesian women artists to prominence takes a similar pattern. Facing discrimination by curators and art historians, they kept silent, as was expected of women in the traditional context. Besides, as one artist revealed, it was beneath their dignity to protest about discriminative selection. Instead, they worked harder, did better and excelled. At the dawn of the new millennium a change was tangible in the world of art, culminating in the first half of 2001 in two large exhibitions by women artists at Galeri Nasional and Bentara Budaya Jakarta. This chapter focuses on change and innovation in art from a women's perspective.

THE GENDER PERSPECTIVE

The independence struggle was perhaps the first step to liberating women from domestic captivity; the 1945 Constitution accorded the same rights and responsibilities to both men and women. In reality, however, women were relegated to domesticity and women's organisations were undermined. The first National Women's Congress was held in 1928 (see Indar Parawansa, Chapter 6). The federation grew, leading to the formation of Kongres Wanita Indonesia (Kowani) in 1946. This umbrella group of over 70 women's organisations was drawn into supporting the male-determined goals of state development, particularly under the Soeharto regime (1966–98). Meanwhile, NGOs focusing specifically on women emerged, producing a new generation of women activists – whose strength increased even more following the economic and monetary crises of 1997 and the mass rapes of ethnic Chinese women that took place in Jakarta in May 1998.

As women stood up and presented a united front, they realised that so-called 'women's concerns' were in fact closely linked to the main game of politics, from which women were largely excluded. It also became clear that atrocities against women had occurred long before the May rapes, in other parts of the country such as Aceh and Irian Jaya.

Nevertheless, gender remained a non-issue in the mainstream of politics until the Indonesian Democratic Party of Struggle (PDI-P) won 34 per cent of the vote in the June 1999 general elections and its leader, Megawati Sukarnoputri, became a possible candidate for the nation's leadership. Suddenly gender was a hot topic, and religious-based arguments against women's leadership erupted. In the heat of the debate it was 'forgotten' that at one point in history women had ruled the Muslim state of Aceh Darussalam for 59 years.

THE VISUAL ARTS

Pioneers

Against this background, it is hardly surprising that the rise of women in the visual arts has followed a similar pattern. The first known woman painter, Emiria Sunassa, was born in north Sulawesi in 1894. She did not seem to have a problem when it came to shining together with her fellow artists in the first indigenous painters' association, Persagi, which had nationalist aspirations. Emiria participated in several exhibitions and was called a genius by peers such as S. Soejojono. In contrast, Tridjoto Abdullah (1917–89), a Javanese and the first known woman sculptor, constructed several sculptures for public places in Yogyakarta, Madiun and even Jakarta, but had only one exhibition in her entire lifetime – and that was with her older brother, the renowned sculptor Basuki Abdullah. In Bali, Ni Made Suciarmi (born 1932) and Dewa Biang Raka (born 1937) have been active as painters, with the latter participating in a youth festival in Romania as early as 1953. Nevertheless, hardly any art historians have conducted extensive research on any of these artists, or included them proportionally in art documentation. Curators of major art exhibitions have displayed little interest in including women artists, supposedly because there were few that could match the generally male-defined standard.

'Awas Bahaya Belakang Kembaang Teratai' (Beware the Danger behind the Lotus Flower), by Emiria Sunassa. Oil on wood, 1943.

Women Artists Associations

Women's desire to expose their art works increased as the number of women involved in the visual arts expanded. The first known initiative came from women who painted as a hobby, when in 1973 Ratmini Soedjatmoko gathered friends, locals and expatriates together in Group Sembilan (Group of Nine). Twelve years later, two professional women painters, Farida Srihadi and Nunung WS, set up Nuansa Indonesia, which organised several exhibitions and even managed to participate in exhibitions abroad. But as its members found their way to a new status as professionals in their own right, Nuansa Indonesia broke up. Another group of artists formed Ikatan Pelukis Indonesia, also in 1985, and other loose associations sprang up as the need arose.

Similar initiatives followed much later outside Java. In Bali it was Mary Northmore who provided an outlet for Balinese women artists by setting up the Seniwati Gallery in Ubud in 1991. In Makassar, South Sulawesi, 20 women artists decided as recently as 1999 to band together in the South Sulawesi Women Artists Association (IPPS), which is led by Nunuk Nurul Chamisany, an artist who is also the head of the provincial Office of the Department of Culture (Taman Budaya).

Breakthroughs

'Women in the world of art' is a fairly new concept in Indonesia, let alone 'women in contemporary art'. For centuries, a destiny of biology that was both natural and divinely ordained has been taken for granted. Kartika Affandi (born 1934), daughter of the great artist Affandi and married to a fellow painter, had to live with her husband's polygamy and the equally painful experience of his possessiveness when it came to sharing the limited paint that was available. Kartika did not say much, but she managed to paint anyway. Her canvases say much about her inner feelings about the culture she was born into.

A great many artists have emerged since then, and many have earned a name in their own right. Towering above them all is Hildawati Soemantri (born 1945). Not only is she Indonesia's first and foremost professional ceramic artist and one of the first women to hold a solo exhibition in her own right, she was also the first Indonesian to obtain a PhD in art history from Cornell University. Her art has lifted ceramics out of the ordinary, positioning it at the level of contemporary fine art.

Hilda was born in Jakarta and graduated from the Department of Art and Design, Bandung Institute of Technology, in 1971. She received her Master of Fine Arts (MFA) from Pratt Institute in New York in 1976, her MA from Cornell University in 1993, and her PhD in art history from Cornell University in 1995 for a thesis entitled 'The Terracotta Art of [the] Majapahit [Era]'. She is currently a lecturer at Trisakti University and the Jakarta Institute of Arts (IKJ), where she founded the ceramics department in 1976.

Hilda was only 30 when she introduced installation art at the Taman Ismail Marzuki arts centre in Jakarta in 1976. It caused quite a stir. The broken pieces and the yellow colour of the ceramics used were all part of the shock, even for her peers, who had yet to become aware of the term 'installation art', and barely understood the profoundly contemplative meaning of a concept that pondered the broken pieces of a person's life, and the process by which the pieces come together at the centre of life itself.

Twenty-five years later, Hilda Soemantri remains at the lonely pinnacle of her profession, producing works of an aesthetic and professional quality that no other ceramic artist has been able to approach, let alone equal, so far. The 27 of her works exhibited at the Japan Foundation in May 2000 (together with those of a former student, Suyatna) confirm the excellence of Hilda's art. Mostly featuring the mountain landscape that had impressed her so much while staying in Victoria, Canada, as an artist in residence and as a teacher at the university, her deeply sensitive works, with their abstract lines, curves and cracks, elucidate the woman as well as the metaphysical dimension of her art. Hilda usually works without predetermination; her works may be called self-creating in that she allows the feel of the texture against her bare hands to determine their shape. But the exquisite images formed of multicoloured glazed slabs suggest meticulous precision and great care.

For Nunung WS (born 1948), to be a painter was a calling, and one that came before being a woman, wife or mother. She was only in fourth grade when she saw the works of Kartika Affandi, but she made up her mind then and there that she would become a painter, and has since worked her way to excellence. Her great determination helped her overcome her father's demand that she pursue religious studies. Nunung persisted on the path she felt to be her destiny and became the first student of the Surabaya Art Academy, later studying with Nashar, noted for his non-figurative art. Initially attracted to abstract expressionism, and subsequently proceeding to planes where colour alone became her mode of expressing the conscious and the subconscious, Nunung surprised everyone when she became preocupied with the subject of the flower. Two recent works show her development. 'Satu Bunga' (One Flower) is still a hesitant line coming from a spontaneous movement of the hand, but 'Bungaku' (My Flower) clearly shows the shaping of form on the canvas. Nuning says the flower has grown within her as a metaphor for her close relationship with her only son. The first woman to succeed in making art her life priority, Nuning admits to a retreat from that determination since turning 50.

Bronze and iron are not usually considered suitable mediums for women, but that does not matter to Dolorosa Sinaga (born 1952), the first woman sculptor to use bronze. Why did she choose this of all materials? 'I like the way it allows exciting colours to come out of the chemical processes and the ample space it provides for self-expression', she says. Her earlier works tended to feature powerless women placed in harrowing positions, although she also made uplifting sculptures of classical dancers. Her recent sculptures show an emerging strength, culminating in her vision of pulling together existing dynamics of women's empowerment. Political and social turbulence, the many cases of violence against women and the sculptor's involvement with the families of missing persons left important traces as Dolorosa matured personally and professionally. Her works have become symbols of humanity's enduring strength, signalling resurrection out of the depths of pain. 'Solidaritas' (Solidarity) (2000), 'Gerak Berlawan' (The Forces Against) (2001) and 'Avante' (Onward) (2001) in particular are reflections of women's strength. They show a further development from one of her earlier sculptures, 'Resistante' (Resistance) (1999), which featured a hand clinched into a fist as a symbol of pain and anger (see back cover). Dolorosa brings to her work what Toeti Heraty has called 'a new metaphysics of

'Theme for Us Today: The Crisis', by Dolorosa Sinaga. Rod iron, 1998.

'False Target', by Astari Rasjid. Mixed media on canvas, 1998.

freedom and re-creation'. Through her, Toeti says, the 'I' can speak. Dolorosa is a sculptor of renown, and certainly not just in Indonesia alone. In 1998 she created a sculpture for the 2nd International Sculpture Symposium in Hue, Vietnam, which has been replicated for the International Sculpture Park in Siena, Italy.

Astari Rasjid (born 1953), who started painting seriously only in the 1980s, finds her major source of inspiration in Javanese culture. Astari was a fashion journalist who had also made a name for herself as a fashion designer when she decided to marry and give priority to her family. Art courses taken in her leisure time, however, stirred up lingering aspirations. After a period of snatching time for the studio and juggling between being a wife and mother and related societal functions, she decided to pursue art full-time. The results have been astounding.

Shattering a cultural glasshouse full of taboos, Astari excels with her insights into the universality of issues encountered in Javanese society. Her excellent command of technique and artistic imagery makes her oeuvres unique and compelling. Included among the 20 best of 22,000 entries in the worldwide

Winsor and Newton Exhibition (1999), her self-portraits in a recent joint exhibition at Nadi Gallery in Jakarta ('Ever Ready Secretary' and 'Formula #1
Perempuan Kuat', or Formula #1 for the Strong Woman) again show her talent
for weaving her story into the larger map of history. In them, she takes a more
humorous tone than usual, playing with and twisting gender-typical concepts
and products popular in the lives of Javanese, and cleverly integrating a subtle
but sharp critique.

Marida Nasution (born 1956) occupies a special place in the Indonesian
graphic art scene. Unlike her peers, who jumped at the opportunity to follow the
more lucrative career of painting, Marida stuck to graphic art. While exploring
other branches of art, she never once deserted the idioms of her beginnings.
Rather, she made graphics an integral part of her innovations, even breaking
away from tradition by making it part of a new development in art – installation
art. Her stirring creativity reached its peak in a spectacular solo exhibition,
'Harkat Perempuan' (Women's Dignity), held at Galeri Nasional in April 2001.
In one of her installations, she positions three circling pyramids made of transparent synthetic fibre at different levels. Each contains a 65–68-centimetre-high
sculpture of a woman at a different phase of her life – as a girl, as a woman in
her prime and as an elderly woman. The notion of women's bondage is emphasised by the placement of dozens of smaller (30-centimetre-high) sculpturines on
either side of the pyramids. Having a heart ailment and an ear infirmity, Marida
went to art school only because that was the closest school to her house. To
everyone's surprise she switched from painting to graphic art, even purchasing
a piece of heavy machinery for her own use. She handles all technical procedures
herself, saying that she loves the sensation of touch and the communicative
vibrations of the materials she works with during the process of creation.

The surrealistic canvases of Lucia Hartini (born 1959) were a new phenomenon on the Indonesian art scene of the 1980s. A virtual autodidact, her brushstrokes – spiralling like hurricanes over the canvas – retain a touch of yearning
and marvel at the same time, and have become a unique feature of her work.
Lucia married a fellow artist at a fairly young age, gave birth to two children and
was then abandoned by her spouse. Fervently making paintings to make ends
meet, she managed to save money for the paint needed to create 'the real thing'
when the day was over. Her tempestuous landscapes of agony and yearning have
travelled the world. Now her life seems to have entered more peaceful waters,
although her style retains its exclusivity, as is evident in recent works such as
'Prahara Televisi' (Tempest on TV) and 'Cakra from the Soul', shown at the
Nadi Gallery exhibition in August 2001.

Arahmaiani (born 1961) said she 'got the shock of her young life' when she
was told she could never be a *nabi* (prophet) like the Prophet Muhammad
because she was a girl. The first well-known woman artist to jump into public
art (in the 1970s), she was expelled from art school because of this and subse-

quently excluded from art exhibitions. When she did participate, the catalogue did not include her name. Increasingly, she has become more involved in performance art, and lately has even used her own body as an artistic medium. Considered one of Indonesia's most radical artists, her artistic explorations now also include photogravure, as seen in 'Migrated Text', a thought-provoking representation of her preoccupation with past experiences and the future.

Erica Hestu Wahyuni (born 1971) stands out as an artist who has made her artisitic 'shortcomings' an asset of sorts, seizing the art market as no other woman artist has been able to do. To the surprise of her critics, her inability to paint figures in the realistic manner has become a hit. Having a retrospective at the age of 30 is unusual, but that is exactly what Erica has achieved. The 89 of her works displayed at Galeri Nasional testify to her enormous achievement, as does the comprehensive documentation that exists of all 600 of her works. Erica's works in the naive mode look disarmingly like endearing fairy tales, yet undeniably gender issues are explored in many of them. In want of protection, Erica has singled out the elephant to act as her mascot in all of her paintings. But a visit to Moscow last year may have effected a turning point; the power of her beloved animal seems to have entered into her very self, as is evident in her Russian masterpiece, 'Mayalubov'.

Since May 1998, Indonesian women have stood together in solidarity. 'Revolution' may be too strong a word to use, but the dynamics of this movement are similar and were showcased, among other things, by a display of art by Indonesian women at the Pontifical Gregoriana University in Rome in October 1998. On the day of the first public meeting of the newly established National Commission on Violence against Women in Jakarta, Professor Toeti Heraty, who accompanied the exhibition to Rome, declared before the Congregation of Papal Excellencies and the Indonesian Ambassador to the Vatican that the works were in homage to the victims.

Many of the works were striking for the visible change in the personal orientation of the artist. This was particularly so in the case of one of the most senior artists, Wiranti Tedjasukmana (born 1933). Best known for her sweet representations of folklore, in this exhibition she is suddenly found using freely swinging brushstrokes. 'Justice Attacked', for example, is a bold comment on the injustice directed at women and in marked contrast to Wiranti's usual work. Ratmini Soedjatmoko (born 1925), best known for her traditional Indonesian fabrics, also presented works showing a strong political concern, exemplified by her painting 'Srikandi Accuses'. Paula Isman (born 1927), a devout Catholic, radically swept aside the traditional image of Eve as temptress and sinner in the history of the human race, to place her in a single statue together with Mary, the mother of God. Astari Rasjid offered her first three-dimensional work of art, linking her personal story with the larger picture of events. This feature has since become her trademark.

'Justice Attacked', by Wiranti Tedjasukmana. Acrylic on canvas, 1998.

THE NEW DYNAMIC

The new dynamic in the Indonesian art world has seen the emergence of numerous exhibitions, both solo and joint. Even in areas remote from the flow of information and new developments in the arts, women artists are on the move.

In Makassar, the 20 women artists in IPPS have vowed to hold regular exhibitions as well as organising travelling exhibitions. Their creative lifeblood includes Andi Musaidah (born 1975), whose pastel paintings tend to lie between the realistic and the surreal. The images in representative works like 'Perkawinan Berdarah' (Bloody Marriage) and 'Wanita Malam' (Night Moth) are symbols perhaps for a woman's hidden dramas. Another notable member of IPPS is the sculptor Tini Martini (born 1964). The bare and simple appearance of 'Buah Hati', which she constructed out of sand and cement, may be a reflection of an austere lifestyle. Equally intriguing is the metaphysical concept in Tini's 'Macrocosmos–Microcosmos', featuring a sculptured head *en face* made of plexiglas, enclosed by a man's profile constructed of wire.

The art installation titled 'Bek Gilhoe Na Lheung' (Forbidden to Tread on the Grass), by the Acehnese ceramist Endang Lestari, attracted much attention at the

'Buah Hati' (Apple of my Eye), by Tini Martini. Sand and cement, 1999.

all-women art exhibition held at Galeri Nasional in April 2001. Recalling the killing fields of her native Aceh, Lestari created ceramic mounds reminiscent of worm casts springing out of the earth, as symbols for the dead that lie buried beneath the grass, while ceramic oblong forms set on sand and continuing against a black cloth intensify the sense of both compassion and gruesomeness. Lestari was born in 1976 in Banda Aceh and obtained her degree in ceramics from Institut Senirupa Indonesia (Indonesia Arts Institute) in Yogyakarta, where she now lives and works.

Also from Aceh is Virsevenny (born 1968), a graduate of Sekolah Tinggi Ilmu Ekonomi (Academy of Economics) in Banda Aceh. She is currently on a two-month training program in art management at the Cemeti Gallery in Yogyakarta. Virsevenny has been concentrating on her art since 1985. Still on the path of discovery, as she herself admits, her paintings appear to apply the realistic, the surrealistic and the abstract. Virsevenny seems most comfortable in the surrealist mode, as it allows her to bring to her canvas something that is real in her vision, though not necessarily in reality.

Bali's I GAK Murniasih (Murni, born 1966) challenges the predominant position occupied by the island's male artists through paintings that bring out her dreams and aspirations in an artistic language that surpasses the imagination. A blend of the abstract and realistic, her voluptuous, often humorous, fantasies based on the sexual organs of the body stand in sharp contrast to the tradition of her Balinese culture.

Diah Yulianti, on the other hand, finds her source of inspiration in the world of spirits of her native Kalimantan. Using unusual imagery and executed in a

Untitled, by Virsevenny. Oil on canvas, 2001.

technique similar to pointillism, her paintings present ghostlike figures that she tries to link to issues or events taking place in the mortal world. Abstractions of spirits appear in elongated vertical form, as if drawing the line between the world above and the world below. This is a belief system of primitive society to which Diah feels exceptionally strongly drawn.

Closer to Jakarta, a new generation of artists has emerged, with several capturing attention through their artistic innovations and new visions. Ironically for a generation that should have experienced a greater degree of freedom to follow its calling, the gender issue seems to be a constant preoccupation. In the all-women art exhibition held at Bentara Budaya in May 2001, Amelia Lestari provocatively underscores the gender issue in her work, 'I Don't Have a Problem with Gender', by putting her male figure in a bra and dumping the woman's face in a shrimp bowl. In another work titled 'I Don't Have Problems with Phallocracy', typical boys' and girls' toys are arranged in boxes. Noteworthy, too, is Tiarma Dame Ruth Sirait (born 1968), a fashion designer by profession who has been seeking new outlets for her artistic urges. In her installation, 'Sweet Lollypop', a manequin is positioned on a carpet to represent a victimised woman, while a poem explains its meaning; the work is a critique on the gratuitous copying of foreign concepts. Tiarma has participated in earlier art exhibitions such as 'Wearable', held in Yogyakarta in June 1999.

'Tali KB-ku di Caplok Ikan' (A Fish Is Pinching my Birth Control Device), by I GAK Murniasih. Acrylic on canvas, 2000.

Wara Anindyah (born 1969) is a relatively new name on the Indonesian art scene. A drop-out of the School of Fine Arts in Yogyakarta, she is a prolific painter whose work often features Chinese-like people. Her inspirations are Chinatown (where she used to live) and her ancestral grandmother, as well as the novels of Pearl S. Buck. Wara is going through a process of self-examination. One is struck by the dark gloom that seems to dominate the atmosphere of her large canvases, in which caricaturist facial traits are like haunting masks in unreal stories.

Judging from her two-dimensional work, 'Jendela Rumah Kita' (The Window of our Home), Rubiati Puspitasari (born 1958) will probably begin to see her name in the papers more often. Her stirring work combines ceramics with glass and wood and inventively brings a three-dimensional aspect to a two-dimensional frame.

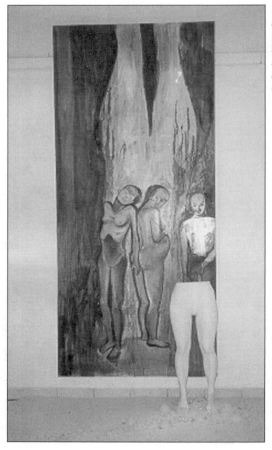

*Tubuh Paradoxikal
Saya, Senyum Regina'
(My Paradoxical Body,
Regina's Smile), by
Regina Bimadona.
Installation, mixed
media, 2001.*

While Regina Bimadona (born 1967) is a painter who presents performance art, it is perhaps her installations that are the most striking, both for their visual attraction as well as their professional quality. Six years ago she was not in favour of having exhibitions specifically for women, saying that this would only widen the gender gap and that gender was not an issue for her. Today, however, it is clear that she has become quite preoccupied with the gender issue, particularly as it relates to restrictions concerning sexuality and the female body. Such concerns are revealed in three large mixed-media installations – 'My Paradoxical Body', 'Body Festivity' and 'The Vagina Resurrection' (300 x 130 cm in size, using oil, canvas, resin, wood, aluminum, plexiglas and sand) – and smaller installations such as 'Phallo' exhibited at Galeri Nasional in April 2001.

Anna Zuchriana (born 1966) made news with a solo exhibition titled

'Kenapa Sih Cina' (What's Wrong with Being Chinese) held in July–August 2000 at Cemara-6 gallery. Originally a graphic artist, she started dealing with the sensitive issue of race in 1997 when she participated in an exhibition together with other teachers from IKJ. From that time stems a painting featuring a bride in ceremonial Betawi (traditional Jakarta) attire, which looks Chinese at first sight. This is an image of her mother, Oey Twat Nio, a woman of Chinese descent who married M. Jusuf Rasjid, a native Betawi. Since then, Anna has continued to paint Chinese people in an Indonesian context, becoming the first artist to highlight racial discrimination on canvas. Whether she will be able to make her work more than just descriptive will depend greatly on her ability to link her exploration of her roots to the universality of contemporary art.

*'Kenapa Sih Cina?'
(What's Wrong with
Being Chinese?),
by Anna Zuchriana.
Mixed media on
canvas, 1998.*

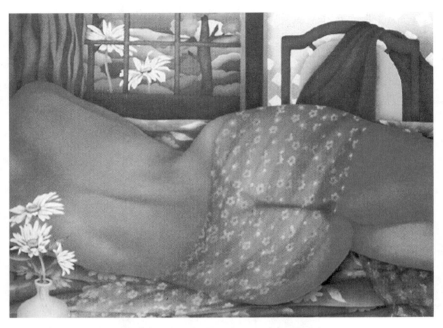

*'Kembangnya Malam' (Indulging in the Fragrance of the Night),
by Reni Hoegeng. Acrylic on canvas, 1998.*

Unusual in the Indonesian art world are the works of Reni Hoegeng (1947), a graduate of the Bandung Institute of Technology whose apple greens and soft pinks, along with her headless figures, have become her trademark. Usually nude, or at most with a transparent cloth elegantly draped around the waist, her headless figures may in the past have denoted a lack of self-confidence. Today Reni Hoegeng is a member of parliament as well as an artist, and this has probably strengthened her personally. This is illustrated by the change in her figures, which now have heads and are usually clothed. However, she still paints them viewed from the back.

Explorations of and experiments with new technology are making an impact, as highlighted by Tris Neddy Santo (born 1949). A graphic artist by training, she uses advanced technology to apply several colours at a time.

Marintan Sirait (born 1960), a long-time ceramist who has earned a name for her installation and performance art, is a versatile artist who also does prints on canvas.

Inda C. Noerhadi (born 1958), who has intensified her painting activities in the past few years, delves into the depths of archeology, her field of expertise. This has had an important impact on her paintings since the May 1998 riots.

Recalling excavations at the Borobudur Temple, Inda recognised features of modern society that once marked the carnal world as expressed in the Buddhist-based Kamadhatu.[1] Further explorations of humankind in relation to pre-historic times – in images presented in her solo exhibition in November 2000 in Bali – lead to the conclusion that not much has changed. Inda, the director of Cemara-6 Gallery, is in the process of completing a PhD in art history at the University of Indonesia.

It is of little importance to women artists whether politically coloured discourses continue – or cease – to question the appropriateness of a woman leading the nation. They are poised to proceed on their path to excellence. There is just no going back.

NOTES

*   For more information about the artists discussed in this chapter, including contact details, please contact the author (carlab@cbn.net.id).

1   In Buddhist teachings as they appear in the temple of Borobudur in Central Java, Kamadhatu is the sphere of desire, and one of the three spheres related to the Buddhist cosmos.

11   LITERATURE, MYTHOLOGY AND REGIME CHANGE: SOME OBSERVATIONS ON RECENT INDONESIAN WOMEN'S WRITING

Barbara Hatley

The dramatic political changes of the last few years in Indonesia undoubtedly have been significant for women. The dismantling of New Order political structures and ideologies has opened up space for varied forms of women's activism. Women's groups have addressed, with enhanced solidarity and agency, problems of economic hardship and political unrest. The horrific rapes of May 1998 and exposure of similar events in regions of military conflict have made violence against women an issue of serious public concern and institutional activity.[1] But the overall effects of change are still unclear. The revival of conservative customary law, particularly Islamic law, as part of new regional autonomy measures is seen as potentially repressive for women (see Noerdin, Chapter 14). Violence against women continues. One might question how developments in the public, political sphere have affected the daily practice of women's lives, and what impact the events of a mere few years might have had on patterns of gender inequality and accompanying ideological assumptions entrenched over centuries.

When and if deep-seated change occurs, a key site of its expression is likely to be cultural forms and the mass media. Numerous studies of New Order cultural expression document the ways in which the conservative, family-centred gender ideology of the regime was reproduced in and reinforced through literary works, magazines, film, television and other media. Through direct government control in the case of state-owned media and a more diffuse reflection of dominant discourse elsewhere, women's roles as male-dependent wives and mothers were valorised, and more autonomous female behaviour queried and criticised (Sen 1982, 1993; Sunindyo 1993; Hatley 1997; Brenner 1999). Such imagery fitted the regime's propagation of an organic model of the state as hierarchically ordered family. Its striking prominence in government propaganda and media is explained by Susan Brenner (1999: 30) as a deflection of attention away from 'real crises of citizenship', wealth inequalities, corruption and ethnic tensions, towards national narratives of moral crisis in the family in which 'the happy middle class family came to stand for a generic Indonesian moral and social order'.

Such practices built upon and developed strategically longstanding patterns of reinforcement of dominant gender ideology through cultural forms. The archetypal ideal of wifely fidelity and devotion embodied in traditional forms of theatre in figures such as Sita and Sumbadra was recalled in novels of the 1970s and 1980s in female protagonists explicitly modelled on these proto-types.[2] Popular films represented both the seductive allure and lethally danger-ous power of the contrasting figure of the autonomous, sexually assertive woman. Nyai Lara Kidul, mythical queen of the South Sea, for example, appeared briefly as voluptuous sex goddess before transforming into a hideous fanged hag reminiscent of Rangda, the widow-witch of Balinese dance drama, emblematic of the frightful power of female sexual energy uncontrolled by male order.[3] Another manifestation of womanly sexual power, the *ledek* female dancer at *tayuban* dancing and drinking parties, became a target of explicit state control, as part of processes of ordering, refining and 'developing' *tayuban* from unruly folk entertainment to an officially sanctioned expression of local cultural identity (Widodo 1995).

To document changes in this picture of cultural reproduction would require a large-scale, wide-ranging investigation of different forms of media well beyond the scope of this paper. It may be too early, in any case, for changes in social practices and attitudes to translate into identifiable trends in media imagery.[4] Where interesting new developments are clearly visible, however, is in the domain of literary writing and performance by women. The range of themes addressed by women fiction writers in recent years has greatly expanded; their freer representation of sexuality includes among other things considerable reference to lesbianism.[5] And several texts by women authors appearing during the last few years challenge the archetypal images mentioned above, of faithful wife, alluring but threatening temptress and monstrous widow-witch. These new interpretations boldly refute accepted, age-old mean-ings. What is suggested is both a perception of the ongoing social force of gen-der assumptions embodied in these ancient symbols, and a commitment to opening up new visions of 'female' and 'male' by dismantling them. Other writ-ers, meanwhile, create new myths for this new time, from the flow of daily life or from futuristic imaginings.

The beginnings of a new spirit may be evident in women's writing, parallel-ing the growth in women's political activism. In this chapter I review these developments, reflecting on their context and potential meanings. The subverted archetypes and new myths, as the most direct expressions of challenge to estab-lished gender ideology, constitute my focus.

HISTORY AND IDEOLOGY: GOOD WIVES AND WIDOW-WITCHES

A brief and necessarily sketchy review of the development of dominant gender
ideology in Indonesia illustrates the historical roles of mythical archetypes of
male and female, their representation in cultural forms and the significance of
their contemporary contestation.

The polarised images of dependent, devoted wife and wild temptress/widow-
witch first became entrenched in Southeast Asia, the historian Barbara Andaya
reports, as patriarchal Hindu states became established. The relatively egalitar-
ian, complementary model of gender relations typical of indigenous Southeast
Asian societies was overlain by new imagery. Female sexuality and fertility,
which in small-scale societies had been celebrated for their centrality to human
survival, in a hierarchical, patriarchal state system had to be properly contained
by male authority. An ideal construction of woman as refined and modest,
dependent and subordinate wife or daughter was contrasted with a demonic
Other. Autonomous womanly power outside male control, threatening the very
basis of social order, was portrayed in terms of a dangerously tempting or
hideously terrifying female figure. Later in Islamic states an understanding of
women's God-given roles as wives and mothers reinforced this picture (Andaya
1994).

The impact of the colonial experience was complex. During the 19th century,
as the masculinity of the Javanese aristocracy was challenged by colonial power,
the celebration of male dominance and female subservience through the imagery
of court art forms intensified (Florida 1996). Later colonial contact, in the form
of European education and ideological influence, exerted a complex impact on
expectations of female behaviour. During the 1920s and 1930s a new vision of
more independent, active social roles for women opened up. At the same time,
the threat of actual sexual miscegenation, or psychological 'contamination' of
Indonesian women by overly free Western ways, prompted reinforcement of the
'traditional', refined feminine ideal by both indigenous leaders and colonial educators. The extent of change had to be contained to prevent moral decline and
societal breakdown if women were seduced too far from their proper roles by
new foreign freedoms.

The gaining of independence saw an expansion of actual social roles for
women, but a decline in ideological attention to gender issues, as masculinist
military and political concerns dominated the national agenda. Later, during the
1960s and 1970s, the definition of national identity in terms of supposedly
essential, indigenous Indonesian cultural values and images had highly conservative implications for women. With the entrenchment of the authoritarian, patriarchal New Order regime, from the late 1960s onwards a narrowly prescriptive
gender ideology was actively propagated and imposed through social policies
and organisational structures (Suryakusuma 1996; Sullivan 1991).

Justifying and reinforcing New Order constructs of women as dutiful wives and mothers was the threat of a horrifying alternative – a monstrous female Other. Central to the anti-left propaganda spread by the Soeharto military regime at the time of its seizure of power were lurid images of acts of savagery supposedly perpetrated by members of the communist-linked women's organisation Gerwani. The communists were said to have encouraged sexual licentiousness as well as political and social assertiveness for women; the New Order, by contrast, was committed to restoring Indonesian women to their essential, 'natural', apolitical role as wives and mothers (Wieringa 1998; Drakely 2000; Tiwon 1996). Such 'othering' of the figure of assertive, independent woman helped justify the regime's resistance to notions of gender equality and female autonomy. The term 'feminist' was identified with sexual boldness, and social assertiveness defined as alien, foreign and contradictory to Indonesian women's inherent, authentic nature.

The impact of this ideological context on cultural representation has been described above. In women's writing of the New Order period the effect was an overwhelming focus on themes of love and domesticity among the contemporary middle class (Hellwig 1994; Woodcroft-Lee 1988; Sumardjo 1982). The protagonists of women's fiction were often educated, professional and well travelled, but always demure, restrained and apolitical. Sometimes an explicit contrast is drawn with the bold, promiscuous behaviour of female characters from Western countries.[6]

SOCIETAL AND LITERARY SHIFTS

But already in the latter years of the New Order period, the hold of dominant, state-generated ideology had begun to weaken. Global currents of thought at odds with conservative state interests attracted the attention of the educated middle class. In the field of gender attitudes, both affluent, career-oriented individual women and non-government organisations espoused their own versions of female 'empowerment'.

In the cultural realm, women's writing began to address a broader range of themes. Occasionally the old stereotypes were challenged. Already in 1987, for example, Leila Chudori's short story *Air Suci Sita*, transposing the Rama–Sita legend to modern-day Canada, had queried the hypocrisy and imbalance of the idealisation of *female* fidelity in the absence of reference to that of men (Chudori 1989). But the protagonist's realisation is a silent, internal one, causing no disruption to her refined, demure outward persona. It is over a decade later before a frontal assault on established gender assumptions and images takes place.

Ayu Utami's work *Saman* was the first of the new women's texts to capture public attention, although not the first to be written. Appearing in May 1998, right at the end of the Soeharto era, this first novel by a young woman writer, awarded a prestigious literary prize, stirred enormous controversy because of its explicit sexual themes. *Saman* simply *assumes* women's equality and autonomy – in work life, in political activism and in love and sex. The four elite, affluent, personally liberated young women who constitute the main female protagonists of the text express their sexuality frankly, and love as they please. The concept of female sexual fidelity seems quite irrelevant to the lifestyle of the free-wheeling, libidinous Cok. Her friend Shakuntala, meanwhile, subverts the myth of priceless female virginity by deliberately breaking the 'precious porcelain' of her hymen with a spoon. And in her imagined role as a fairy princess in a fortressed castle, instead of waiting for a handsome knight to claim her in marriage, she falls in love with a barbarous demon from the surrounding forest. In secret trysts with him Shakuntala happily commits the 'crime' of which Sinta, the legendary faithful wife of shadow play and dance drama, must prove her innocence in a trial by fire after her long imprisonment by the demon king Rahwana.

While undermining classical images of the refined, chaste feminine, Ayu's text also celebrates the contrasting archetype of female power, grounded in nature and the supernatural. The mother of the main male protagonist (Wisanggeni or Saman), referred to only by the generic title of 'Ibu' (Mother), has a mysterious and dangerous connection with the spirit world. Sometimes she is psychologically 'away', unresponsive to her surroundings – she communes with the creatures and plants of the forbidding jungle behind the family home. Three times she becomes pregnant, but the unborn or just-born child dies or disappears, without explanation. Ibu is distraught, contrite but silent. Sometimes, at the edge of his consciousness, her son Wis hears the children, and the voice of an unknown man talking with his mother. But he never sees them, or talks about them. And Wis's father remains devoted to his wife, despite his grief over the lost children. For Ibu is warm, vivacious and beautiful, beloved by all – essential Woman.

Such archetypal reference is both local and universal. It recalls Eve in the primal garden, and Durga–Umayi, the alternately benign and destructive consort of the Hindu god Siva, as well as Javanese/Balinese images of the dangerous power of female sexuality – that of Nyai Lara Kidul of the South Sea, witchcraft by scheming wives and the temptations of *ledek* dancing girls. The unique aspect of this manifestation is that Ibu is not reviled or punished for her actions; her 'bad' side is accepted as part of her overall character.

Just as Ibu, the local embodiment of the dangerous power of sexual Woman, is cherished by husband, family and community, so too the four young urban protagonists, who in another context might be labelled brazen and overly Westernised, are portrayed without blame or criticism. The dichotomy of good woman/bad woman, and of pure, virtuous Indonesian womanhood versus threat-ening, sexualised Western 'Other', is ignored.

One incident in the narrative playfully subverts the whole issue of the East/West racial and sexual divide. Shakuntala imagines herself as a native maiden bathing in a river. In this instance her encounter is with a *foreign* 'demon', an early European adventurer. The pair embrace and talk. The man pro-duces a 17th century almanac to illustrate European impressions of bizarre Asian sexual preoccupations, including the shameless demand by women that men wear penis decorations for their pleasure. Laughingly, Shakuntala recounts her country's beliefs about the refinement of the East versus the crassness of the West, about European women wearing bikinis in the street, ignoring virginity and having sex on television. The narrator comments on the absurd irony of a man and woman debating the propriety of Eastern versus Western cultural sys-tems – while sitting naked.[7]

Demons, foreign and local, portrayed as sensitive and thoughtful conversa-tionalists, constitute one pole of Ayu's subversion of standard male archetypes. Another is the reinterpretation of the knightly 'hero'. Wis or Saman, the undoubted hero of the novel, displays enormous courage and tenacity in defend-ing the dispossessed community of rubber tappers, culminating in brutal torture by the military on their behalf. But in physique and personal style he is the antithesis of the strong, virile *satria* (warrior), magnetically attractive to women but coolly resistant to their seductive wiles. Saman is small, thin and not partic-ularly prepossessing. As a Catholic priest he is inexperienced with women, and though responsive to Yasmin's seduction, barely able to 'perform'. Earlier, when held by the military, he had had electric wires attached to his penis. 'Cut it off if you like', Saman had joked with his torturers. '... I only use it for peeing. I don't need much length. But leave my fingernail. I need that for picking my nose.' Brave and virtuous Saman may be, even Christ-like in his combination of courage and compassion, but without a hint of macho masculinity. And in this period of swaggering militias, military terror and neighbourhood violence, such an alternative vision of maleness is surely a positive contribution.

EMBRACING THE DARK

In addition to the range of age-old archetypes highlighted and reworked in *Saman*, several other recent texts take up and indeed embrace the most powerful and fearful of female mythic images – Calon Arang or Rangda, the widow-witch of Javanese/Balinese legend and performance. Long viewed with dread as the personification of evil and destruction, sometimes theorised as elemental male fear of women,[8] what alternative meanings might Rangda's image hold for today?

Goenawan Mohamad's opera libretto *The King's Witch* and Toeti Heraty's long prose-poem *Calon Arang: Kisah Perempuan Korban Patriarki* [Calon Arang: The Story of a Woman Victim of Patriarchy] highlight Calon Arang's marginalisation and trickery by King Airlangga and his priestly advisor, Mpu Bharada. For Goenawan, Calon Arang is a victim of centralised political power. In Toeti Heraty's poem, as the title indicates, the problem is patriarchy.

The immediate inspiration for this work, Toeti explains, came from a photograph by Rio Helmi of the Calon Arang character in a Balinese performance. This image, hung in Toeti's bedroom and pictured on the cover of her Calon Arang text, shows a strong, sympathetic, middle-aged face, not at all the monstrous fanged mask of standard representation. Ideas she had held for a long time – about baseless, unjust prejudices against widows and divorcees, and the suffocating restrictions placed on women by the patriarchal system – coalesced around that image.

Her poem begins with the standard image of Rangda as a horrifying symbol of evil, with her tongue of fire, wild hair, talons and pendulous breasts. The story is quickly summarised of her destructive revenge on the people of Kediri over the lack of marriage proposals to her daughter, Ratna Manggali, and her eventual defeat by King Erlangga and his priest in the name of preservation of the order of the state. Thus ends this 'myth about the love of a mother and the power of the state'. But 'history is not as simple as this'. We look more closely at Calon Arang's persona. Remarkably, the angry old woman, stereotypically portrayed with wild hair and pendulous breasts, becomes a figure of sympathy and identification. No one recognises now that she has ever lived a different life, as a child, as a young woman who was as pretty as her daughter, as a wife, and now, disastrously, as a widow. At 67, Toeti Heraty, accomplished poet, scholar and cultural figure, mother of six, writes (Heraty 2000: 6–7):

Apakah Anda tahu apa artinya menjadi janda apakah tahu artinya menjadi perempuan tua	Do you know what it means to be a widow? Do you know what it is like to become an old woman?

and

Ah, kini aku mengerti sekali bahwa dalam geram menjadi korban patriarki marah dan berang membakarnya	Ah, now I know very well that in her fury At becoming a victim of patriarchy Anger itself consumed her

In conversation Toeti observes that she can empathise with the fury that Calon Arang would have felt at what had happened to her, and imagine how she may have vented that anger through her magical powers.[9]

At the launching of Toeti's poem in November 1999, another reinterpretation of the Calon Arang legend was staged to celebrate the event – a dramatised monologue titled *Pembelaan Dirah* [The Defence of Dirah] by Cok Sawitri, a Balinese woman writer, performer and journalist. Accompanied by two male musicians and another female dancer, Cok Sawitri performed her vision of the story of Calon Arang, a widow of the district of Dirah, as a victim of political violence perpetrated by centralised, male-controlled state power. With her wild bloodied hair and piercing glance, the widow is a fearful figure, capable of breeching the king's fortress and slaying thousands of his men. But she retreats into the forest to avoid bloodshed, to carry out 'perlawanan dalam bentuk moral dan budaya' (moral and cultural resistance). Even when the king's forces pursue her and attack her followers' quarters, she advises her supporters not to resist. But the king's men spread tales of her evil magic and destructive acts, to blacken her image with the people. The power holders of today, the narrator reports, are similarly oppressive and violent. The ordinary people may indeed have turned against the 'king' and forced him to step down, but lies spread by his regime, and those before it, live on. After four centuries of reinforcement, the myth of Calon Arang's evil nature is deeply engrained in the popular imagination (Asmaudi and Dwikora 1999).

In Cok Sawitri's vision, as in Goenawan Mohamad's libretto, Calon Arang's struggle is not against universal patriarchy but totalitarian state power. The inspiration for this work, the artist reports, was the July 1996 attack by Soeharto regime thugs on the headquarters of Megawati Sukarnoputri's party. For Cok Sawitri, Megawati at this time was a symbol of the nation's suffering – 'negeri saya jadi janda' (my country had been made a widow) – abused and marginalised. She studied various versions of the Calon Arang story in palm-leaf manuscripts, developing a view that she had represented a sect that opposed King Airlangga and his priest Mpu Bahrada on religious grounds. When attacked by the king, the Dirah group defended themselves spiritually rather than physically, in similar fashion to Megawati's moral and legal resistance to the Soeharto regime after the routing of her party base. The performance drew on several Hindu mantras expressing peace.

Though conceived and developed in 1996, the performance was not presented publicly until 1999. The dangers of taking on and personally re-creating the magically powerful Calon Arang role, heightened presumably by the anti-government, political suggestion of this new interpretation, were too great. Cok Sawitri fasted for months in preparation for the first performance; her own mother tried to dissuade her, fearing she would die, and huge crowds gathered to watch. By the time of this presentation, in August, Megawati had won a majority in the general elections but was being sidelined in the political manoeuvring for the presidency, as Islamic religious leaders declared illegitimate the concept of a female head of state. By November, when the monologue was performed at the launching of Toeti Heraty's poem, Megawati had lost the presidency to Abdurrahman Wahid. Like Calon Arang, she was experiencing ongoing slander and marginalisation. Cok Sawitri is quoted in a review of the performance as suggesting that her work also has a wider reference, to all kinds of situations of repression. And her message is one of resistance: 'What I want is for everyone to carry out resistance in her own space'.[10]

The association of the Calon Arang myth with Megawati provides an intriguing variation on her usual portrayal in political discourse as 'Ibu' – both exalted by her followers as nurturant mother of the nation, and scornfully dismissed by her critics as unskilled housewife, unprepared for political leadership. The comparison with Calon Arang rests on Megawati's experience of oppression by a central, patriarchal state, and bears the positive suggestion of a deep-seated power, suppressed all the more ruthlessly because of its threat to the status quo. No direct connection is made in Cok Sawitri's work with the infamous Calon Arang-like images of the monstrous female which the New Order state itself produced and propagated. But new tellings of the tale emerge, and new workings of the image.

As mentioned earlier, the Indonesian military justified its elimination of the left and seizure of political control in the mid-1960s by fabricating lurid images of licentiousness and barbaric cruelty supposedly perpetrated by members of the communist-linked women's organisation Gerwani. Such propaganda tapped into archetypal male fears of women's demonic power, long embodied in literature and theatre in figures such as Calon Arang, to represent the threatening potential of politically mobilised woman. Yet even this most darkly intimidating invocation of the Calon Arang myth has now been reworked by a woman author: in Ayu Utami's *Larung* (2001), a Balinese grandmother deliberately assumes the terrifying persona of widow-witch cum Gerwani activist in order to protect her family.[11]

The old woman addresses her now-adult grandson, recalling the past. When he was very small she had taught him to eat beetles and flying ants, drawing on the earth at a time of famine in the land, ignoring the voices branding her as a sorceress and inducting her grandson in the ways of a *leyak* (evil spirit). Later, she recounts, the little boy had been heartbroken when his beloved playmate, a young Chinese girl, disappeared after a brutal raid on her father's rice store by starving peasants. The next year the mobs came to take away his father, an army officer, as part of the anti-communist violence of that time. The old woman had opened the door and stood before them unafraid, armed with awareness of her reputation for the possession of powerful black magic. The soldiers left her alone, but captured, tortured and murdered her son. Then they came again for her daughter-in-law, whom they branded as a member of Gerwani. This time the grandmother was waiting, and confronted the gang outside the door. 'I am the oldest in this neighbourhood', she said. 'My daughter-in-law is not Gerwani ...

I am Gerwani.'[12] With her reputation for dark powers, dressed in a waist cloth reputedly harbouring a snake, the old woman was clearly a formidable presence. The mob retreated and the young mother was saved. Here, age-old conceptions of Calon Arang's destructive power are not refuted or reinterpreted but invoked for strategic purposes, to a successful end. The key issue is survival.

The three authors, Toeti Heraty, Cok Sawitri and Ayu Utami, have each approached the Calon Arang/Rangda figure in a different way – explaining and justifying the witch's fury; refuting, as male slander, her standard portrayal; making strategic use of the fear she evokes. What is novel and remarkable is that their works should have appeared almost at the same time, embracing the most hated and feared, but also the most powerful, of mythical female archetypes. These woman writers publicly identify with and defend the horrifying male fantasy of powerful woman, Rangda, unafraid of such association.

MYTHS OF THE EVERYDAY

Rather than contesting established stereotypes, another recent text creates its own mythic quality through evocation of the ongoing, timeless quality of female experience. *Tarian Bumi* [Dance of the Earth] by Oka Rusmini (2000) focuses intensely on the interwoven stories of four generations of women, living within the tight spatial and psychological boundaries of the walled family compound of village Bali. The text moves back and forth in time, from an opening conversation between the main protagonist, Telaga, and her small daughter, to recollection of the lives of Telaga's paternal grandmother, mother and mother's mother, to Telaga's own childhood, adolescence and young adulthood, and back to the present day. For all these female lives the determining constraints are the same – the rules of caste and patriarchal custom as they intersect within marriage. And for all of them the result is suffering.

Telaga's paternal grandmother, the daughter of a wealthy upper-caste *brahmana* family, feels tragically betrayed when her unstable only son takes as his wife not a high-born woman like herself but a mere commoner. This woman, Telaga's mother, through her beauty, skills in dance and driving ambition, has attracted a *brahmana* husband, but at the expense of complete separation from her own family, and humiliatingly low status within his aristocratic home. Telaga, by contrast, falls in love with a low-caste man, upsetting her mother's plans for a spectacular aristocratic match. Her husband dies, but she lives on with his family, unwelcome and lonely. Finally she attempts to resolve the conflicts of this situation by ceremonially repudiating her *brahmana* identity and assuming that of a low-caste *sudra*.

The wider social and historical context of these events is indicated only in passing references.[13] The key focus is dialogue between female figures –

between mother and daughter, grandmother and granddaughter, woman teacher and girl pupil, and young female friends. Always the subject is the roles and life experiences of women. Mothers and grandmothers advise and instruct young girls, attempting to prepare them for adulthood and marriage; the latter question and protest against the restrictions they must undergo.

The picture on one level is of constant frustration and pain. In this situation women may turn on one another, venting their feelings on someone of lower status, a daughter-in-law. But another striking aspect of womanly experience is enormous strength, courage and endurance. Daughters and granddaughters admire the courage and strength of their female elders. A remarkable example is Luh Dalem, Telaga's mother's mother. Left widowed and impoverished, then attacked and blinded in a vicious rape, resulting in the birth of twin girls, Luh Dalem speaks of life as a continuing adventure, and its troubles as challenges. She also gives explicit voice to the notion of women's strength:

> Balinese women are not given to complaining. They prefer to sweat and toil … Their sweat is fire. From that sweat the smoke of the kitchen is maintained. Their milk feeds not only the children they bear. It also feeds men. Sustains life itself.[14]

Here, one might argue, is a core theme and image of the novel. Throughout the text the fire of women's strength, intelligence and courage has been amply illustrated, along with the frustration and unhappiness caused by the narrow limits of its expression. If and when that energy bursts out of the kitchen and into the wider world, what a conflagration will result! In this context the closing motif of the novel, the assumption by the protagonist Telaga of *sudra* status, perhaps takes on particular significance. Though bringing no practical benefits, the symbolic potential of this act of separation from the high-caste family and its past is arguably profound.

The author of this text, Oka Rusmini, is a Balinese of *brahmana* caste, raised in Jakarta. Coming to live in Bali when her family returned there during her junior high school years, she recalls her deep shock at the differences in lifestyle from the world she had known. The rules of caste and patriarchal family custom seemed frighteningly restrictive. At the ceremony for her first menstruation she learnt that only a man of *brahmana* caste could become her husband. In the event Oka Rusmini married a Javanese fellow journalist at the *Bali Post* newspaper. Though still able to visit her parents, she is estranged from the extended family over this offence. Many *brahmana* women fail to marry, she reports, because of the prohibition against 'marrying down'. Some become involved in lesbian activity; some younger women defy the rules. But the sanctions remain severe.

Concern over these issues motivates a focus in Oka Rusmini's fiction on women's lives. Before writing both *Tarian Bumi* and an earlier novel, she carried out 'research' on her subject. In the case of *Tarian Bumi* she went to live in the district of Tabanan, in a village famed for its dancers. Her intention was to experience and write about village women of all social levels. Concentration on *village* life, in contrast to the middle-class, urban settings typical of women's writing, and the sense of authenticity in its spare yet intense descriptions and conversations, are the great strengths of Oka Rusmini's work.

POTENTIAL FUTURES

In its dramatic contrast to Oka Rusmini's novel, another new text testifies to the variety of contemporary women's writing, and may indicate positive new directions. *Supernova: Ksatria, Puteri dan Bintang Jatuh* [Supernova: Knight, Princess and Falling Star] is set worlds away from the physically and psychologically enclosed space of village Bali, in cosmopolitan Jakarta and cyberspace. A professional, highly educated gay couple embark on a novel within a novel about three urban, educated, hyper-modern Indonesian yuppies like themselves – a woman, her husband and her lover. The 'knight, princess and falling star' of the title refers to a myth one of the male protagonists, Ferre, has read as a boy; in this text he becomes the knight who loses the princess, his lover, but thereby encounters the star, the wondrous Diva, top-class prostitute and super-intellect. As her alter ego, Supernova, Diva dispenses advice on the internet about life, philosophy and science; she can read minds and enter others people's dreams. The text moves back and forth between narrative, protagonists' dialogue and writers' commentary, Supernova's discourses and the gay couple's discussions about cybernetics, science and philosophy. All is artifice, riddles, story within story. And yet there are serious messages, too, in Supernova's advice about understanding one's own completeness, in the love relationships, and in the person of Supernova as the embodiment of woman as freedom and power.

The work of a 24-year-old female singer from Bandung, Dewi Lestari or Dee, *Supernova* was launched with a great flourish of publicity and controversy. Celebrated as the expression of new dimensions of consciousness, emblematic of a new generation and enthusiastically espoused by young readers, the novel was also judged by some to be contrived and pretentious, its scientific content dismissed by experts as factually incorrect. But there seemed to be relatively little emphasis on the work as *women's* writing, with all of the associated presumptions. Within the novel itself, although Supernova could be interpreted as a new mythical image of woman, confronting old stereotypes, no explicit emphasis is given to this reading, amid the various themes and dimensions of the text.

Critical judgements of this text aside, it is surely positive that women's fiction is taking diverse paths – challenging dominant gender archetypes, locating the mythical in the everyday, addressing previously taboo political issues, engaging with fashionable new scientific and philosophical discourses, appealing to different generations – rather than following predictable, stereotypical patterns. Certainly the hold of longstanding gender imagery and New Order ideological constructs has loosened. Such developments did not begin with the demise of the New Order regime, but they appear to have flourished in the new climate. What influence they may have on broader popular culture will depend on many factors, in media production and social life. But certainly models for more varied cultural expression by and about women are available, in the skills and confidence of contemporary women authors and the works they create.

NOTES

1   These developments are mentioned in a number of other contributions in this volume, and are addressed in detail in Budianto (2002).

2   Sumbadra is the wife of the hero Arjuna in the Mahabharata epic and Sita the wife of Rama in the Ramayana. Both are icons of wifely fidelity and devotion in the Javanese versions of these epics played out in theatrical performance. Recent works of modern literature drawing on these models include Umar Kayam's short story *Sri Sumarah* (Kayam 1975) and Linus Suryadi's *Pengakuan Pariyem* (1981). See Hatley (1997) and Clancy (1988) for more detailed discussion of these and similar works in their social and literary context.

3   Stephen Atkinson (1993) analyses the appeal of horror films of this type popular in Indonesia during the 1980s.

4   One recent study of popular media, Pam Nilan's work on magazine stories and young Balinese women's views of romance and marriage, indicates little perceived 'liberation' as a result of modern, global social trends, but rather new anxieties and pressures for women in relation to 'free choice' marriage (Nilan 2001).

5   Lesbian themes are mentioned in a number of the works discussed here, particularly *Tarian Bumi*. A recently published volume called *Lines* consists entirely of short stories with lesbian protagonists.

6   An example of this occurs in N.H. Dini's novel *La Barka* (1976). Here an Indonesian woman living in Europe, undergoing similar experiences of marital separation and divorce to those of a group of European friends, explicitly distances herself from certain aspects of their behaviour. 'Our Eastern customs are so different', as she explains (Dini 1976: 78).

7   A number of the points discussed here are examined in more detail in an article on post-coloniality and Indonesian women's writing (Hatley 2002).

8   The philosophical and cosmological meanings of the Rangda figure are complex and various, as Michele Stephen illustrates in a richly detailed, intensively researched recent article (Stephen 2001). Uncontested, however, is the association of Rangda with femaleness, destructive power and witchcraft, the intense fear she inspires, and the understanding that through confrontation with a *male* counterpart, this terrible power is capable of containment and redirection.

9   This conversation took place at Toeti Heraty's home in Jakarta in July 2001. In the

same month I also met Oka Rusmini in Bali and later spoke with Cok Sawitri by phone. Information about the writers is drawn from these conversations.

10 'Yang saya inginkan setiap orang melakukan pelawanan dengan ruang sendirinya' (Dian 2000).

11 A short story by Ayu Utami entitled *Larung* first appeared in Indonesian in the journal *Kalam* and was reprinted in the English-language journal *Latitudes*. The same text forms a section of the author's recently published novel *Larung*, the sequel to *Saman* (Utami 2001: 60–70).

12 'Aku yang tertua di kampung ini. Menantuku bukan Gerwani ... Tapi akulah yang Gerwani' (Utami 2001: 70).

13 Telaga's mother's family suffers particular hardship because of her father's alleged connections with the Indonesian Communist Party (PKI). His disappearance, presumably during the 1965 anti-communist reprisals, leaves her maternal grandmother alone to earn a living, and leads indirectly to a brutal attack and rape as she returns from the market. But this issue is mentioned only briefly.

14 'Perempuan Bali itu, Luh, perempuan yang tidak biasa mengeluarkan keluhan. Mereka leibih memilih berpeluh ... keringat mereka adalah api. Dari keringat itulah asap dapur bisa tetap terjaga. Mereka tidak hanya menyusui anak yang lahir dari tubuh mereka. Mereka juga menyusui laki-laki. Menyusui hidup itu sendiri' (Rusmini 2000: 19).

12   WOMEN AND THE LABOUR MARKET DURING AND AFTER THE CRISIS

Lisa Cameron

This chapter seeks to examine the labour market experiences of Indonesian women during and since the financial crisis. In particular, it seeks to investigate in what way women's experiences have differed from men's. Several studies were conducted in the year or two following the onset of the crisis, with the aim of examining the labour market impact. Few, however, focused specifically on women's experiences. By using the National Labour Force Survey (Sakernas) data for all years from 1996 to 2000, this study attempts to lay out comprehensively the impact the crisis had on women's labour market opportunities and experiences, and also examine to what extent the market is returning to its pre-crisis state and whether the crisis looks like having a lasting impact on women's roles in the labour market.

DATA

The Sakernas is conducted in August each year.[1] It consists of a stratified random sample of the population. The sample size has varied over time. Over the period used in this paper it varies from over 70,000 households in 1996 to about 31,500 households in 2000. Sampling weights are provided that allow the samples to be weighted up to represent the entire Indonesian population. These weights vary by province and urban/rural status and are applied in all of the calculations below.

The Sakernas is a standard labour market survey. Respondents are asked some basic demographic questions about their gender, age, educational attainment, marital status and their relationship to the household head. They are then asked a number of questions aimed at establishing their labour market status. If an individual works, then information is collected on the type of work done, the number of hours worked and, if the person is an employee, the wages received. Those not working are asked whether they are searching for work and, if so, what search methods they are using. Since 1997 some questions have been asked about work transitions. This allows us to examine the characteristics of those who lost their jobs during the crisis period and those who have been able to find new positions since the economy began to recover. The Sakernas is not a panel survey and so it is generally not possible to examine the same individual's labour market experience over time.

The tables that will be presented below contain summary statistics for the period 1996–2000. I will focus largely on the changes from 1997 through to 1999 (the crisis period) and the subsequent start of the recovery, 1999–2000. The 1997 data are 'pre-crisis' because they were collected in August. Although the rupiah began to depreciate in mid-July 1997, by the end of August it had reached only Rp 3,000/US$ (compared with its original value of Rp 2,500/US$) and the real consequences of the depreciation were yet to be felt in the labour market.[2] The 1996 figures are included in the tables so that the reader can get a sense of the trends before the onset of the crisis.

I will first examine the crisis impact and then the evidence of recovery.

CRISIS IMPACT

Labour Force Participation

Previous studies of the labour market impact of the crisis have shown that in response to the large decreases in real labour income, labour force participation increased between 1997 and 1999, and that women's labour market participation increased to a greater extent than men's (Sigit and Surbakti 1999; Gilligan et al. 2000).[3] Table 12.1 presents the labour force participation rates of men and women from 1996 to 2000.[4] The national figures show a smallish increase in participation for both women and men between 1997 and 1999, of 1.5 and 1.4 percentage points respectively. This translates into an addition of about two million people to the workforce over this period.

Previous studies of the impact of the crisis have established that it varied widely across regions, and hence it is important to disaggregate the data. Urban areas, particularly in Java, were more severely affected because of their strong formal labour market. The low value of the rupiah caused mayhem, resulting in many lay-offs in the financial sector (where foreign currency-denominated loans ballooned in rupiah terms), the construction sector (particularly in Jakarta, where businesses put large-scale construction on hold) and the formal manufacturing sector (which relied heavily on imported inputs). In contrast, the export-oriented agricultural sector benefited from its enhanced competitive advantage, and some

Table 12.1 Labour Force Participation Rates, 1996–2000 (%)

Year	Total		Urban		Rural	
	Females	Males	Females	Males	Females	Males
Indonesia						
1996	52.1	87.9	43.6	80.6	57.4	92.4
1997	51.2	87.4	44.5	80.6	55.5	91.9
1998	52.6	88.3	44.7	81.4	58.0	92.9
1999	52.7	88.8	46.6	82.8	57.0	93.1
2000	53.1	88.5	45.1	82.7	59.3	92.9
Change						
1997–99	1.5	1.4	2.1	2.2	1.5	1.2
1999–2000	0.4	−0.3	−1.5	−0.1	2.3	−0.2
Java						
1996	49.9	86.8	43.8	80.8	54.7	91.5
1997	48.9	86.3	44.7	80.6	52.4	91.0
1998	51.4	87.0	45.1	81.2	56.8	92.0
1999	52.2	88.3	47.5	83.0	56.5	93.2
2000	51.7	88.1	45.7	83.0	57.6	93.2
Change						
1997–99	3.3	2.0	2.9	2.4	4.1	2.2
1999–2000	−0.5	−0.2	−1.9	0.0	1.1	−0.1

rural areas, particularly in the Outer Islands, also benefited from the 'crisis'. Although the crisis may not have had a direct adverse impact on rural areas, it did have an indirect impact through the return of villagers who had been laid off in the cities, and through price increases.

Table 12.1 disaggregates the labour force participation data by urban/rural status at the national level and within Java. At the national level, the increase in participation during the crisis period is greater in urban than in rural areas, for both women and men. In Java the increase in participation is much more pronounced, and is greater for women than for men. Women's labour force participation in Java decreased just before the crisis (1996 to 1997) but then increased quite sharply from 48.9 per cent in 1997 to 51.4 per cent in 1998. It continued to increase to 52.2 per cent in 1999. Hence from the onset of the crisis to 1999 there was a 3.3 percentage point increase in the number of women either working or looking for work in Java, compared with a 2 percentage point increase for men. The greater increase in women's labour force participation is evident in both urban and rural areas. Female labour force participation increased by 2.9 percentage points in urban areas relative to men's increase of 2.4 percentage points. The gender difference was even more marked in rural areas, where women's labour force participation rate increased by 4.1 per cent and men's by 2.2 per cent.[5]

Unemployment Rates

Labour force participation signifies the person's desire to work but doesn't reflect the demand side of the labour market. The crisis induced people to look for work as a means of increasing the real value of their earnings, which fell rapidly as a result of the increasing price levels. Table 12.2 shows how successful they were by presenting the unemployment rates. Unemployment rates are not as useful a measure in developing countries as in developed countries because, without social service unemployment payments, few people can afford to be unemployed for any period of time. Below, I supplement these measures with another measure of the deficiency of labour demand, underemployment.

The figures presented in Table 12.2 clearly indicate that the crisis increased unemployment, and that unemployment rose more markedly among men than among women. This is true for both urban and rural areas, in and outside Java, but is most clearly seen in urban Java (Figure 12.1). Male unemployment in urban Java increased by 3.8 percentage points from 7.6 percent in 1997 to a high of 11.4 per cent in 1999. Female unemployment also increased, but by a smaller 1.9 percentage points. Before the crisis, unemployment was highest among women. By 1999, male unemployment rates were higher than female unemployment rates in Java, although still lower nationally.

That men experienced higher increases in unemployment than women can be explained by their greater involvement in the formal sector.[6] In 1997 only 22.7 per cent of working women were engaged in the formal sector compared with 50 per cent of men. In addition, the lower representation of women in the construction and financial sectors shielded them, at least initially, from the crisis. The first casualties were in these sectors. Retrenchments then followed in those manufacturing sectors that were dependent on imported inputs. These included electronics, metal products and machinery manufacturing, which are male-dominated, but also the sectors in which women are concentrated – textiles, garments and leather goods (Oey-Gardiner and Dharmaputra 1998). However, women are also concentrated in agriculture, trade and the services sector, which were less severely affected.

In industries where women and men work side by side, gender-biased

Table 12.2 Unemployment Rates, 1996–2000 (%)

Year	Total		Urban		Rural	
	Females	Males	Females	Males	Females	Males
Indonesia						
1996	6.1	4.4	10.7	7.5	3.9	2.8
1997	5.8	4.3	10.0	7.4	3.6	2.5
1998	6.3	5.4	10.9	9.2	3.9	3.1
1999	7.1	6.4	11.7	10.7	4.4	3.8
2000	6.9	6.0	10.7	8.9	4.6	4.0
Change						
1997–99	1.3	2.1	1.7	3.2	0.8	1.3
1999–2000	−0.2	−0.4	−1.0	−1.8	0.2	0.2
Java						
1996	6.0	4.7	9.5	7.2	3.8	2.9
1997	5.8	4.9	9.0	7.6	3.5	2.8
1998	6.6	6.2	10.5	9.6	4.0	3.6
1999	7.2	7.6	10.9	11.4	4.4	4.5
2000	6.9	6.7	9.9	8.9	4.6	4.7
Change						
1997–99	1.4	2.7	1.9	3.8	0.9	1.7
1999–2000	−0.3	−0.9	−1.0	−2.5	0.2	0.2

retrenchments can result in women bearing the brunt of unemployment. For instance, women were widely laid off before men in Korea during the crisis. However, Oey-Gardiner and Dharmaputra (1998) report that there is little evidence of this having occurred in Indonesia.

The Sakernas data support this view. The 1998 Sakernas asked individuals whether they had stopped working between July 1997 and August 1998 and, if so, why. Of those who reported having been laid off, 28 per cent were female. This is a little less than their proportional representation among all employees, of 31 per cent.[7] Women may have been kept on because they are often paid significantly less than men and so offer firms cost savings.

The government was criticised over the fact that its public works programs (*padat karya*) were originally not open to women. In response to the criticism at

Figure 12.1   Unemployment Rates in Java, 1996–2000 (%)

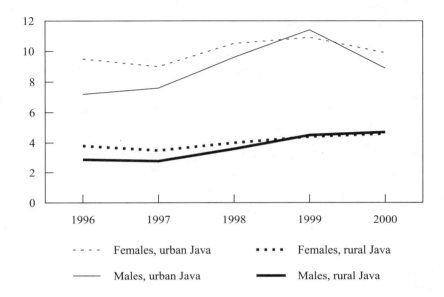

least 20 per cent of new jobs under these programs were to be allocated to women (which still results in an underrepresentation of women relative to the number of women unemployed).[8] Although these programs are now theoretically open to women, their focus on manual labour acts as an implicit barrier to women's involvement.

Underemployment

Many people who lose their source of employment and who cannot afford to be unemployed for any length of time will turn to the informal sector for employment. They may, for instance, set up their own small trading or services business. Hence, many people will maintain some form of employment and so will not appear in the statistics as 'unemployed'. Underemployment is an alternative measure of the insufficiency of labour demand. It is defined here to be the percentage of the workforce working less than 35 hours per week. Table 12.3, which presents the underemployment rates, shows that women experience much higher underemployment than men. This reflects, at least in part, that many women *choose* to work less than full-time. The changes in underemployment over time are consistent with the unemployment results. Men have experienced greater increases in underemployment than women. Unlike the unemployment results, however, the larger increases in underemployment for men are driven by the

Table 12.3 Underemployment, 1996–2000 (%) [a]

Year	Total		Urban		Rural	
	Females	Males	Females	Males	Females	Males
Indonesia						
1996	54.1	29.3	31.6	16.0	63.8	36.2
1997	51.6	27.3	31.0	16.0	61.5	33.4
1998	55.0	30.7	34.9	19.1	64.7	37.0
1999	52.7	30.1	34.1	18.7	62.5	36.8
2000	50.3	27.4	30.2	15.2	61.4	35.3
Change						
1997–99	1.1	2.8	3.1	2.6	1.1	3.4
1999–2000	−2.4	−2.7	−3.9	−3.5	−1.1	−1.5
Java						
1996	50.2	27.3	28.3	15.3	62.6	35.0
1997	48.7	25.9	28.5	15.7	61.6	33.0
1998	52.6	29.5	33.2	18.7	64.8	37.0
1999	50.2	28.8	32.4	18.3	62.5	36.7
2000	47.1	26.2	27.5	15.1	61.5	35.4
Change						
1997–99	1.5	2.9	3.9	2.7	0.9	3.7
1999–2000	−3.0	−2.6	−4.9	−3.3	−1.0	−1.3

a   Underemployment is defined as working less than 35 hours per week.

rural sector. In the urban sector, women have experienced larger increases in underemployment.[9]

Leaving the Labour Force

The labour force is defined to include both those who are currently working and those who are searching for work. During economic downturns many people choose to leave the labour force because they see no hope of attaining work. The unemployment rate is defined as a percentage of the labour force and so those who choose to leave the labour force do not appear in the official statistics. One of the most startling indicators of the crisis impact is the number of people who reported having stopped looking for work because they had lost hope of getting a job. In 1997, before the crisis, only 1.1 per cent of women and 2.0 per cent of men reported that they had stopped searching for this reason. This jumped to 8.3 per cent of women and 9.6 per cent of men in 1998. If these people had been included in the official unemployment figures, then unemployment in 1998 would have been 19.0 per cent for women and 14.8 per cent for men.[10]

Wage Earnings

That male employment was more adversely affected by the crisis than female employment suggests that the demand for male labour was more deficient relative to its supply than the demand for female labour. One would thus also expect that male wages may have suffered more on average than female wages. Table 12.4 presents average hourly wages from 1996 to 2000.[11] Large decreases are recorded between 1997 and 1999 for both men and women, particularly in urban areas. As anticipated, the declines for men are larger than those for women. The difference is generated in urban areas where men's real wages dropped by 25.1 per cent and women's by 20.9 per cent. In rural areas, however, women's earnings decreased more than men's. There is some evidence to suggest that women were displaced by men as manufacturing employees in rural areas. The percentage of female wage workers working in manufacturing decreased by 2.72 percentage points between 1997 and 1999 in rural areas, whereas for men it increased by 1.27 percentage points. This could explain the larger wage decrease for rural women.

Variation in Crisis Impact across Socioeconomic Groups

As we have already seen, the labour market was more adversely affected in Java than off-Java. Of those who stopped working during the crisis, a disproportionate number were among the younger and better educated. This no doubt reflects their greater involvement in the formal sector. The concentration of job losses among the young and better educated was higher for women than for men. For example, women with a tertiary education were 2.3 times more likely to have lost a job between 1997 and 1998 than their representation in the population would suggest. The corresponding ratio for men is 1.26. Similarly, women under 30 years of age had a higher chance of losing a job relative to older women, than young men relative to older men.

Household Dynamics

As shown above, more people are in the labour force now than before the crisis

Table 12.4 Hourly Wages, 1996–2000 (1996 Rp) [a]

Year	Total		Urban		Rural	
	Females	Males	Females	Males	Females	Males
1996	4,090	5,428	4,728	6,345	3,299	4,438
1997	4,546	5,910	5,195	7,029	3,710	4,697
1998	3,873	4,704	4,049	5,412	3,639	3,887
1999	3,692	4,695	4,108	5,267	3,114	3,983
2000	4,111	5,456	4,544	6,114	3,427	4,511
Change (%)						
1997–99	−18.8	−20.6	−20.9	−25.1	−16.1	−15.2
1999–2000	11.3	16.2	10.6	16.1	10.1	13.3
Wage gap (%)						
1997	23.1		26.1		21.0	
2000	24.7		25.7		24.0	

a   Figures are deflated using the price indices for the capital city in the relevant province.

and the increase in labour force participation has been greater among women than among men. Why has women's labour force participation increased to a much greater extent than men's? An understanding of the relationship between men's and women's hours of work within the household offers an explanation. An examination of working hours and labour force participation shows that women's labour force participation is much more responsive to that of male householders than vice versa. In 1996, an urban (rural) female household member was 8 (6) percentage points less likely to work if there was a male working in the household than if there were not. In addition, an urban (rural) female who worked was likely to work about 7 (5) hours less per week if a male worked in the household than if there were no working male. In sharp contrast, men's labour force activity is largely independent of that of female household members.[12] Although this relationship remained fairly static from 1996 to 2000, what did change over the period was the number of men who were unable to find work. With increased male unemployment, women entered the workforce to try and make up the shortfall in earnings. Although there are more unemployed women now than before the crisis, households do not tend to respond by increasing the participation of male household members – probably because most men are already working and possibly too because of the smaller contribution women's earnings make to total household income.

RECOVERY AND RETURN TO PRE-CRISIS CONDITIONS

The Sakernas data show clear signs of a recovery in the labour market by August 2000, after the continued decline up to August 1999. Unemployment, although still higher in 2000 than in 1997, began to drop. Like the rise, the fall in unemployment was greater for men than for women. Female unemployment in Java returned to being higher than male unemployment, but constituted a smaller percentage of total unemployment than before the crisis. Underemployment similarly decreased for both men and women. The ratio of female to male underemployment also remained lower than before the crisis.

The 2000 Sakernas asked whether respondents started their current main job between July 1999 and July 2000. Categorising these new jobs in terms of the educational status and age of the respondents shows that it is largely the same group that lost jobs immediately following the crisis – that is, the young and better educated – that has obtained new jobs since the economy started its recovery.

The increase in labour demand resulted in average wages increasing sharply between 1999 and 2000, although they remained below their pre-crisis levels. Men's hourly wages had decreased more sharply than women's during the crisis and rebounded more quickly between 1999 and 2000. In fact, they rebounded to such an extent that nationally the wage gap is higher now than it was in 1997, immediately before the crisis (measured as 1 minus the average female wage over the average male wage). The increase in the wage gap is being driven by the widening wage gap in the rural sector. As mentioned above, this may be due to the displacement of women from wage employment in rural areas. In contrast, the urban wage gap has fallen, as fewer men are in the formal sector.

The unemployment, underemployment and wages figures cited above suggest that the economic downturn has swung into reverse. However, a more detailed picture of the economic recovery is gained by looking at changes in the work status of workers (Table 12.5) and these don't show such a clear-cut reversal. For men, although unemployment had decreased, in August 2000 there was little sign of movement back into the wage sector and away from self-employment. The recent increases in work opportunities are being generated largely in the self-employment sector. The percentage of working men who were employees continued to decline in both rural and urban areas and self-employment to increase.

Women's experiences have differed from men's. In urban areas female wage employment has picked up, although it is still below its pre-crisis share. As a

Table 12.5 Work Status, 1996–2000 (%)

Year	Females			Males		
	Self-employed	Employee	Unpaid	Self-employed	Employee	Unpaid
Indonesia						
1996	38.72	27.16	34.12	53.16	37.87	8.97
1997	34.78	28.71	36.51	51.88	38.9	`9.22
1998	35.16	27.42	37.42	54.29	35.6	10.11
1999	37.32	27.81	34.87	54.77	35.77	9.46
2000	32.62	28.1	39.28	55.48	35.46	9.06
Change						
1997–99	2.54	−0.9	−1.64	2.89	−3.13	0.24
1999–2000	−4.70	0.29	4.41	0.71	−0.31	−0.40
Urban Indonesia						
1996	35.78	49.72	14.5	38.29	58.07	3.64
1997	33.98	49.67	16.35	38.38	57.53	4.09
1998	34.35	47.86	17.79	41.45	53.97	4.58
1999	36.36	46.39	17.25	42.02	53.43	4.55
2000	32.50	48.34	19.16	42.34	53.27	4.39
Change						
1997–99	2.38	−3.28	0.90	3.64	−4.10	0.46
1999–2000	−3.86	1.95	1.91	0.32	−0.16	−0.16
Rural Indonesia						
1996	39.99	17.48	42.53	60.7	27.6	11.70
1997	35.16	18.73	46.11	59.16	28.9	11.99
1998	35.55	17.60	46.86	35.55	25.59	13.13
1999	37.82	17.96	44.22	62.23	25.4	12.34
2000	32.69	17.02	50.29	63.95	24.0	12.07
Change						
1997–99	2.66	−0.77	−1.89	3.07	−3.42	0.35
1999–2000	−5.13	−0.94	6.07	1.72	−1.45	−0.27

result there has been a movement out of self-employment to the wage sector. There has also been a move to unpaid work. It is not clear how to interpret this increase in unpaid work. With the onset of the crisis, the percentage of females engaged in unpaid work in urban areas increased, presumably due to the lack of paying jobs. Now, with some signs of recovery in the formal economy, there has been a further increase in unpaid work. It is possible that this reflects an increased ability by some households to afford to have women working in the household business rather than needing to be out earning another income. It thus may reflect gains in household welfare. Alternatively, it could be that although some women have been able to move back into wage employment, others (maybe those with lower educational attainment and work skills) have been struggling to make self-employment pay and are still turning to unpaid work.

In rural areas the number of women working as employees has continued to decrease. There has also been a large increase in the proportion of working women engaged in unpaid labour in rural areas. In contrast to the urban experience, the proportion of rural women working in the unpaid labour force had decreased during the crisis. Between 1999 and 2000 it increased sharply, however – by more than 6 percentage points to well above the pre-crisis level. Most of this unpaid work is in the agricultural sector and it corresponds with a large decline in the proportion of women who are self-employed.[13] This result, coupled with the increases in female unemployment in rural areas, suggests that the rural areas are yet to share fully in the recovery.

With the increased availability of work, one might have expected to see a reversion in the labour force participation rates to the pre-crisis levels. For men this is the case. Although still higher than pre-crisis levels, male labour force participation has decreased in both urban and rural areas (but with no change in urban Java). Women's experience here is again quite different. In urban Indonesia, women's labour force participation declined quite sharply between 1999 and 2000. In rural areas it continued to rise. Much of this rise is accounted for by the aforementioned large increase in unpaid agricultural workers. As a result, at the national level female labour force participation has increased.

CONCLUSION

In summary, women were sheltered somewhat from the full crisis impact due to their underrepresentation in the formal sector of the economy. Women did, however, suffer increases in unemployment (and underemployment) – although to a lesser extent than men. Possibly the main way in which women were affected by the crisis was indirectly – through its effect on labour market opportunities for the men in their families. In response to high male unemployment and underemployment, women increased their participation in the labour market.

The Sakernas data clearly show that labour demand has increased since 1999. Male unemployment and underemployment have decreased more rapidly than for women but the ratios of female to male unemployment and underemployment remain lower than before the crisis. These trends suggest that as the economy continues its recovery the relative labour market positions of men and women are likely to return to their pre-crisis positions. Male wages have already increased relative to women's such that the wage gap is now greater than before the crisis. Although labour demand has picked up, there has not yet been a strong re-emergence of the formal sector. In urban areas women have gained relative to men in terms of their share of wage employment, whereas in rural areas they seem to have been displaced from the formal sector.

To the extent that women were somewhat protected from the crisis in the labour market, that protection resulted from their underrepresentation in the most lucrative sector – the formal sector – much in the same way that rural areas and the Outer Islands were protected by their lesser reliance on this sector. Increasing women's access to the formal sector is, however, necessary if women are to participate fully in the development process and gain an equal share of the benefits.

Women went backwards during the crisis in rural areas in terms of their share of wage employment. Whether women can hold on to the small gains they made relative to men in urban formal sector employment and make up the ground lost in rural areas remains to be seen.

NOTES

1   The survey has been conducted since 1976. Originally it was conducted on a quarterly basis, but since 1994 has been conducted annually. In that year it was conducted in July. In every subsequent year it has been conducted in August.
2   Comparisons of the 1997 figures with those from 1996 and 1998 confirm this.
3   The labour force participation rate is defined as the percentage of the population currently working or looking for work.
4   All calculations are for individuals aged at least 15 years. Other studies have examined the impact of the crisis on child labour and found that it decreased over the crisis period. See Cameron (2001).
5   It is not clear why there was a much larger increase in rural areas. The increase in participation was spread pretty evenly across the industries in which women are typically involved. It may be that it was easier for women who had not previously been working to enter the labour force in rural than in urban areas. Markets are more congested in urban areas, and having contacts may play a larger role in obtaining work.
6   The Sakernas data do not allow us definitively to identify people as working in the formal or the informal sector. The 1997 survey does, however, provide quite

detailed information on job types. I used these data, along with the work status information, to define formal sector employees as those who are wage employees or who are self-employed with permanent paid help. From this group I excluded farm labourers, those involved in small-scale trade or the provision of petty services and those who are self-employed in the trades. Some studies treat the wage sector as the formal sector.

7   These figures will also capture the differential impact of the crisis on male and female sectors and so it is difficult to determine categorically whether or not lay-offs were gender-biased. Ideally we would compare lay-offs within narrow industry bands.

8   In 1998, 34 per cent of unemployed were women.

9   Both men and women worked fewer hours in 1999 than in 1997. The mean decreases in hours worked, while small, are larger for men, particularly in rural areas. Kernel density estimates of the distribution of hours of work show very little change pre- to post-crisis. Hence, it is not the case that some people are working much longer hours and others are working much shorter hours, leaving the average relatively unchanged.

10   Up from 7.0 per cent for women and 4.7 per cent for men in 1997.

11   The Sakernas only collects information on wage earnings.

12   These figures are the marginal effect estimates from probits of women's labour force participation on a dummy variable that equals 1 if at least one male in the household works, 0 otherwise, controlling for the age, educational attainment and marital status of the woman, how many children aged less than or equal to ten years there are in the household and the local unemployment rate. The hours equations were tobits of the hours worked by women as a function of the same set of control variables. Analogous equations were estimated for men.

13   The sheer size of the increase in unpaid labour is large enough to give rise to questions as to the accuracy of the data. However, all other aspects of the 2000 Sakernas data appear reliable and it is not clear why there would suddenly be a considerable amount of measurement error in this one figure. The Sakernas questions on work status did not change between 1996 and 2000.

13   WOMEN'S INTERNATIONAL LABOUR MIGRATION

Graeme Hugo

The involvement of Indonesian women in international labour migration has increased substantially over the last two decades. This chapter traces the movement of women – both legal and undocumented – to work overseas. It discusses the processes of recruitment, training and deployment, and the reasons why women choose to work abroad. There is a focus on the impact on the women themselves, and on the families and communities they leave behind. It is clear that while for many women working abroad is a negative and disempowering experience, others gain from it. All signs indicate that women's migration will increase. This chapter examines existing policies and practices on the protection of international women labour migrants from Indonesia and makes a number of recommendations for urgent consideration.

TRENDS IN LABOUR MIGRATION OF WOMEN: DOCUMENTED MIGRATION

Indonesian female labour migration can be divided into that which passes through official channels and that which does not. Table 13.1 shows the annual changes in the numbers of Indonesian overseas contract workers (OCWs) that have occurred over the last quarter-century. There is a clear pattern of growth in the numbers of workers deployed overseas, most of whom are women.

The apparent downturn in 1995/96 was due to the exclusion of some workers from the data, while the exceptional figures for 1996/97 include a large number of workers already in Malaysia who received an amnesty (Hugo 2000). Bearing these special circumstances in mind, it is apparent that there was an upturn in deployment of workers following the onset of the Asian economic crisis in mid-1997 (Romdiarti, Handayani and Rahayu 1998: 23). Indeed, the number of official OCWs sent overseas between the onset of the crisis and the end of 1999 was greater than all those sent under the country's first five five-year plans (Repelita I–V).

The dominance of women in the official outflow of labour migrants has been consistent over the last two decades. Of the OCWs deployed under Repelita VI (1994–99), 1,021,103 were women and 440,133 were men. Three-quarters of Indonesian labour migrants went to two nations: Malaysia (38.1 per cent) and Saudi Arabia (37.7 per cent). In both cases women migrants outnumbered men, only slightly in the case of Malaysia but by twelve to one in the case of Saudi Arabia. Females also dominate migration to Singapore and Hong Kong, whereas migration to South Korea and Taiwan is dominated by men.

Table 13.2 shows that domestic workers make up the majority of official migrant workers. A report from the Indonesian Embassy in Saudi Arabia indicates that 92 per cent of Indonesian women workers in the country are in domestic service (Anon. 1997). It has been reported that there are 150,000 Indonesian women working as foreign maids in Peninsular Malaysia (*Migrant News,* March 2000), 58,000 in Hong Kong (*Deutsche Presse-Agentur*, 23 October 2000) and a similar number in Singapore.

Women labour migrants are not drawn randomly from across Indonesia. Figure 13.1 shows the distribution by province of origin of OCWs deployed from Indonesia during Repelita VI. Java – and West Java in particular – is the origin of the majority. One survey of the 16,361 returning OCWs arriving at Jakarta airport in October 1997 indicated that 47 per cent had been born in West Java (Hugo and Bohning 2000).

TRENDS IN LABOUR MIGRATION OF WOMEN: UNDOCUMENTED MIGRATION

Undocumented labour migration is almost certainly greater in scale than documented migration, with Malaysia the main destination. This movement has a long history which pre-dates the formation of Indonesia and Malaysia as independent nations, or even as colonies of European countries (Hugo 1993). The numbers involved are unknown, but 1.4 million Indonesian citizens resident in Malaysia voted in the 1997 Indonesian elections, and the Malaysian government has estimated the number of Indonesian workers resident there at 1.9 million (Kassim 1997). Much of the undocumented migration involves the OCWs taking up low-paid, low-status jobs eschewed by Malaysians.

There are two overlapping systems of undocumented migration, the first involving Indonesians largely from Sumatra, Java and Lombok to Peninsular Malaysia, and the second movement from eastern Indonesia to Sabah and, to a lesser extent, Sarawak in East Malaysia. Broadly, there are three ways in which these undocumented migrants are able to work abroad.

*Table 13.1 Overseas Workers Processed by the Ministry of Labour,
1969–2001* [a]

Year	Middle East		Malaysia/ Singapore		Other		Total	Change over Previous Year	Sex Ratio
	(no.)	(%)	(no.)	(%)	(no.)	(%)	(no.)	(%)	(males per 100 females)
2000	128,975	30	217,407	50	88,837	20	435,219	2	46
1999	154,327	36	204,006	48	69,286	16	427,619	6 [b]	41
1999/2000	153,890	38	187,643	46	62,990	16	404,523	–2	44
1998/99	179,521	44	173,995	42	58,153	14	411,609	75	28
1997/98	131,734	56	71,735	30	31,806	14	235,275	–55	20
1996/97 [c]	135,336	26	328,991	64	52,942	10	517,269	328	79
1995/96	48,298	40	46,891	39	25,707	21	120,896	–31	48
1994/95	99,661	57	57,390	33	19,136	11	176,187	10	32
1993/94	102,357	64	38,453	24	19,185	12	159,995	–7	36
1992/93	96,772	56	62,535	36	12,850	7	172,157	15	54
1991/92	88,726	59	51,631	34	9,420	6	149,777	74	48
1990/91	41,810	48	38,688	45	5,766	7	86,264	3	73
1989/90	60,456	72	18,488	22	5,130	6	84,074	37	35
1988/89	50,123	82	6,614	11	4,682	8	61,419	1	29
1987/88	49,723	81	7,916	13	3,453	6	61,092	11	35
1986/87	45,405	66	20,349	30	2,606	4	68,360	23	61

a   In 2000 the Indonesian government changed over from a financial-year (1 April–31 March) to
    a calendar-year system of accounting.
b   Percentage increase between 1999/2000 financial year and 2000 calendar year.
c   This was the year in which over 300,000 labour migrants to Malaysia were regularised (194,343
    males and 127,413 females).

1   Migrant workers enter the destination countries clandestinely and do not pass
    through any official border checkpoint. These include the large numbers of
    Indonesians who enter Malaysia by crossing the Malacca Straits from Riau
    to the coast of Johore.
2   Those who enter the country legally but overstay their visa, for example, the
    large numbers who enter Sabah from East Kalimantan.
3   Those who enter the destination country under a non-working visa but sub-

Table 13.1 (continued)

Year	Middle East		Malaysia/ Singapore		Other		Total	Change over Previous Year	Sex Ratio
	(no.)	(%)	(no.)	(%)	(no.)	(%)	(no.)	(%)	(males per 100 females)
1985/86	45,024	81	6,546	12	4,094	7	54,297	21	44
1984/85	35,577	77	6,034	13	4,403	10	46,014	57	79
1983/84	18,691	64	5,597	19	5,003	17	29,291	38	141
1982/83	9,595	45	7,801	37	3,756	18	21,152	18	
1981/82	11,484	65	1,550	9	4,570	26	17,604	11	
1980/81	11,231	70	564	4	4,391	27	16,186	56	
1979/80	7,651	74	720	7	2,007	19	10,378		
1977							3,675		

Repelita		Target	Total Deployed
VII	(1999–2003)[d]	2,800,000	862,838
VI	(1994–99)	1,250,000	1,461,236
V	(1989–94)	500,000	652,272
IV	(1984–89)	225,000	292,262
III	(1979–84)	100,000	96,410
II	(1974–79)	none set	17,042
I	(1969–74)	none set	5,624

d   Covers 1999 and 2000 only.

Sources: Suyono (1981); Singhanetra-Renard (1986: 52); Pusat Penelitian Kependudukan (1986: 2); Departemen Tengara Kerja (1998: 14).

sequently obtain work, such as the (mainly women) Indonesians who obtain an *umroh* (pilgrimage) visa to enter Saudi Arabia, but once there obtain work. In most cases, work is arranged in advance. One estimate of the number of Indonesians in this category is 150,000, 80 per cent of whom are women (*Jakarta Post*, 11 November 1997).

While some undocumented flows are dominated by women (such as those to Saudi Arabia), on the whole it would seem that – in contrast to documented

*Table 13.2 Sector of Employment of Official Workers Deployed Overseas,
Repelita IV–VII*

Sector	Repelita IV (1984–89)		Repelita V (1989–94)		Repelita VI (1994–99)		1999–2000 (Oct.)	
	(no.)	(%)	(no.)	(%)	(no.)	(%)	(no.)	(%)
Plantations	34,398	11.8	144,403	22.1	158,994	10.9	189,397	22.0
Transport	41,438	14.2	92,882	14.2	103,097	7.1	41,424	4.8
Construction	4,409	1.5	624	0.1	102,920	7.0	7,995	0.9
Energy and water	760	0.3	6,151	0.9	1	–	57	–
Hotel/catering	958	0.3	124	–	1,808	0.1	198	–
Commerce/finance	5,189	1.8	349	–	305,286	20.9	105,433	12.2
Mining/oil	19	–	3,385	5.2	4	–	–	–
Manufacturing	12	–	13,863	2.1	199,390	13.6	189,945	22.0
Domestic service	205,079	70.2	389,706	59.7	589,736	40.4	358,439	41.5
Other	–	–	785	0.1	–	–	–	–
Total	**292,262**	**100.0**	**652,272**	**100.0**	**1,461,236**	**100.0**	**862,838**	**100.0**

Source: Indonesian Department of Labour, unpublished data.

migration – men probably outnumber women among undocumented migrant workers. There are, however, indications that the numbers of women are increasing; this is evident in the outflow of migrant workers from East Flores to Sabah. A study of a village in East Flores, East Nusa Tenggara, in the late 1980s traced migration by village men back to the 1940s, whereas the movement of single women did not begin until the late 1970s. The first female migrants accompanied their husbands to Malaysia, or in some cases went to look for long-absent husbands (Graham 1997).

A similar finding emerged from a survey by Raharto et al. (1999) of outmigration from another village in East Flores.[1] Figure 13.2 depicts the years in which each of the migrants surveyed first went to Malaysia. Whereas just over half of the men had left since 1990 (53 per cent), almost three-quarters of the women (72 per cent) had left since that time. The increasing involvement of women in migration to Sabah is also evident in the data on deportations of illegal migrants from Sabah to East Kalimantan (Table 13.3).

Establishing which parts of Indonesia undocumented migrants come from is difficult, but the deportation data for Sabah show a concentration from the

Figure 13.1 Province of Origin of Official Overseas Migrant Workers, 1994–99

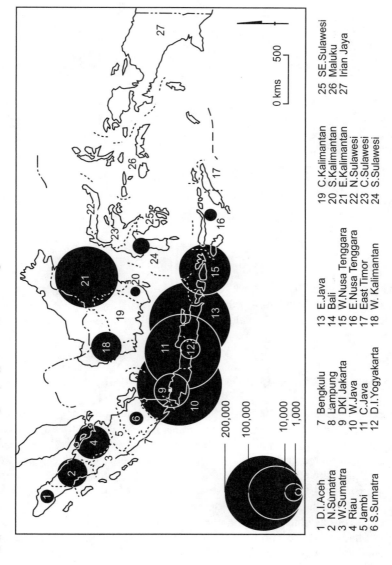

1 D.I.Aceh	7 Bengkulu	13 E.Java
2 N.Sumatra	8 Lampung	14 Bali
3 W.Sumatra	9 DKI Jakarta	15 W.Nusa Tenggara
4 Riau	10 W.Java	16 E.Nusa Tenggara
5 Jambi	11 C.Java	17 East Timor
6 S.Sumatra	12 D.I.Yogyakarta	18 W. Kalimantan

19 C.Kalimantan	25 SE.Sulawesi
20 S.Kalimantan	26 Maluku
21 E.Kalimantan	27 Irian Jaya
22 N.Sulawesi	
23 C.Sulawesi	
24 S.Sulawesi	

Source: Indonesian Department of Labour, unpublished data.

Figure 13.2 Overseas Labour Migrants in Surveyed Village by Sex, 1976–96 (no.)

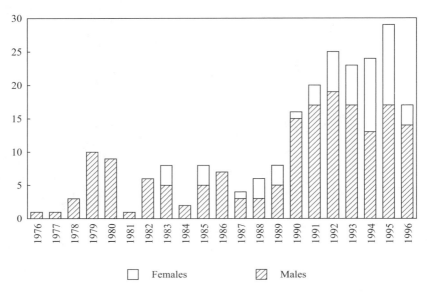

☐ Females   ▨ Males

Source: Raharto et al. (1999).

provinces of South Sulawesi, East Nusa Tenggara, West Nusa Tenggara and East Java (Table 13.3). Table 13.4, showing the results of two surveys of undocu-mented women migrants in Kuala Lumpur, indicates that most came from Java and Sumatra.

CHARACTERISTICS OF WOMEN LABOUR MIGRANTS

Surveys of female labour migrants from Indonesia, both documented and undoc-umented, find that the women tend to be in their 20s or early 30s and have rela-tively low levels of education. The East Flores survey (Raharto et al. 1999) indicates that migration is certainly selective of the better educated population, even in this relatively undereducated area – of the migrant workers still away, 96.7 per cent of the males were literate, as were all of the women. This is sig-nificantly above the average for East Nusa Tenggara where, in 1990, 21.9 per cent of persons aged ten years and over were illiterate. The majority of migrant workers had completed primary school. This was especially evident among women and the more recent migrants who were still away. Male migrant work-

Table 13.3 Province of Origin of Undocumented Indonesian Workers Deported from Tawau (Sabah) to East Kalimantan, January 1994 – June 1996

Province of Origin	Males (no.)	Females (no.)	Females (%)	Total (no.)
Entered Malaysia with documentation [a]				
South Sulawesi	8,604	4,798	35.8	13,402
East Nusa Tenggara	6,871	3,923	36.3	10,794
East Java	2,428	1,512	38.4	3,940
West Nusa Tenggara	4,180	808	13.3	4,988
Southeast Sulawesi	1,029	244	19.0	1,283
Central Sulawesi	152	52	25.4	204
East Kalimantan	343	279	53.4	522
Other	594	275	31.6	869
Total	24,111	11,891	33.0	36,002
Entered Malaysia without any documentation				
All Indonesia	14,033	3,897	22.4	17,430

a   But subsequently overstayed their visas or worked on a visiting pass.

Source: Provincial Development Planning Office of East Kalimantan, Samarinda, unpublished data.

ers were more represented in both the lowest and the highest educational attainment categories than was the case for women. Overall, however, the bulk of migrant workers from East Flores had quite low levels of educational attainment and hence took up unskilled work in Sabah. Further evidence of their educational profile is provided by unpublished data from the Samarinda Provincial Development Planning Office. These data indicate that the educational attainment of all migrant workers deported from Sabah was somewhat higher than found for migrants from East Flores. Some 86.4 per cent of the deported workers were classified as unskilled. There is a similar profile for women who move overseas legally.

Another interesting characteristic of migrant workers was their relationship to the head of the household, with differences emerging between those still away and those who had returned. Table 13.5 shows that, in the former group, children of the household head were predominant. This was especially true of women,

Table 13.4 Place of Origin of Female Overseas Migrant Workers according to Three Studies (%)

Place of Origin	Kuala Lumpur (Dorall & Paramasivam 1992)	Workers Registered with Indonesian Embassy, Kuala Lumpur (Nasution 1997)	Returnees Arriving at Jakarta Airport (Pujiastuti 2000)
Java	50.3	70.0	87.5
Sumatra	43.2	13.1	–
Flores	0.7	–	–
Lombok	1.4	14.4	12.5
Other	–	2.5	–
N	141	397	40

Table 13.5 Relationship of Migrant Workers to Head of Household in Community of Origin (%)

Relationship to Household Head	Migrants Still Away		Returned Migrants	
	Males	Females	Males	Females
Household head	23.9	–	87.9	8.8
Wife/husband	3.3	–	2.2	55.9
Child (not yet married)	58.7	91.7	8.8	8.8
Child (married)	4.3	4.2	1.1	5.9
Parents (in law)	1.1	4.2	–	5.9
Other family	8.7	–	–	14.7
N	92	24	91	34

Source: Raharto et al. (1999).

Table 13.6 Educational Background of Female OCWs according to Three Studies (%)

Level of Education	Kuala Lumpur (Dorall & Paramasivam 1992)	Returnees Arriving at Jakarta Airport (Pujiastuti 2000)	East Java (Rural Development Foundation 1992)
No education	13.4	20.0	–
Primary	57.4	42.5	64.8
Lower secondary	19.9	18.5	27.5
Upper secondary	9.2	20.0	13.7
N	141	40	71

reflecting a pattern of female migration whereby movement to Sabah usually occurs before the women marry.

While that is also the pattern for young men, there is a significant movement among married men as well. More than one-quarter of the migrant households interviewed in Flores were *de facto* female-headed households as defined by Hetler (1989, 1990). Among returned migrants, the bulk of males were house-hold heads. The pattern for women is more mixed: almost one-tenth of returned migrants were household heads of *de jure* female-headed households (Hetler 1989, 1990), reflecting perhaps some tendency for marriages to be put under strain by the absence of women (and men) in Sabah for long periods. This was frequently reported during fieldwork in other villages studied in East Flores as well (Graham 1997).

The three surveys covered in Table 13.6 indicate that the bulk of female OCWs have low levels of educational attainment.

TRAFFICKING OF WOMEN AND THE SEX TRADE

Little is known about the trafficking of people in Indonesia, although it most certainly exists as an element in the high level of undocumented migration out of the country. One part of people-smuggling/trafficking activities in Indonesia focuses on the East Malaysia–Philippines–Kalimantan triangle in northern and central Indonesia (Scalabrini Migration Centre 2000: 13). Sabah in particular has a rapidly expanding entertainment and sex industry that involves women from both the Philippines and Indonesia, some of whom have been trafficked. There is also a well-established movement of women from Sumatra into Singapore and West Malaysia to be involved in the sex industry. For example, sex workers from Riau travel to Singapore each evening to conduct business, returning home the next day.

Trafficking as a particular subset of international migration is increasing in scale, complexity and impact. Indonesia, like other Southeast Asian nations, is increasingly affected by it. Trafficking takes many forms but there are two basic categories: where the migrant is voluntarily engaged, usually paying large amounts of money to a trafficker; and where the migrant is not moving of her own free will but is effectively enslaved by the trafficker, sometimes to repay debts incurred by her family. The distinction is often blurred. Migrant workers may engage a trafficker to facilitate entry to another country, only to find on arrival that the promised job does not exist. They are then forced to take a job they do not want to do, at remuneration well below that promised. There are many cases of women being offered jobs in offices, factories or the so-called entertainment industry only to find they have to work as prostitutes in the desti-nation country (*Asian Migration News*, 15 May 2001).

Part of the undocumented migration from Indonesia to Malaysia has involved the trafficking of women. As Jones (1996: 18) points out:

> The rise in the Malaysian demand for Indonesian maids has been accompanied by an apparent increase in cases of trafficking of Indonesian girls and women into Malaysia for prostitution – apparent because no statistics are available on such a sensitive issue, and the number of articles appearing in the press of both countries is a guide.

Jones (2000: 77) observes that most women trafficked from Indonesia to the sex industry of Sabah are from East Java, although there is also some involve-ment of women from Kalimantan. Jones cites several examples of women and girls being forced to work in the sex industry against their will.

In 2001, Khofifah Indar Parawansa, the Indonesian State Minister for Women's Empowerment, expressed alarm at the trafficking of Indonesian chil-dren into the sex industry (*Asian Migration News,* June 2001). Two-thirds of the estimated 6,800 sex workers in Malaysia are Indonesians, some of them chil-dren. Indonesian authorities had gathered information on child trafficking in 40 cities around the nation.

THE MIGRATION PROCESS

The Indonesian Department of Labour, through its Overseas Worker Placement

Agency, regulates the recruitment, placement, training, deployment and return of officially registered overseas workers from Indonesia. A typical pattern is for a woman to be recruited by a registered recruiting company (PJTKI), which then arranges placement, training and deployment, and registers the potential migrant with the Department of Labour for a fee. This process often takes several months, and there are many stories of women being overcharged, or receiving limited training and information about what awaits them and what is required of them at the destination.

There is also a substantial immigration industry operating outside of the official system. It is extremely rare for an OCW to go overseas without the assistance of an agent of some kind (usually several such agents), or of family members or friends already working abroad (Spaan 1999). In the case of women moving from East Flores to Sabah, the process is highly organised. Boats leave at regular intervals from particular offshore locations and proceed to Pare Pare or Makassar in South Sulawesi. There agents arrange passage to Nunakan in East Kalimantan, where the women obtain passports and border passes to enter Sabah. They seek work through middlemen (*calo*) or through a friend or family member already working there. In effect, an 'industry' has developed to facilitate each stage of the migration process.

Very few migrant workers are able to fund their migration from their own resources. In Raharto et al. (1999), the proportion was higher among the sample of returned migrants than among those still away, because the former included many who had migrated more than once (42.4 per cent) and so had earned enough to fund their own remigration. The bulk of migrant workers relied on their families for the money. This could involve the family taking out a loan and incurring a debt. Around one-fifth borrowed the money from *calo* or friends. Most (94.7 per cent) took 6–12 months to pay back the loan. Often the *calo* had an arrangement with the employer in Malaysia to deduct loan repayments from the salary of the worker.

The process of obtaining work in the destination country relied heavily on family and friendship linkages. Some 62 per cent of female migrant workers obtained their first job through a family member and 21 per cent through a friend. Moreover, female migrants were more likely to travel to Sabah with other family members than was the case for males: of the 58 female migrants surveyed, only four reported travelling to Sabah alone.

Jones (2000: 39) makes the important point that in Indonesia 'exploitation and abuse of migrants [begins] before the migrant ever sets foot abroad'. Potential migrant workers are obliged to progress through several stages involving agents, travel providers, government officials and trainers and so on, most of whom will charge a – sometimes excessive – fee.

There is a great deal of evidence that Indonesian female OCWs experience exploitation and abuse while overseas. The fact that the bulk of them work as domestic servants means that they are often not covered by labour laws at the destination. If they are undocumented, they are particularly vulnerable. Their documents may be held by the employer and they are often not free to leave the house or seek alternative work. In addition, the power relations in the work situation may mean that they are vulnerable to overwork and exploitation, including sexual exploitation (Anderson 2000). Low levels of education, lack of training, and limited preparation for and knowledge of the destination and working situation can exacerbate the problems confronted by migrant workers.

One indicator of the bad experiences overseas of many Indonesian female migrant workers is the high rate of premature return among some groups, especially women working in Saudi Arabia. According to several surveys of OCWs returning from the Middle East, a substantial proportion return within one year even though most contracts run for at least two (Table 13.7). Women who return before their contracts expire may also experience a substantial financial loss. Most first-time migrant workers have borrowed large sums of money to finance their travel overseas. Given the high interest rates charged and the fact that they have worked for only a short period, they are likely to retain a large debt that will take a long time to repay. Premature returns also have a negative impact on Indonesia's reputation as a reliable supplier of labour, and on the recruiting agencies' credibility with their employer clients.

Table 13.8 shows the reasons given for premature return by migrants from West Java (Hugo 2002). In this survey, only 53 per cent of all respondents returned home because they had completed their contract. Further evidence of the high rate of premature return of OCWs is provided by data collected at Jakarta airport upon their return. In 1998 the government established a special terminal at the airport purely for OCWs (terminal 3). All returning OCWs are required by the Department of Labour to fill in a questionnaire asking for their name, address, passport number, type of work, name of the recruitment agency that had sent them overseas, date of departure and return, country of destination and employer's details. They are also asked to outline any problems they had experienced.

Data collected for December 1998 and September–October 1999 are presented in Table 13.9. The majority of OCWs processed at Jakarta airport were women from Java who had worked in the Middle East. Of these more than one-third were returning prematurely – more than one-quarter in less than a year and more than one-tenth within three months. This represents a very high rate of premature return. It is apparent that most had returned before completing their contract because of difficulties they had experienced at the destination.

The files of non-government organisations (NGOs) are bulging with the horror stories of women who have worked in the Middle East, where they are not protected by local labour laws because they work in private homes. Solidaritas Perempuan (Women's Solidarity), for example, has published a dossier of

Table 13.7 OCWs Returning to Indonesia within One Year (%)

Province of Origin	Destination	Year	Source	Away Less than One Year	
				(%)	(no.)
Central Java	Middle East	1986	Mantra, Kasnawi and Sukamardi (1986)	18.1	167
Yogyakarta	Middle East	1986	Mantra, Kasnawi and Sukamardi (1986)	63.4	93
West Java	Middle East	1986	Mantra, Kasnawi and Sukamardi (1986)	21.0	100
West Java	Middle East	1992	Adi (1996)	12.2	90
Java	Middle East	1999	Pujiastuti (2000)	60.0	40
Java	Middle East/ Malaysia	1991	Spaan (1999)	31.0	18

Table 13.8 Reasons Given by Migrant Workers from West Java for Their Return

Reason	Number	%
Completed contract	78	53
Salary wasn't high enough	2	1
Work was too hard	4	3
Missed family	26	18
Sick	13	9
Evil influences	1	1
Recruitment agency brought them home	5	3
Deportation	1	1
Other	16	11

Source: Hugo (2002).

Table 13.9 Profile of Returning OCWs Arriving at Jakarta Airport, December 1998 and September–October 1999 (%)

	December 1998	September–October 1999
Total (no.)	**8,690**	**32,483**
Females	99.2	96.7
Returning from Middle East	93.4	70.2
Length of stay		
< 3 months	15.6	11.4
4–11 months	12.3	14.2
12–23 months	12.7	19.9
24+ months	59.4	54.5
Reason for return		
End of contract	59.4	55.5
Holiday	2.9	4.7
Sick	4.8	2.4
Experienced problems	15.6	12.9
Other	17.3	24.5
Place of origin		
West Java	–	49.2
Central Java	–	23.6
East Java	–	18.1
Outside Java	–	9.1

Source: Ministry of Labour.

complaints made by 172 returning migrants between 1995 and 1998, and Jones (2000) has documented a large number of cases of abuse and exploitation among Indonesian migrant women in Malaysia. The Indonesian media frequently report on cases of abuse and exploitation. In June 2001, for instance, it was reported that '37 Indonesian domestic helpers have accidentally fallen to their deaths from apartment buildings in Singapore during the past three years. All of them fell while cleaning windows' (*Asia Migration News*, 30 June 2001). *Media Indonesia* reported that at least 90 Indonesian migrant workers had died in 2000, most in Saudi Arabia. Reports of rape and sexual assault are common (*Hong*

Table 13.10 Reasons Given by Returned Migrants for Leaving the Village

Reason	Males		Females	
	(no.)	(%)	(no.)	(%)
Restricted opportunities in the village	74	81.3	24	70.6
Lack of funds	11	12.1	1	2.9
To help family	1	1.1	4	11.8
Family too restricted	2	2.2	4	11.8
Other	3	3.3	1	2.9
Total	**91**	**100.0**	**34**	**100.0**

Source: Raharto et al. (1999).

Kong Mail, 18 June 2001; *Straits Times*, 21 February 2001; *Asian Migrant News*, 15 March 2001; *Media Indonesia*, 12 April 2001).

IMPACTS OF FEMALE LABOUR MIGRATION

In assessing the effects of labour migration in Indonesia, it is important to con-sider both the women themselves and the families, communities and regions they leave behind. Table 13.10 shows the reasons given by respondents from East Flores for going overseas to work; the perception of restricted opportunities at home was the main factor (Raharto et al. 1999). It is interesting that women migrants were more likely than men to cite family-related reasons for leaving the village. The reasons for this are two-fold.

First, many women migrate as part of a strategy for the family to spread its labour resources in order to earn sufficient income. Such women saw migration as a response to the income needs of the family. This is in line with the findings of other research that women migrants are often considered more reliable remit-ters than men (Hugo 1995a).

Second, many women view migration as an escape from the constraints of the family. Again, this has been found in other research to be an important moti-vation for young Indonesian women to leave rural areas (Wolf 1990; Sunaryanto 1998).

The effects of female labour migration on families and communities of origin involves adjusting not only to the absence of mothers, wives and daughters, but also to the influences of newly acquired money, goods, ideas, behaviour and innovations sent and brought back by the migrant workers. Remittances during the first six months of 2001 have been estimated at US$4 billion (*Asian Migration News*, 31 July 2001). But official remittance figures are only the tip of the iceberg, with much money flowing back with friends and when the migrants themselves return at the conclusion of their contracts. Many women also bring back expensive goods when they return (Mantra, Kasnawi and Sukamardi 1986). Adi (1996: 266), in a study of a village in West Java, found that households with a member working overseas had an income of Rp 495,000 per month (US$147 at the time), more than twice that of households without a worker overseas. Some two-thirds of this income was attributable to remittances. He also found that 80 per cent of the remittances were spent on consumption, such as house building or home improvements, paying off debts, educating children and meeting the daily needs of the family. The remainder was invested in land or small businesses. This pattern of level and use of of remittances is repeated in a large number of studies (see, for example, Mantra, Kasnawi and Sukamardi 1986; Heyzer and Wee 1994; Pujiastuti 2000).

The impact of remittances on family and village economies is immediately apparent when one enters rural communities with large numbers of OCWs in East Nusa Tenggara. Houses tend to be made of brick or stone rather than wood or *atap* (thatch), and there is an air of prosperity despite the often poor agricultural potential of the land. In East Flores the contemporary success symbol is a *parabola* (satellite dish) to receive television from Hong Kong, Malaysia and Australia, as well as Indonesia. The cost of installation is Rp 1.35 million (US$675), or almost three times the local average annual income, but one finds *parabola* dotted all over the villages with substantial numbers of migrants in Sabah.

There has been some examination of the effects of female labour migration on families (Hugo 1995b, 2001), including on marriage and divorce. The women who work as labour migrants tend to be unmarried or divorced (Pujiastuti 2000; Adi 1996; Hugo 2001), although married women predominate among migrants to Saudi Arabia (Heyzer and Wee 1994). A significant form of female movement to Malaysia from Indonesia involves women seeking husbands who have been absent for extended periods. It was reported in 1995 that of 226 undocumented migrants deported from Peninsular Malaysia to Dumai in Riau a few days earlier, 43 were women looking for their husbands (*Riau Post*, 20 August 1995).

It would appear that separation of family members for the often extended periods involved in international labour migration can lead to marital instability and the consequent permanent break-up of the family unit. In fieldwork in East Flores, this was one of the most frequently voiced comments about the impact of migration to Sabah (Raharto et al. 1999). Indeed, in some cases both men and women had taken another spouse in the destination country. Studies have generally found a higher incidence of divorce among migrant than non-migrant households. However, this was not the case in Adi's (1996) study of female domestic workers migrating from West Java to the Middle East.

A major question concerns the relationship between labour migration and changes in the role and status of Indonesian women. One study of returning female overseas workers (YPP 1992) found that the women increased their involvement in the family's affairs after returning from employment overseas. Other relevant findings of the study are as follows.

- Husbands' respect for their OCW wives often increased.
- Men took a greater role in childrearing while their wives were absent, and there was a breaking down of the traditional division of family labour along gender lines.
- There was little evidence of negative effects on children due to the mother's absence.
- The extended family did many of the tasks that would normally have been done by the OCW women.
- Most returning women considered their main role to be that of a homemaker.

While some Indonesian women improve their status as a result of labour migration, not all are so empowered. Many simply exchange one patriarchal structure (in their home village) for another in the destination country; others – particularly domestic servants and sex workers – are caught in unequal power relationships with their employers. Some women succeed only in enhancing the economic status of their family, without experiencing any increase in their own overall status. This would appear to be particularly the case for women working as domestic servants in the Middle East (Adi 1996). There may also be certain threshold effects operating, so that one two-year stint in the Middle East by a West Java woman may not be enough to produce a change in her status whereas two such periods may be sufficient to produce a change.

There can be no doubt that while migration often results in women gaining a range of new freedoms, in some cases the opposite can occur. For some women, migration can mean the loss of important and valued village support systems. Robinson (1991: 50) points out that for Indonesians working as domestics in Saudi Arabia:

> The conditions of work – often in isolation in the employer's home – have great potential for exploitation. Within Indonesia the women have access to some resources, in particular their families and their social networks, giving them a limited degree of power in negotiating work relations and work conditions – something which is lacking in international migration.

It is of interest that in the study of East Flores there was little evidence of abuse and exploitation of the females moving to Sabah, although many were employed as domestic workers (Raharto et al. 1999). This appears to be because most women move as part of a group, usually including male family members.

SOME ISSUES IN FEMALE INTERNATIONAL LABOUR MIGRATION

The involvement of Indonesian women in labour migration, especially to work as domestics, has attracted considerable controversy in Indonesia, especially among religious and women's groups. Cases of mistreatment, excessively heavy workloads, abuse, rape and sexual harassment are given prominent media coverage. However, this has had little apparent impact in depressing the level of demand among Indonesian women to work overseas. As Robinson (2000b: 251) has pointed out:

> The situation of these women has given rise to a highly contested public debate in which the government's policies have been subjected to trenchant criticism. The public debate, which engages the ethical, moral, economic and political issues involved in labour export, has been widely reported in the Indonesian press. The rhetoric of the debate indicates these women have become pawns in the economic strategies of the Indonesian government and in its political relations with Saudi Arabia.

A growing number of NGOs in Indonesia are becoming involved in providing support services to female labour migrants and in lobbying the government to improve support and protection for them. There can be no doubt that there needs to be greater commitment to the protection of OCWs at each stage of the labour migration process, including the following.

- Field surveys indicate that potential female OCWs make the decision to depart based on limited and often incorrect information. Timely provision of comprehensive, relevant and accurate information about the costs and conditions of migration, remuneration and conditions at the destination, and the rights and responsibilities of both migrants and employers would help equip women to resist exploitation. Such information would also assist potential migrants to decide whether or not to migrate, and to choose between destinations.
- Many Indonesian female OCWs are subject to exploitation in the process of recruitment. The protection of the rights of migrant workers demands the establishment of an effective complaints procedure, effective regulation of the myriad agencies involved in the migration process and development of a range of protective structures.

- Too often the issue of protection of OCWs in the destination country is side-stepped by Indonesian officials, who claim they cannot interfere in the affairs of a foreign country. However, Indonesia could follow the example of the Philippines, which appoints labour attachés in a large number of countries to protect and support its OCWs. Indonesia has only two such attachés, and there is little evidence that they are active in supporting Indonesian women working overseas. Support could also be provided through bilateral and multilateral efforts, including ensuring that OCWs are protected by labour legislation in the destination country (Chin 1997). Similarly, it is apparent that NGOs can and do play a significant role in the protection of OCWs in destination countries.
- Many of the problems faced by OCWs relate to their undocumented status. Every effort needs to be made to regularise their movement. In doing this, however, care must be exercised not to penalise the OCWs themselves, since regularisation could result in greater financial costs to the women themselves.
- The answer to improving the situation of OCWs does not lie in placing bans on migration. A ban on the deployment of Indonesian women to work as domestics was applied for three months in 1998 (*Asian Migration News*, 21 October 1998), and in 2001 the government announced a temporary ban on sending domestic helpers to Singapore (*Asian Migration News,* 31 July 2001). Such bans usually only result in women OCWs being forced to move as undocumented migrants, increasing their vulnerability.
- There is also scope for greater protection of OCWs on their return to Indonesia. There is evidence that women arriving home, often to the specially dedicated terminal at Jakarta airport, are prey to exploitation and in need of protection. They may also need assistance in adjusting to life back in Indonesia.
- Indonesian female OCWs are often unfairly given the total blame for the problems they experience. Officials in destination areas cite their unskilled status and low education levels as reasons for their problems.
- Women moving overseas are often exposed to greater health risks than would be the case if they remained at home. They should be given the knowledge and the means to protect themselves against diseases, especially HIV/AIDS and other sexually transmitted diseases.

CONCLUSION

Indonesia is already one of the world's major suppliers of OCWs and the numbers it sends overseas will increase over the next few years. Indeed, the onset of the financial crisis has led to an upturn in the number of international migrant workers. The government has set targets for the numbers sent overseas since Repelita III (1979–84). Repelita VI (1994–99) set a target of 1.25 million overseas workers, but 1.46 million were deployed. The target for Repelita VII (1999–2004) was more than doubled to 2.8 million (Departemen Tenaga Kerja 1998: 14). This recognises the increasing contribution that OCWs are making to the nation's well-being through foreign exchange earnings, reduced unemployment and underemployment, and regional development. However, these benefits come at a considerable human cost, especially to women migrant workers, and there is a need for the government to demonstrate the political will and commitment to protect and support the rights of its OCWs effectively. This opportunity was provided with the introduction of a new set of labour laws in 2000 containing provisions on the control and regulation of recruiting agencies and middlemen, protection of workers and provision of information to intending OCWs. Putting these innovations into operation will demand a high order of government commitment. It will require the development of an effective complaints procedure within Indonesia and at the destination, effective control of recruitment intermediaries and proper punishment of exploitation of intending workers, and the provision of relevant, high-quality training for OCWs, support systems at the destination and health and other insurance.

NOTE

1   This study was done in collaboration with the Centre for Population and Manpower Studies, Indonesian Institute of Sciences (PPT-LIPI).

14 CUSTOMARY INSTITUTIONS, *SYARIAH* LAW AND THE MARGINALISATION OF INDONESIAN WOMEN

Edriana Noerdin

In Langsa Aceh Timur, on 2 October 1999, a group of unidentified masked men stopped a bus carrying women workers of PT Wira Lanao. The women were made to get off the bus, and the men cut off their hair by force … According to the perpetrators, the women workers were wrong to go out without covering their hair (*Serambi Indonesia*, 5 October 1999; Noerdin 2000: 8).

Alifah (not her real name), a high school graduate from Garut (West Java), was asked by her mother to visit her grandmother who lived on the border of Tasikmalaya and Ciamis district in West Java. Because of the distance, Alifah, who wore a *jilbab* to cover her hair, started very early in the morning. However, because the roads and transportation links were not very good, at around 7 in the evening Alifah had only got as far as the city of Tasikmalaya … After waiting for around one hour at the bus terminal, she eventually found a public pick-up car that was going to the village. To her utter bewilderment, as the car was leaving the terminal, a group of men stopped the vehicle and forced Alifah out of the car … Alifah heard some of them saying that she had violated a regional regulation of *syariah* law by going out at night without being accompanied by her husband or a male relative. They took off her *jilbab* and shaved off her hair as a punishment (*Suara Rahima*, No. 2, 1 August 2001: 34).

The implementation of regional autonomy in Indonesia since 2001 has opened the door for people in the regions to breathe new life into customary institutions that had been repressed by the Soeharto government for more than three decades. As both Islam and customary institutions had suffered under Soeharto as he sought to homogenise the country and extend his control, it is not surprising that in certain regions the current resurgence of customary institutions is closely linked to demands for the implementation of *syariah* law. This chapter looks at the relationship between regional autonomy, the revitalisation of customary institutions and discriminatory measures against women contained in provincial regulations for the implementation of *syariah* law. Currently, none of these regulations have any legal standing because they have not been endorsed by the national parliament (DPR). Despite this, in some regions they have been enforced on the streets by their proponents.

DEMANDS FOR *SYARIAH* LAW

Apart from Aceh, there are at least ten other regions in Indonesia (West Sumatra, Riau, Palembang, Makassar, Bone, Gorontalo, Ternate, Banten, Tasikmalaya and Sukabumi) that have passed or are about to pass regulations allowing the implementation of *syariah* law. There is a history to the increasing demands for the introduction of *syariah* law in Indonesia.

In the lead-up to independence, there was fierce debate and political struggle surrounding this issue. On 1 March 1945 the Investigating Committee for the Preparation of Indonesian Independence was established under the auspices of the Japanese occupation authority. It was composed of prominent Indonesians representing diverse social, ethnic, regional and political groups in the Japanese-occupied Netherlands East Indies. In addition, distinguished religious leaders representing Islam and other religions were present at committee meetings (Rammage 1995: 10, 35). Sukarno, who was later to become the first president of Indonesia, argued that the new country should be based on a belief in God. It would then be neither an Islamic nor a secular state but a 'religious' state in which religion and the state were kept separate, and people of all religions would be free to fulfil their respective religious obligations.

On 22 June 1945, however, a compromise was adopted. In a draft preamble to the constitution, the state ideology, Pancasila, was adopted, but the ordering of its five principles was altered to put belief in God first. In addition, the words, 'with the obligation for Muslims to follow *syariah* law' were added to this tenet. Islamic leaders also sought to stipulate in the constitution that the president must be a Muslim.

This draft preamble became known as the Jakarta Charter. But its proponents failed to gain the upper hand, and the constitution that emerged after the proclamation of independence in August 1945 did not contain the concession laid out in the charter, nor a requirement that the president must be a Muslim. It was Mohammad Hatta, later to become the first vice-president, who had succeeded in persuading the constitutional drafting committee to omit the references to Islam in the final draft of the preamble and in the constitution. Hatta was afraid that the predominantly Christian, eastern parts of Indonesia would not join the united republic if it adopted Islam as its ideological basis (Rammage 1995: 14). The passion to implement *syariah* law did not die with the political defeat of the Jakarta Charter. Although low profile, it lived on, waiting for the right political configuration to emerge.

More than half a century later, following the fall of Soeharto in 1998, efforts to revive the Jakarta Charter have strengthened. In the current fluid political situation, the forces competing for power include Islamic groups, nationalists, the military and Golkar (the last two representing the forces of Soeharto's New Order).[1]

THE REPRESSION OF ISLAM AND CUSTOMARY INSTITUTIONS UNDER SOEHARTO

Throughout the New Order period, both customary institutions and Islam experienced repression. Soeharto and the military used violence to subjugate the diverse political, economic and social groups in Indonesia to the state ideology, Pancasila, using the slogan 'Bhineka Tunggal Ika' (Unity in Diversity). In order to promote uniformity, village governments based on customary institutions and traditional conflict resolution mechanisms were formally replaced with a centralised, uniform and bureaucratic structure of government that extended from local neighbourhood and citizen associations to village, subdistrict, district and provincial tiers of government.

Under Soeharto there were five-year cycles of repression, echoing the national five-year development plans, Repelita. Five years after gaining power, he exercised a clever political strategy to undermine Islamic groups. In 1973, the government forced political parties, including many Islam-based political parties, to merge. The various Islamic groups that made up the newly formed United Development Party (PPP) soon became preoccupied in an internal power struggle to gain control of the party. Five years later, in 1978, Soeharto introduced another ideological offensive designed to further specify and control the parameters of political discourse in Indonesia. On 22 March 1978 the People's Consultative Assembly (MPR) approved a decree called 'Guide to the Full Comprehension and Practice of Pancasila' (known in Indonesia as P-4). This enforced the nationwide propagation of Pancasila through rigorously implemented ideological education courses. All new students entering university had to study Pancasila. In addition to promoting political uniformity, this move was designed to prevent the PPP and other Islamic groups from gaining legitimacy by using Islam as the ideological basis of their organisations. Another five years later, in July 1983, Soeharto announced that all organisations, especially political parties, must formally adopt Pancasila as their sole ideology. He argued that the unconditional acceptance of Pancasila was essential for continued national stability, unity and economic growth.

All seemed quiet on the religious and ethnic fronts for the three decades of Soeharto's presidency. But appearances can indeed be deceptive. As we have learned from the experience of the former Republic of Yugoslavia and the Soviet Union, the use of state violence to repress plurality does not eradicate difference.

In Indonesia, it was not plurality that was eliminated but the ability to tolerate difference – the ability to empathise with people of a different ethnicity and religion. Revitalising suppressed ethnic identities was done aggressively, with many people projecting their own dissatisfaction and frustration violently on others. On the religious front, we have not only witnessed the eruption of communal violence, but also a resurgence of demands for the implementation of *syariah* law, more than half a century after it had apparently received a lethal blow.

ISLAM, CUSTOMARY INSTITUTIONS AND THE MARGINALISATION OF WOMEN

The implementation of regional autonomy that began in 2001 is intended to give the regions more authority to manage their own development and affairs. It is also intended to restore customary institutions, in the hope that traditional conflict resolution mechanisms will be able to prevent further outbreaks of communal violence. Article 104 of Regional Autonomy Law No. 22/99 stipulates that 'the Village Representative Body (BPD) (or similar institutions named differently in different regions) should work to safeguard customary relations, formulate village regulations, channel people's aspirations and monitor the running of village government'. The law allows people either to form a new BPD or to revitalise customary institutions to carry out the role of a BPD. Unfortunately, article 104 is not accompanied by a regulation to prevent the revitalisation of the feudal and patriarchal values embedded in many of these customary institutions.[2]

For example, the matrilineal character of the Nagari system traditionally followed by the Minangkabau ethnic group in West Sumatra does not guarantee women's participation in decision-making, which is dominated by the *ninik-mamak* (male elders) (*Kompas Minggu*, 2 September 2001: 30). Matrilineal kinship, though often described as *matriarki*, in fact gives Minangkabau women little control over their lives. Wieringa (1995: 257) points out that if, for instance, a *mamak* (uncle) were to register a piece of clan land under his own name and then sell it – which is illegal according to customary law – his sister would have no legal way to retrieve her land. This is because the inheritance rights of West Sumatran women under customary law have not been translated into the national code of law. Along with the erosion of their communal rights, women are hardly represented at all in the regional parliament and local councils, and have no access to state courts. Thus a woman whose communal land rights had been violated by her brother would not be able to take him to court.

Under the Nagari system, it is the uncle who authorises a niece's marriage and the brother who decides whether or not a woman should sell her inheritance. The customs of the Minangkabau stipulate that women should be under the supervision and protection of a man – whether a brother or uncle – and that women must fulfil their obligations as set out in customary rules (Radjab 1969: 57). The matrilineal system in West Sumatra has produced a high polygamy rate. Radjab states that at the end of the 1960s, 45 per cent of married men in Nagari Sumpur had more than one wife, 19 per cent in Agam Tua and 15.7 per cent in Maninjau (p. 47). The drive to revitalise customary institutions within the context of providing greater regional autonomy will only encourage a return to the Nagari system in West Sumatra. Patriarchal in character, it fits well with the conditions promoted by *syariah* law.

The regional legislature of West Sumatra has recently issued a draft regulation on the 'Banning and Eradication of Amoral Behavior'; this is closely associated with the revitalisation of customary Nagari institutions in the region. The draft regulation does not use the term '*syariah* law' but in essence it is the same thing. Among other things, it strictly regulates how women should dress and bans them from going out after 10 p.m. unless accompanied by a *muhrim* (close male relative). The draft regulation specifically bans women from wearing miniskirts, sleeveless shirts and tight clothing that men might find sexually arousing. In West Java, a similar regulation gives power not just to the police but to community members as well to enforce the regulation, allowing them to arrest, harass, assault and publicly humiliate suspected violators. This was the regulation used in Langsa Aceh Timur to justify the assault on women workers described at the start of this chapter.

It is not just the women of West Sumatra and West Java who are denied their rights in the name of revitalising customary institutions and *syariah* law: as the second quotation at the beginning of this chapter shows, women in Aceh are also suffering discriminatory treatment. In their desire to turn Acehnese women into a symbol of Islam, Acehnese *ulama* seem to think that women do not know what is best for them, and need to be made to do things for their own good. Ameer Hamzah, a well-known Acehnese *ulama* and columnist, expresses support for the use of violence to discipline Acehnese women as follows.

> It is necessary that we all support the success in making women cover their hair. At first, women will feel obligated to do this. But after they realise its benefits, they will feel happy and get used to it. Hair that is shaved off will grow back. Miniskirts that are cut off do not cost much. What is important is that women now dress in Islamic clothing, practising Syariah Islam. Say goodbye to decadent clothing' (*Serambi Indonesia*, 3 November 1999; Noerdin 2000: 10).

Taking its example from West Sumatra, the local legislature in the district of Karimun in the province of Riau is currently preparing a similar regulation but, in order to avoid controversy, without calling it *syariah* law. Meanwhile, the districts of Cianjur in West Java and Surabaya in East Java have passed regional regulations concerning the prevention of amoral activities. The targets of such regulations are always women. In Karimun, police have arrested women as they went about their daily business on the grounds that they were wearing clothing that did not fit the criteria set down in the new regulation. In Cianjur, Karimun, Yogyakarta, Jakarta and many other places, Muslim groups have intimidated women and burned down buildings used for entertainment and prostitution. Increasingly, women are being banned from going out after 8 p.m. in order to prevent them from 'conducting amoral activities' (*Kompas*, 13 August 2001: 34, 5 September 2001: 26).

Dr Musda Mulia, a Muslim intellectual, has pointed out that, historically, every country that implements *syariah* law has begun its political program by repressing women's rights. She sees this as a political shortcut to gain legitimacy by creating a symbol of Islam, given the time it would take to establish legitimacy through social and economic development to improve the welfare of the people. Women have been easy targets because they were unorganised and still subjugated to patriarchal values. According to Dr Mulia, Islam in general and *syariah* law in particular has been deliberately misused to discriminate against women (*Suara Rahima*, No. 2, 1 August 2001: 17).

Mernisi (1991: viii) takes the same position, arguing that Islam was originally responsive to the needs of subjugated women. According to her, in the 7th century thousands of women fled into the city of Medina because the Prophet and Islam promised equality and dignity for all – both men and women, masters and servants. Every woman who came to Medina while the Prophet was the political leader of the Muslims could gain access to full citizenship and the status of *sahabi*, companion of the Prophet. These women, called *sahabiyat*, enjoyed the right to enter into the councils of the Muslim *umma*, speak freely to the Prophet, dispute with men, fight for their welfare and be involved in the management of military and political affairs. Mernisi concludes:

> When I finished writing this book I had come to understand one thing: if women's rights are a problem for some modern Muslim men, it is neither because of the Qur'an nor the Prophet, nor the Islamic tradition, but simply because those rights conflict with the interests of a male elite (Mernisi 1991: ix).

What is particularly disturbing is that many Muslim men, acting in a chauvinistic way, are ignoring the legal process for the implementation of *syariah* law. In order to have legal force, a regional regulation approved by the regional legislature needs the endorsement of the DPR. However, as we saw in the case of Alifah in West Java, some men are not bothering to wait for this endorsement but are taking the law into their own hands. The men who assaulted Alifah were not punished because this would have been considered to be going against Islam.

In Cianjur district in West Java, there has been a continuing debate about the implementation of *syariah* law. Some people say that this should be preceded by a regional regulation (*perda*) that would need to be endorsed by the DPR. Others argue that a letter from the regent of Cianjur would be enough to legalise *syariah* law, and that there is no need to obtain the endorsement of the national parliament. In the midst of this controversy, the regent of Cianjur has already issued a letter to all government offices in the region instructing them to intensify the implementation of *syariah* law. At present, all Muslim women working in government offices in Cianjur – and even women working in private banks such as Bank BCA – wear a *jilbab* to cover their hair (*Kompas*, 30 August 2001: 21). Resistance could lead to women being branded un-Islamic.

The lack of women's participation in the revitalisation of customary institutions and formulation of *syariah* law is a reflection of the wider problem of the exclusion of women from the political process. NGOs and other organs of civil society have shown a lack of interest in including women in their efforts to facilitate citizens' participation in the implementation of decentralisation and regional autonomy, and local government is still very much perceived as the domain of men. Thus, for example, Regional Regulation No. 5/2000 of the Special Region of Jakarta (and a similar regional regulation in the district of Kendal, Central Java) states that only the head of the family can become a member of a village council (BPD), while the national Marriage Law explicitly says that the head of the family must be a man ('Otonomi Daerah Bisa Merugikan Perempuan', *Kompas*, 14 June 2001).

Research and policy analysis carried out by various women's organisations show that women are not just excluded from BPDs, but also face tremendous obstacles in the struggle to participate in decision-making and planning in the regions. For instance, despite the pressing needs of women, who make up more than 50 per cent of the population and are among the poorest of the poor, they have little say in regional budget planning. From a women's perspective, many customary institutions are in need of reform because they promote male domination. They should therefore be democratised at the same time as they are revitalised, in order to allow women to be represented in the new, custom-based institutions of local government.

The danger is that the revitalisation of customary institutions will simply reinforce the patriarchal tendencies of the current male-dominated system. Under the Nagari system, for example, only the chief of a clan can become a *wali nagari* (regional representative). Since no woman has ever been selected to become a clan chief, none has ever been selected to become a *wali nagari* (*Kompas*, 18 June 2001: 27). As women do not have access to decision-making, it is not surprising that the revitalisation of the Nagari system of social relations has been undermining their rights and interests.

There is an increasing awareness that the women's movement in Indonesia needs to learn from the success of women's movements in a number of other countries. In India, women secured places on local decision-making bodies following amendments to the 1992 Constitution; the Women Reservation Bill guarantees that at least 33 per cent of all such seats are reserved for women. In Uganda, the 1987 Constitution reserves 30 per cent of local council seats for women. In Tanzania, 25 per cent of elected councillors at the district level should be women. Meanwhile, in the Philippines, the Local Government Code (1991) provides a legal basis for the participation of low-income earners in the planning and implementation of development programs that affect their communities. Because a high percentage of women are in this group, such legislation can provide them with a voice in decision-making power. In Indonesia, women's organisations need to focus their advocacy on the revision of Regional Autonomy Law No. 22/99 to allow women at the local level to exercise decision-making power (Kaukus Ornop 17, 2001).

While working to reform regulations and laws, the women's movement in Indonesia must continue its efforts to raise the consciousness of women who are still subjugated under patriarchal customary relations. Otherwise, Indonesian women will not be able to utilise the opportunities offered by legislative reform to struggle for women's rights. Faced with a resurgence of patriarchal values embedded in many customary institutions, and a stepped-up campaign for the implementation of *syariah* law at the regional and even possibly at the national level, Indonesia's disparate women's groups must unite and work closely together. Unless the relationship between the revitalisation of customary institutions and the demand for the implementation of *syariah* law is taken seriously, the women's movement in Indonesia may suffer a severe setback.

NOTES

1   Of the Islam-based political parties, the National Mandate Party (PAN), Justice Party (PK) and United Development Party (PPP) are considered more radical, while the National Awakening Party (PKB) is considered more moderate. Amien Rais heads the PAN and is currently the chair of the MPR; Vice-President Hamzah Haz leads the PPP; and Abdurrahman Wahid, the ousted president, is the leader of the PKB.
2   This is not always the case. Efforts to revitalise Sasak customary relations in the northern part of West Lombok, for example, have been characterised more by the attempt to democratise feudal values. The Sasak communities have no intention of implementing *syariah* law in West Lombok.

15 WOMEN'S GRASSROOTS MOVEMENTS IN INDONESIA: A CASE STUDY OF THE PKK AND ISLAMIC WOMEN'S ORGANISATIONS

Lies Marcoes

There have been significant changes to religious and secular women's organisations in Indonesia as a consequence of political changes since 1998 – the ongoing social and political process known as *reformasi* (reform). This chapter reports on a case study of the Family Welfare Movement (PKK) and some Islamic women's organisations operating at the grassroots level in the post-Soeharto era.[1] The PKK was for many years considered an important vehicle for the implementation of government development programs in rural areas, in particular through one of its most 'successful' programs, the establishment of Posyandu (Integrated Health Posts)[2] in villages across the nation for new mothers, babies and children. Its social networks reached many women nationwide. The issues addressed by the new Islamic women's organisations established only in the last two decades are quite different from the traditional concerns of the older Islamic organisations, and also of the PKK.

Recent political changes have generated the question as to whether New Order institutions like the PKK and Posyandu remain viable: can they continue to act as the machinery of development, and are they still capable of carrying out their programs? If so, what elements have contributed to their survival? If they do wither away, will the Islamic women's organisations – especially those associated with the two major Islamic organisations, Nahdlatul Ulama (NU) and Muhammadiyah – be able to take their place and support development from below at the grassroots level? If not, what other kinds of organisations can best fulfil the needs of women in rural areas?

Many of the once strictly social Islamic organisations are now also political institutions. The election of the leader of the NU, Abdurrahman Wahid, as president in 1999, and of Amien Rais, Muhammadiyah's representative, as speaker of the People's Consultative Assembly (MPR), points to the growing political power and influence of Islamic groups in Indonesia. One of the most notable developments has been the entry of the NU and Muhammadiyah into the political arena as powerful and fully fledged political parties. Under the New Order these had become principally social organisations with an Islamic background, although together their membership totalled around 50 million. Since 1999, however, they have been positioned at the centre of political power. Consequently, the women's organisations affiliated with the NU and Muhammadiyah – Muslimat, Fatayat and Aisyiyah – have also come to occupy an important and potentially powerful position.

To understand the role of the various Islamic women's organisations in Indonesia today – particularly in rural areas – it is necessary to look more closely at their activities, aims and vision. Would they be capable of assuming the role formerly played by the PKK, and acting as reliable supporters of government development programs? Could they adapt their missionary endeavours, usually focused on matters of the hereafter (*akhirat*), to include activities of a more secular nature – by, for example, developing programs to address social, health and other problems?

The findings presented here are based on research conducted recently in Java. The data from our fieldwork and interviews concern the development of women's organisations in rural areas, including Muslimat, Aisyiyah and several hybrid Islamic women's non-government organisations (NGOs) as well as the semi-governmental PKK and Posyandu.

THE PKK AND POSYANDU

The nationwide network of locally active, semi-governmental organisations known collectively as the PKK was set up in the 1970s with the support of Indonesia's New Order government. Kardinah Soepardjo Roestam was influential in the development of the PKK during the latter half of the decade. Her husband was the governor of Central Java from 1974 to 1983, so Kardinah automatically became the head of the provincial branch of the then still fledgling PKK program. She became the national head of the PKK when her husband was given the post of Minister for Internal Affairs in 1983. The PKK developed as a social organisation emphasising activities of particular interest to women. Local cells were established virtually everywhere in Indonesia, from the most remote village to the poorest urban neighbourhood. Nurtured and sustained by the New Order government, these cells developed into a vast network encompassing most of Indonesia's regions.

The social programs carried out under PKK auspices were aimed primarily at improving the standard of living of families and households in rural areas. The PKK conducted a number of successful campaigns, including the nationwide health scheme known as Posyandu, a program to combat illiteracy called Kelompok Belajar (Kejar) Paket A and B, and economic schemes directed at increasing the family budget.[3]

The health services provided by the Posyandu were directed in particular at pregnant women, new-born babies and infants. They included practical measures to improve the health of small children, such as the provision of nutritional foodstuffs and regular weighing of babies, physical check-ups for pregnant women, an immunisation program, information on family planning and advice on contraceptive use. PKK members in a community would organise a regular cycle of activities under which Puskesmas (Community Health Centre) staff would visit the locality to provide specialist services such as immunisation and pregnancy examinations. Members would assist with such activities as weighing children and charting their growth, providing advice on nutrition and health to mothers, and providing supplementary food to children.

The PKK has also been active in education – its intensive literacy program, Kejar Paket A, has been particularly successful. Programs on household economics have had a more limited impact, with economic success at the household level still depending largely on the active involvement and enthusiasm of individual families. The PKK's efforts to improve household income have focused on providing modest financial support to individuals and groups to enable them to set up small businesses and cooperatives in such fields as dressmaking, cooking and catering, manufacturing, animal husbandry and small stalls (*warung*).

Almost from the beginning the PKK has attracted criticism. Its regional bias towards Java (where it was first established and where its programs were at first concentrated) and the uniformity of the rules and regulations covering the implementation of its programs were blamed for the disappearance of pre-existing local schemes and seen as a threat to regional potential. Particularly in the early years its programs were strongly influenced by the interests of urban middle-class Javanese women, and showed a strong bias towards that group. Increasingly, too, the PKK began to be seen as a vehicle for the government's overall development policies. Another point of criticism concerned the observation that, although it was supposed to be a women's organisation, in reality the PKK acted on behalf of the interests of men. Under the PKK's organisational structure, the wife of any male head of office, from the highest (that is, the president) down to the lowest (the village head), automatically became the head of her husband's allocated PKK branch. Thus it was the position of her husband within the national bureaucracy rather than her own ability that determined a woman's position within the PKK. Furthermore, the PKK was frequently accused of active collusion with the ruling government party, Golkar. Allegedly the heads of the organisation tried to influence participants in PKK programs (that is, nearly every family with children in the whole of Indonesia) to vote for the government party, Golkar.

The most severe criticism, however, was the accusation that the PKK's health programs acted as a vehicle to enforce the nation's family planning program. It was alleged that the organisation was ignoring women's basic human rights and denying them autonomy over their bodies and reproductive health.

The PKK acted as a nationwide mass organisation. It functioned as a valuable and efficient vehicle to promote the government's development policies, especially in rural areas. It was seen as particularly effective in implementing programs that depended on massive nationwide support, such as the almost complete mobilisation of the population required to yield success in immunisation programs.

As is the case with the Islamic women's organisations (discussed below), the PKK depends heavily on the active involvement of individual women in implementing its various programs. Over the past decade participation has been declining. As a result the PKK has become less visible, though not necessarily less influential.

The Ministry of Home Affairs, which is responsible for the PKK, doesn't seem willing to just give up on it. But the effects of political reform – which have been felt throughout the country, affecting all layers of society – can be felt here too. A visible symbol of this is that the letter 'P' in PKK no longer stands for *pembinaan* (guidance, instruction) as before, but for *pemberdayaan* (empowerment). The new name can therefore be translated as 'Family Welfare Empowerment Movement' (see Indar Parawansa, Chapter 6). The PKK is also said to have softened its formerly authoritarian and pro-government stance to include an element of the – still rather abstract – concept of empowerment of family welfare in its policies. It is hoped that the change in name and policies will bring about a better, more intimate relationship with the population – and in particular that the PKK will prove more sensitive and attentive to the interests of women.

Our case study found that some branches of the PKK and Posyandu are functioning quite well, contributing actively to the development of the communities in which they are stationed. For example, in *kelurahan* Klojen in Malang – a densely populated urban community with many elderly people and pensioners (*lansia*) as well as a group of transvestites (*waria*) – Posyandu staff have developed a health and activities program for the elderly (including a physical exercise program), and an arts (karaoke singing) and AIDS prevention program directed at the *waria*. In other parts of the country, however, the Posyandu have had to discontinue their programs. According to a recent UNICEF report, about half of Indonesia's 250,000 Posyandu should be regarded as dysfunctional (UNICEF 1999). The same report includes the observation that a growing number of formally self-sufficient Posyandu are becoming increasingly dependent on funding from the Puskesmas.

We found that a number of factors are crucial in ensuring the continued relevance and existence of the Posyandu and PKK. These are:

- a jointly owned asset, such as credit facilities or revolving funds, to be managed by the members themselves;
- a program of scheduled, routine activities that are supported by professional health officials from, for instance, a Puskesmas in the same area;
- a trustworthy local head who is actively involved in supporting and developing activities and programs;
- creativity among officials, to make activities meaningful to all local members, even if this sometimes means diverging from the more generally formulated government guidelines (as was the case in Malang);
- willingness to cooperate with other local NGOs; and
- the ability to obtain structural financial support from one or more sponsors from the private sector (local enterprises).

Because of their close involvement with local communities, revitalising the PKK and the Posyandu would seem to be a viable way of staying in touch with and defending the interests of women in rural areas. This could be achieved in a number of ways – by establishing better schemes for cooperation with other locally active social organisations, for example, or by intensifying programs specifically developed to meet and maximise local needs, demands and potential.

Their nationwide representation, widespread support and inclusive approach position the PKK and Posyandu for success in offering assistance to needy groups, individuals and local communities in the present era of regional autonomy. Although the system is in place, there are several issues that need to be addressed. The first of these is the association with the former New Order regime: this should give way to a structure in which democracy, social reform and relative independence from the country's political institutions can develop more freely than is presently the case. Second, these organisations need greater resources – although the selection of resources should be made in consultation with other local NGOs. Finally, local groups need to be involved more directly in the decision-making process of their local PKK and Posyandu, to ensure that they respond to community needs and not just to national interests.

ISLAMIC WOMEN'S ORGANISATIONS

The first Islamic women's organisation in Indonesia was formally established in Yogyakarta in 1917. This was Sapa Tresna, which in 1920 became known as Aisyiyah. Other Islamic women's organisations developed in the context of the nationalist movement, including Muslimat NU, founded in 1946. Over the last decade a number of new Islamic women's organisations have sprung up. The organisations that are active in rural areas and villages are all affiliated with one of the two major religious organisations: the traditionalist NU (Muslimat and

Fatayat) or the modernist Muhammadiyah (principally Aisyiyah, which is also active in urban areas). We can safely assume that, unlike the PKK and Posyandu, the Islamic women's organisations were not directly involved in the government's development programs, although they were required under the New Order to act in accord with the Broad Outlines on State Policy (GBHN).

The Traditional Islamic Organisations

The traditionalist/modernist distinction theoretically concerns differences in the interpretation of religious jurisprudence and law (*fiqh*). The NU and Muhammadiyah take different approaches to the education of their followers. Historically, the NU's educational system has been based on the *pesantren* (Islamic boarding schools and teaching centres). *Pesantren* tend to be located in rural areas and are headed by locally appointed Islamic scholars (*kyai*). Teaching emphasises individual competence and comprehension rather than group lessons in a class. Muhammadiyah schools, by contrast, are more likely to be located in urban areas and are organised in a more modern way. Students are educated according to standardised curricula incorporating both secular and religious subjects, and are taught in classes divided according to age group. The Muhammadiyah system places less emphasis than the *pesantren* on classical scholarship.

This seemingly strict distinction between the NU and Muhammadiyah is becoming increasingly blurred, since the majority of *pesantren* now adhere to the more general rules on education put forward by the Ministry of Religious Affairs. It is therefore becoming more and more problematic to speak about 'modernist' versus 'traditionalist' Islamic groups in Indonesia.

The same can be said of their respective women's groups. Most organise regular sessions to recite passages from the Qur'an, usually at a *majlis taklim* (assembly for the religious instruction of women). Discussion at these sessions is limited to basic questions of theology and such topics as the duties of a wife as laid down in *fiqh*. Other activities concern the schooling of children attending the Islamic kindergartens, primary schools and girls' schools (Marcoes 1992).

Along with their religious and educational activities, both Muslimat (NU) and Aisyiyah (Muhammadiyah) have set up development programs for women, backed by small-scale financial assistance. They offer social activities for women and children; study of Qur'anic texts at a basic level; support for small-scale economic development schemes and pilot projects aimed at generating income for individuals and groups; and a program for the home care of orphans and the elderly. In addition, Aisyiyah has established a relatively wide network of vocational education centres. The main women's organisations claim to have a large number of members. The NU-affiliated groups – Muslimat and Fatayat – reportedly have a joint membership of over ten million. Aisyiyah is estimated to have about five million members. However, these are 'theoretical' data only, as many members are not actively involved in any of the programs provided by these organisations.

Fatayat regards itself as an organisation for young Muslim women. With an estimated six million members, it seems to offer more progressive schemes and programs than Muslimat. Some of these are concentrated in 'traditional' fields and are similar to Muslimat programs, but Fatayat has also set up reproductive health programs in line with its long-term commitment to women's empowerment. For many years Fatayat has collaborated with UNICEF in providing information and education on family planning, nutrition and family health, as well as advocating the importance of women's reproductive rights.

Since 1997 Fatayat has begun to extend its activities to advocacy on matters related to women's empowerment and political participation. With the support of the Asia Foundation and the Ford Foundation, it has established a network of institutions known as LKP2 (Institute for Women's Consultation and Empowerment), designed to provide advocacy and support for the victims of domestic violence in rural areas. So far Fatayat has established 25 such units across Java and Bali. It provides gender awareness and advocacy training for LKP2 staff and holds annual conferences on domestic violence and gender issues. LKP2 staff also carry out training sessions in the regions for local women.

Compared with the NU-affiliated organisations, women's groups associated with Muhammadiyah have initiated relatively few programs for the empowerment of women. Nevertheless, a small yet meaningful step was taken with the appointment – for the first time ever – of a woman, Ruhaini Zhuhayatin, to the Assembly for Decisions on Islamic Law (Majlis Tarjih) in 1995.

The 'New' Islamic Organisations

The impetus for the new Islamic women's organisations was discontent with the perceived inadequacy and inefficiency of the established organisations, and with the conservative outlook of their older members. The new organisations are more concerned with 'modern' issues such as domestic and public violence, reproductive health, political rights and equal access to economic means. In short, they address openly and directly the issue of justice for women in the public as well as domestic sphere. The theme uniting these organisations is women's empowerment and the advocacy of women's rights within the context of Islamic teachings. This has necessarily meant addressing a number of complex and sensitive issues, such as public and domestic violence, women's reproductive health and sexuality, and women's equal access to economic resources and education. The new organisations have also made efforts to formulate less gender-biased and discriminatory interpretations of religious texts.

One of the first organisations to address explicitly the relation between Islam, gender and women's reproductive health rights was FN-P3M (Organisation for the Development of Pesantren and Society), set up in Jakarta in 1995. Although not formally linked to the NU, most of its members and activists are connected in some way to the NU or its *pesantren*, and reside in *pesantren* communities.

Another new organisation, Forum Kajian Kitab Klasik Islam (Forum for the Study of Classical Islamic Texts), was established in Jakarta in 1997 by a group of progressive women activists, the majority of whom are alumni of a State Institute for Islamic Studies (IAIN). Its Islamic and religious specialists, as well as sociologists, anthropologists, gender specialists and other professionals, are attempting to formulate less gender-biased and more just interpretations of the classical Islamic texts as they pertain to the rights and responsibilities of women. These explicitly gender-biased and strongly discriminatory texts still circulate among the pupils of *pesantren* as part of the general curriculum.

During the 1990s Fatayat developed a more extensive social program for women incorporating gender analysis and focusing on women's reproductive health, with the support of the Ford Foundation. Its Yogyakarta branch established a new NGO called the Fatayat Health Foundation, an independent body without any formal association with the NU that concerns itself with the issue of women's reproductive health within the context of Islamic teaching.

The riots and violence that broke out in Indonesia in May 1998 were followed by widely published and shocking accounts of acts of cruelty and sexual violence against women. These developments instigated the establishment of several women's organisations focusing specifically on social and humanitarian aid, and in particular of one nationwide social Islamic organisation advocating women's empowerment. This was Puan Amal Hayati (PUAN), established in Jakarta in 1999. PUAN was the brainchild of Sinta Nuriyah Abdurrahman Wahid, the wife of the former president. Its overall objective was to reduce violence against women, particularly in the domestic sphere, through the revision of gender-based rights and the training and education of women in *pesantren* communities. Given the important role played by the *pesantren* as a formative educational system with strong sociocultural norms and values, and their role in shaping the intellectual and moral values of most of Indonesia's religious and community leaders, these centres can be considered strategic institutions for the introduction of new ideas. They are thus an important entry point for developing men's sensitivity to women's rights, particularly their personal security and other basic human rights. The PUAN has pilot projects in five areas: Jakarta, Cirebon in West Java, Jember and Madura in East Java, and Mataram in West Nusa Tenggara.

The membership of the more recently founded Islamic NGOs is quite small. Forum Kajian Kitab Klasik Islam, for instance, has only 10–20 participants, and Fatayat's YKF counts a mere 200–300 members. However, from the outset these organisations wanted to establish relatively small, exclusive organisations with a limited membership as an effective way of addressing the issues at stake for them. By restricting the number of members, they believe they can develop their programs to the full while supporting their members and making extensive use of their potential. The aims and goals of these organisations are thus allegedly well served by such a restricted and exclusive approach.

Funding Issues

In general, the Islamic women's organisations are entitled to run their own financial affairs. Funds are received from members, who may make individual donations or contribute as part of their religious obligation (*zakat, sadakah*). Funding is therefore not structural, and is limited. Muslimat and Fatayat, despite their close links to the NU, are expected to manage their own funds and seek additional income. Here the creativity and capability of executive board members is of the utmost importance. In many cases these organisations request additional financial support from foreign donor agencies such as UNICEF and the Ford Foundation.

Aisyiyah is not quite as willing to request additional funding from outside sources. Its executive board selects carefully the organisations with which it is willing to work. In Aisyiyah circles the organisation's independent status is highly valued, and it seems to be able to obtain most of its funding from members, subsidiaries and the Islamic community in general.

The PKK and Posyandu are largely dependent on the government for funding. Until three years ago all their funding came from the government, but since the demise of the New Order, they have been trying to find additional sources of finance and make their numerous small and localised organisations more self-sufficient. This change in approach is mainly due to the introduction of a greater degree of regional autonomy. As well as looking for sponsors, the PKK and Posyandu have found themselves working with NGOs as a way of obtaining additional funds. Ideally they would be able to set up a modest – perhaps crude – but effective financial system, based on a savings and loan mechanism attracting individual donations and contributions from members and the general community. Slowly they would be able to amass a small amount of capital on which to depend.

CONCLUSIONS

Based on the findings of our study of women's organisations in Indonesia, it is our conclusion that many of the recently established, non-governmental Islamic women's organisations are specifically addressing gender-related issues. An increase in funding from donor agencies has been important in this development.

The PKK is being forced to reconsider seriously its mission and future in the reform era. With the transformation of New Order structures – or even, at times, their displacement by new political constellations – the question remains as to whether the PKK and Posyandu can continue to function. If they cease to exist, will the women's organisations affiliated with the NU and Muhammadiyah be able to take over their role and provide support from below at the grassroots level? If not, what kinds of organisations could step in to fulfil the needs of women in rural areas?

Most of the activities organised by Muslimat, Fatayat and Aisyiyah involve their own members only or are limited to a particular *pesantren*, and can thus be labelled exclusive. This is very different from the PKK and Posyandu, which in theory at least were set up to benefit all members of the community, no matter where they lived. In contrast to the Islamic organisations – both old and new – they can therefore be regarded as open and receptive. All women are entitled to join the PKK and benefit from the services offered by the Posyandu, particularly when they have very young children. However, at present the level of communal involvement in these organisations is limited, for it is still the wives of village officials who are expected to play a leading role. This policy has definite drawbacks because, while many of the PKK's leaders are committed to implementing its social and health programs, others lack the enthusiasm to support and successfully implement these local schemes and activities.

The new Islamic women's organisations have succeeded in a relatively short period in establishing an open and public forum for discussion of women's rights and empowerment, although the number of women reached through their programs is limited. It has been difficult for these organisations to remain free of the political pressure and expectations exerted on them by the NU and Muhammadiyah, which are now two of the most powerful political forces in Indonesia. While Muslimat, Fatayat and Aisyiyah, the older women's organisations, are not formally linked to the NU and Muhammadiyah in terms of organisational structure, in reality they can be viewed as a division of their 'parent' organisations. Although they are clearly distinguishable from the all-male NU and Muhammadiyah, their closeness to them places constraints on their ability to develop programs.

The same can be said of the PKK and Posyandu as well. Although they are autonomous organisations in name, fending for the interests of women, at the same time they too are part of a larger, all-male organisation (that is, the government).

The nationwide health care schemes carried out by the PKK and Posyandu have been successful in reaching millions of women and children throughout the country. However, a serious shortcoming of these organisations has been their susceptibility to mass mobilisation by the government. On more than one occasion the New Order government took political advantage of this.

Our research leads us to conclude that the PKK and Posyandu network could be extended to become the basis for a general national health care system in Indonesia. This would, however, require a thorough revision of programs and a clear formulation of the development aims to be pursued and issues to be addressed.

NOTES

1   This article is taken from my study, 'A Review of Women's Grassroots Movements in Indonesia: A Case Study of the PKK and Islamic Women's Organisations in the Post-Soeharto Era', sponsored by the Asian Development Bank (ADB), Manila. I would like to thank the ADB's Lisa Kulp, who gave me the oportunity to undertake this research, as well as Professor Mayling Oey-Gardiner and Dr Peter Gardiner of Insan Hitawasana Sejahtera for their support and supervision. Nevertheless, responsibility for the study remains my own.
2   Posyandu are run on a regular basis in village communities by PKK volunteers who weigh babies, give nutritional advice and coordinate the visits of Puskesmas staff. The latter provide medical services such as antenatal care, immunisation and simple medication.
3   Interview with Kardinah Soepardjo Roestam (8 March 2001); see also Sudaryanto (1996).

16 WOMEN'S ACTIVISM AGAINST VIOLENCE IN SOUTH SULAWESI

Zohra A. Baso and Nurul Ilmi Idrus

Violence against women was a neglected issue in Indonesia before 1998 (Blackburn 1999). The women's movement in the reform era has focused on the issue of violence against women in both the public and the domestic sphere, including harassment of female labourers. Street demonstrations have been organised by women's groups to protest against violence, including the widespread campaigns across Indonesia following the May 1998 riots in which over a hundred Chinese Indonesian women were brutally raped. The exact numbers are unclear, but Sumardi (1998: 20) claims that 168 women were raped, 152 from Jakarta and its surrounds and the rest from Solo, Medan, Palembang and Surabaya. Blackburn (1999) argues that the May riots enabled Indonesian women's organisations to draw public attention to the issue of violence against women. Heryanto (2000: 59) says that although the state was not solely responsible for all that took place, state violence was the dominant factor in the May riots.

This chapter examines the efforts of women activists in South Sulawesi to end violence against women, from the time of Soeharto's New Order to the era of 'Mutual Help' (Gotong Royong) under Megawati's presidency. As well as examining the national dimensions of violence against women, it looks at the specific kinds of violence that arise in the dominant Bugis–Makassar society. The chapter stresses the importance of national-level discourses and national political coalitions in finding ways of dealing with violence and in arguing for social and legal changes to address violence against women.

GENDER RELATIONS IN SOUTH SULAWESI

In South Sulawesi, it is often argued that women enjoy high social status. This may be because it is believed that some of the first rulers, who descended to earth and whose superior status was acknowledged, were women. Röttger-Rössler (2000) has demonstrated the aspects of gender and authority among the Makassar that are significant for the traditional leadership role of women, particularly in the daily practice of traditional religion. She bases her argument on the local belief that the first divine ruler of Bontoloe was a woman, Bombong Koasa, who emerged from a bamboo trunk to become the leader of the former kingdom of the Makassar in Gowa.

Abdullah (1985), in his book on the Bugis and Makassar, raises the question of whether women's high status in South Sulawesi is because the first divine ruler in Gowa was a woman. How do these mythic representations of the high status of women impact on everyday gender relations?

Gender relations in Bugis society are illustrated by a popular saying, 'A woman's domain is around the house; a man's domain reaches to the borders of the sky', implying a clear-cut division of roles between men and women in domestic life (Pelras 1996: 161–2). The wife is considered to be the 'boss' at home because household management is under her authority, including the control of household money in line with women's function as a *pajaga bili'* (housekeeper).

Bugis women are considered to be *intang paramata* (jewellery), which means that they are held in an honoured position as the symbol of the 'magnificence and high status' of the family. This is the reason why the honour of the family is attached to women. Women are also the primary symbol of *siri'* (honour) (Millar 1983: 484), and therefore have to be protected at all times by their male relatives.[1] This is supported by *adat*. Can the view that women are the symbol of family *siri'* be used to legitimate violence against women in South Sulawesi? Other questions may follow from this. For instance, what is the community response to violence against women in South Sulawesi? And what efforts have been made to eliminate such violence?

NON-GOVERNMENT ORGANISATIONS AND THEIR ACTIVITIES IN SOUTH SULAWESI

The women's movement in Indonesia is not a new phenomenon; it emerged before Indonesia gained its independence (see Indar Parawansa, Chapter 6). However, its activities have not always been acknowledged, especially in relation to 'taboo' private issues or traditional values.

The contemporary women's movement in South Sulawesi began in 1977 when 10 female student activists from Hasanuddin University protested against discrimination against female students in campus organisations. One of their main concerns was women's subordinate role in the management of campus activities – the female students were always given stereotypically female positions such as secretary or treasurer, whereas leadership was dominated by the men. The campus protest was followed by discussions aimed at broadening women's horizons, and several leadership training sessions were conducted for women activists. The activities and ideas that began on campus were continued, developed and disseminated on campus and in the wider community over the next decade.

In 1987, the South Sulawesi Consumers' Association Foundation (YLK-Sulsel),[2] led by Zohra A. Baso, held a seminar on women and children as the objects of advertising and product marketing. This was followed by the emergence of several new non-government organisations (NGOs), such as the Institute for the Study of Coastal Communities (LP3M) led by Sufri Laode, which aimed to give coastal communities economic power; Yayasan Jati, a centre for the environment, women and children formed in early 1998 by students from various institutions in South Sulawesi; and the Centre for Community Research (Lekmas), set up by Bahtiar Mashud to focus on community development.

Among the more recently established NGOs are Forhati, Yayasan Fatayat and Yayasan Pa'bata Ummi, all of which were set up by young activists. Although these are not purely women's NGOs, an important aspect of their activities has been the empowerment of women and children. In 1994, as the AIDS epidemic intensified, YLK-Sulsel held seminars on women and AIDS designed to counter the assumption that women in particular were carriers of AIDS, and raise women's awareness of the disease. YLK-Sulsel conducts consumer advocacy with a gender perspective, focusing on grassroots education and workshops on women's rights.

Some districts in South Sulawesi have local women's NGOs, formed to achieve women's empowerment. These include the Centre for Women's Empowerment (LPP), with its branches in Bone and Soppeng (LPP-Bone and LPP-Soppeng), the Consortium of Concerned Torajan Women (KPPT) and other local organisations in Bulukumba and Wajo. All of these were established by women concerned to strengthen women's rights in the renewed freedom of the post-Soeharto era. In its early phase LPP-Bone focused its activities on campaigning against prostitution in the local area. Its activities now range from advocacy and campaigning to grassroots education on women's rights in collaboration with other NGOs in Makassar and, at times, the government.

The Activities of LBH-P2I

In the last five years, women's NGOs in South Sulawesi have focused particularly on the issue of violence against women. One example is the Law Service for Indonesian Women's Empowerment (LBH-P2I), led by local activist and lawyer Christina Joseph. LBH-P2I was established in 1995 with funding from the Canadian International Development Agency (SGIF-CIDA). Three years later it established the first women's crisis centre in South Sulawesi, with a 24-hour hotline for victims of violence. Since its establishment the centre has handled 141 cases: 17 in 1998, 41 in 1999 and 83 in 2000.[3] These ranged from cases of domestic violence and rape to state-sponsored violence, but the largest single category was marital violence, known in Indonesia as KDRT (*kekerasan dalam rumah tangga*, or 'violence in the household'). LBH-P2I provides women with legal assistance when cases are filed with the police, because women are notoriously *buta hukum* (literally, 'unseen' in regard to the law). The staff also provide other forms of assistance, such as counselling, help in reporting incidents to an offender's superior at work and support for women in refuges.

LBH-P2I's promotional activities have been carried out under the slogan 'Anda Tidak Sendiri' (You Are Not Alone), accompanied by the following statement:

Jika anda, sahabat, keluarga, tetangga, atau siapapun yang anda ketahui, dengar, saksikan, atau mengalami pelecehan seksual, perkosaan, diskriminasi, atau bentuk kekerasan lainnya terhadap perempuan. Jangan malu, jangan takut, tak perlu ditutupi. Itu bukan masalah pribadi, atau masalah orang lain, tetapi masalah perempuan. Laporkan ke polisi, hubungi LBH-P2I – Women Crisis Centre.

If you, your close friend, family, neighbour, or whoever you know, hear, witness, or experience sexual harassment, rape, discrimination or other type of violence against women. Don't be ashamed, afraid, don't hide the case. It is not a personal problem, or someone else's problem, but a women's problem. Report to the police, or contact LBH-P2I – Women Crisis Centre.

The aim of this statement is to encourage all people – victims as well as witnesses – to 'break the silence' by reporting any case of violence against women either to the police or to the crisis centre. LBH-P2I also hopes to raise awareness that violence against women is a societal rather than an individual problem.

The Activities of the FPMP

Another significant women's NGO in South Sulawesi is the Women's Forum (FPMP). This was set up in Makassar in 1995 – that is, in the New Order period – by three local women activists, Christina Joseph, Zohra A. Baso and Nina Angraini. The FPMP gathers together women of different backgrounds to strengthen capacity to eliminate violence against women. As well as monitoring and advocating against violence directed towards women, it campaigns on issues such as women's political rights.

Following the fall of Soeharto, the FPMP was poised to join the movement for political reform by increasing its level of activity. In the lead-up to the 1999 general election, it conducted training sessions to educate women and campaign for their political rights as voters. This was considered vital because women had become a 'political tool' under the Soeharto regime, with major women's organisations such as the Family Welfare Movement (PKK) and Dharma Wanita mobilising them to support Golkar, the party of the regime. The campaign, conducted throughout May 1999 both in the city of Makassar and in the *kabupaten* (districts) of South Sulawesi, was supported by several other NGOs.

One of the FPMP's educational efforts during the election campaign was the creation of a poster containing the following statement:

Makkunraie Mappattentu   **Women Determine**
Pusa ppilei parettei?   Are you confused about which party to
                               choose?

Maccamaneng mattale' janci   People easily promise
makkabettangeng maccalowo   compete to persuade

Nasaba' makkunraie   Because women
seddito awatangeng   are also powerful
pappile kaminang maega   as the dominant voters
ianaro riaseng   that is to say
makkunraie mappattentu   women determine
werena wanuae   the dignity of the nation

Pusa ppilei parettei?   Are you in doubt who to choose?
Ati-atiki mangkalinga janci   Be careful to listen to the promise
atutuki ripappalecena tauwe   be careful of people tempting you

Nasaba' makkunraie makkuasatongi   Because women are powerful
de'tau makkulle pinrai   no one can change
iya kipileiye   what women choose

The statement on the poster was endorsed by the 48 political parties formally recognised by the Indonesian government. The accompanying illustration showed a woman casting her vote, accompanied by an official of the Commission of General Election Observers (Komisi Pemantau Pemilu).

The FPMP monitors reports on public as well as domestic violence. From October 1999 to May 2001, it carried out a detailed analysis of reports of violence against women appearing in the local newspapers (*Fajar, Berita Kota* and *Pedoman Rakyat*). During this period the newspapers reported on 190 cases of public violence: 21 cases of cruel treatment or battering, 12 murders, 14 cases of deception by a male partner, 20 cases of economic deception, two cases of verbal abuse, two kidnappings and 53 cases of sexual harassment and rape). In July 2001, the FPMP established a self-supporting women's crisis centre with a working team of 10 young female activists. In handling cases of violence against women, it sometimes collaborates with LBH-P2I, particularly when legal consultation is needed.

Other activities of the FPMP related to the abolition of violence against women include a major campaign in the aftermath of the sexual violence of the May 1998 riots, and a dialogue on political and gender inequality held on 21 May 1999. On 7–8 August 2000, the FPMP and other east Indonesian NGOs collaborated with the provincial government in discussing how to implement a program to reduce the level of violence against women in Makassar. This program was devised under the Ministry for Women's National Plan of Action to empower women (see Indar Parawansa, Chapter 6).

The activities in Makassar to mark the International Day against Violence against Women on 25 November 2000 were coordinated by the FPMP. More than 100 women from various organisations gathered and peacefully distributed stickers, brochures and posters. In their speeches, women activists endorsed the 'zero tolerance policy' on violence against women proclaimed by the government (*Fajar*, 27 November 2000).

On Hari Kartini (Kartini Day) on 21 April 2001, women's NGOs, with support from grassroots organisations in South Sulawesi, conducted a *teater rakyat* (people's theatre) as an alternative way to campaign against violence. The following day, the FPMP, in collaboration with the Centre for Electoral Reform (CETRO) and Anging Mammiri' Community for Women's Solidarity (SPKAM), conducted a seminar on women's representation in parliament.

VIOLENCE, THE MEDIA AND COMMUNITY RESPONSE

Media reporting on women, especially rape cases, gives cause for concern. In addition, negative portrayals of women are used for entertainment purposes and in pornography. The Women Journalists Forum for South Sulawesi (FWPSS) was established in 1998 to promote greater professionalism in press reporting on women.[4] Newspaper reports describing a rape victim as, for instance, 'beautiful' or 'sexy' insinuate that she deserved to be raped. Raped women are portrayed as *diobok-obok* (ruined), indicating how language has become a tool to insult women through the media. But it is not only language that is problematic; often the images presented in the mass media amount to a 'second rape'.[5]

An article in a Makassar daily newspaper has questioned whether a case of sexual harassment has ever reached the courts ('Malu Ungkapkan Pelecehan' [Ashamed to Report Harassment], *Fajar*, 9 July 2000). Women are reluctant to report sexual harassment, let alone rape – particularly rape in marriage. This unwillingness is due to several factors. First, raped women often experience a 'second rape' when police officers insinuate that they invited the rape through their actions, physical appearance or clothing. Media reports reveal similar assumptions, for instance: 'three young men ruined the beautiful body of the girl' (*Fajar*, 12 January 2000); 'four men raped a beautiful woman in the garden' (*Fajar*, 7 August 2000); and 'a teacher denied that he had touched her plump and full breasts (*buah terlarang*)' (*Fajar*, 23 August 2000). Second, the police may further harass the victim with questions like, 'You enjoyed it, didn't you?' Fear of being stigmatised significantly influences women in their decision as to whether to report a rape.[6] Third, lack of awareness of the law means women are unprepared for the reality of a public court case and media publicity. Fourth, rape cases are unlikely to proceed unless there is a witness or physical evidence to prove that the victim had been attacked. Such evidence may be obtainable through a medical examination, but finding a witness is almost impossible, except in cases of gang rape in a public place (as occurred during the May riots).

It is notable that since the women's movement opened up the issue of violence against women to public discourse, the number of cases reported by local newspapers in South Sulawesi has increased. Although there are no firm quantitative data, newspaper clippings collected by the FPMP indicate an increase in such reports over the last five years, whether this is rape of teenage girls, marital violence or other kinds of violence against women.

As in other cities in Indonesia during the reform period, Makassar has witnessed several large demonstrations protesting against sexual violence and/or sexual abuse of women. On 24 November 1999, for example, students of the University of 45 Makassar organised a large demonstration following the attempted rape of a university student. This incident happened at around 9 o'clock at night as the student was going to the office of the Islamic Students' Association (HMI) in the city centre. The driver of the *pete'-pete'* (public minibus) in which she was travelling turned off the official route and took the student to a dark place on the other side of town, where he and his two male 'passengers' attempted to rape her. The student managed to escape with the assistance of a passing taxi driver, who drove her to the HMI office. The woman's friends at the office tried to report the incident to the local police in the middle of the night, but could not persuade them to take any significant action.

The unresponsive behaviour of the police sparked anger the following day, with students expressing their rage by taking hostage hundreds of *pete'-pete'* drivers along the route travelled by the student. Drivers who tried to fight back were attacked violently. The *pete'-pete'* drivers responded by bringing all local transportation to a halt – any driver who tried to operate as usual was attacked by other drivers.

The student protesters claimed that they took their action through disappointment with the police, who had failed to act on what they probably considered a 'trivial' incident. The coordinator of the organisation of *pete'-pete'* drivers said that the students should have reported the incident to his organisation; if they had done so, he felt sure they could have worked together to solve the problem by 'peaceful means'. The students wanted to publicise the case as part of a broader agenda of exposing violence. The *pete'-pete'* coordinator, on the other hand, wanted to keep it hidden, arguing that a resolution away from the public eye would be to the advantage of both sides – meaning that the student would not face shame and the three perpetrators would be arrested without violence.

The attempted rape of the student was completely forgotten as public attention focused on how to solve the transport problem caused by the stand-off between the drivers and the students. Local newspapers viewed this as far more important than the attempted rape, presumably because it inconvenienced a far greater number of people.

There is, nevertheless, evidence that sexual violence against women is becoming less tolerated. For instance, on 1 May 2000, *Berita Kota* reported that a widower accused of kidnapping and raping a girl had been burned to death by a 'crowd of people' in Takalar.[7] This case resulted in a breach of *siri'*, bringing shame to the family of the victim and surrounding community, including the family of the man. The act of mass punishment occurred not only to defend *siri'* but also because many previous such cases had not been treated seriously by the police. In this case the actions of the girl's family were due to a feeling of *asse're siri'* (sharing one's *siri'*),[8] and the community response was motivated by feelings of *pacce* (social solidarity).[9] In such cases, the concepts of *siri'* and *pacce* are used as a normative law for the family and the community to manifest *siri'*.

From October to December 2000, *Fajar* reported on an extreme case of marital violence which ended in murder in Pare-Pare, 200 kilometres from the metropolitan city of Makassar. In response, the community not only conducted an investigation itself but also demanded that the police take action against the husband. Community pressure continued until the victim's body was examined and the husband arrested.

Fajar (7 July 2000) reported that Jamila Nompo – a police chief in the city sector of Bontoala Makassar – challenged the view that the police are unwilling to respond seriously to allegations of violence against women. She encouraged women to report incidences of violence, saying that the police would respond sensitively. In the new political climate in Indonesia, she said, police are now aware of how to handle such cases quickly and compassionately.

In August 2000 the regional police of South Sulawesi, in collaboration with a local women's NGO, introduced a Special Investigation Room where women could report cases of violence in confidence. This was part of a nationwide scheme introduced by the former Minister for Women's Empowerment, Khofifah Indar Parawansa (see Chapter 6). The initiative needs to be promoted if it is to be effective and if it is to motivate victims to report instances of violence.

RAISING AWARENESS OF WOMEN'S RIGHTS

Local daily newspapers such as *Fajar*, *Binabaru* and *Pedoman Rakyat*, and radio stations such as Telstar FM, Sentosa FM, Bharata FM, Smart FM and Mercurius FM, can be influential in raising awareness of women's problems and campaigning against violence.[10] Sentosa FM, for instance, broadcasts several programs directed at women. One of these is 'Visi Wanita' (Women's Vision), which seeks women's views on topics such as women and politics, and women and violence. Another of its programs, 'Bincang Masalah Wanita' (Discussing Women's Problems), uses a talkback format for women to air their problems. Another talkback program that discusses issues of concern to women is produced by YLK-Sulsel in collaboration with local radio stations such as Al-Ihwan and Gamasi-Delta.

Smart FM has a very popular daily program called 'Harmoni Keluarga' (Family Harmony). On this talkback program, experts like Christina Joseph and other young activists offer advice on such problems as violence, dating and marriage. The presenters are both male and female.

The response to these programs varies. One of the discussions on Smart FM, concerning whether there should be a regulation banning sexual violence in marriage (marital rape), triggered heated debate. Opposition to the introduction of such a regulation was based on religious and cultural beliefs: callers said that it was sinful for a woman to refuse her husband sex; that rape within marriage was a Western concept; and that there was no such thing as rape in marriage. Callers supporting such a regulation said that it was sinful for a husband to force his wife to have sex; and that men needed to recognise that they could not treat their wives arbitrarily (Smart FM, 17 January 2000).

Marital rape has been a subject of debate since early 1993, when a draft law that would have made it illegal failed in the legislature (DPR). While there were no street demonstrations, as occurred when the 1974 Marriage Law was passed, public debate on this issue has continued. One national magazine, for instance, has regularly published news tending to undermine rather than support the legislation. During the Soeharto era one Minister for Women's Affairs, Sulasikin Murpratomo, commented in its pages that the concept of marital rape was not appropriate under the state ideology, Pancasila, and did not fit with Indonesian 'culture'.[11] In the same article Aisyah Amini, a member of parliament, maintained that rape necessarily occurs outside marriage and argued (like many of Smart FM's callers) that marital rape was a 'Western concept' that could not be applied in the Indonesian context (Hafidz 1993: 18–20).

CONCLUSION

Violence against women in South Sulawesi can be viewed as being bound up with local values about appropriate female behaviour, and the connection between female virtue and family honour (*siri'*). However, especially in the reform era, South Sulawesi has followed other parts of Indonesia in experiencing an explosion of concern about violence against women as a public issue. While women's NGOs have been at the forefront of protests challenging men's perpetration of violence against women, increasing media reports of violence, student protests and mass anger directed towards rapists indicate that men too are beginning to confront the problem. The growing public debate has led to an increase in media reporting of violence and sexual assaults against women, providing the means by which violence is challenged.

NOTES

1   The Bugis/Makassar word *siri'* has multiple meanings – shame, shyness, fear, humility, disgrace, envy, self-respect, honour, morality – as described in Rahim (1981/82: 109–10).
2   YLK-Sulsel was originally the South Sulawesi branch of the national consumers' organisation YLKI, but became an autonomous organisation in 1995.
3   These data are based on an interview in December 2000 with a staff member of the LBH-P2I Women's Crisis Centre in Makassar.
4   Myra Diarsi, a member of the National Human Rights Commission (Komnas HAM) and an activist in the organisation Voice of Concerned Mothers (SIP), has said that, in the reporting of rape cases, a raped woman is raped again by the media. The implication is that the media play a significant role in perpetuating women's subordination in society.
5   For example, the medical examination of the body of Bidan (Midwife) Satirah in Pare-Pare, whose husband was suspected of murdering her, was conducted in public. *Fajar* ran a photo of her 'naked body' being examined in an 'open space ... witnessed by a crowd of people' (16 October 2001). In this case, the 'second rape' was perpetrated not only by the media, but also by the medical team. The examination should of course have taken place at the nearest hospital.
6   Articles in daily newspapers such as *Fajar, Berita Kota* and *Pedoman Rakyat* indicate that significant numbers of women do report cases of rape to the police. Although there is still a social stigma attached to rape, women are becoming more confident in reporting it.
7   Such crowds do not usually include women. Although women can defend their *siri'*, it is more usual for male relatives to do this on their behalf.
8   This Makassar term is similar in meaning to the Bugis term, *masse'di siri'*.
9   The Makassar word *pacce* (in Bugis, *pesse*) literally means 'smarting' or poignant' (Andaya 1979: 367); it expresses the attitude of making a sacrifice in someone else's interest (Mangemba 1977: 1). In Bugis as well as in Makassar, the concept of *siri'* is in alignment with *pacce* (Mangemba 1977: 2). Consequently, there is a Makassar saying, 'Punna tena siri'nu, nia tosseng paccenu' (similar to the Bugis saying, 'Kode' siri'mu engka mussa pessemu'), which means that if you don't have *siri'*, at least you have a feeling of solidarity.

10 Telstar is the only radio station to have had a popular, long-running program specifically on 'social problems' since the mid-1990s. The other stations have sprung up
since 1998, often using a talkback format for their women's programs.

11 Pancasila sets out the five basic principles of the Republic of Indonesia: belief in
one God; a just and civilised humanity; the unity of Indonesia; democracy guided
by the wisdom of representative deliberation; and social justice for all Indonesians.

17 GENDER MAINSTREAMING AND SEX-DISAGGREGATED DATA

Soedarti Surbakti

THE GENDER GAP IN INDONESIA

In Indonesia, women comprise slightly more than half the population. Yet they remain seriously underrepresented in higher education, political decision-making, the judiciary and upper echelons of the civil service. In this chapter I examine what sex-disaggregated statistics tell us about gender equity and development in Indonesia. I then discuss policy responses to the underrepresentation of women, focusing on the concept of gender mainstreaming, which became part of national development policy under a Presidential Instruction issued in 2000. Finally, I examine the various data sources necessary for gender mainstreaming, and the important role played by the Central Statistics Agency (BPS) in the collection and dissemination of data. I argue that reliable, sex-disaggregated data are central to gender mainstreaming and, ultimately, to promoting gender equality.

Sex composition in Indonesia has not changed much over the last decade: on average there are around 99 males for every 100 females. The sex ratio, however, is not equal across all age groups: it is over 90 for people aged under 60 years but lower than this for older age cohorts, implying that women have a longer life expectancy than men. Based on the preliminary results of the 2000 population census, there are around 102 million females in Indonesia and 101 million males (BPS 2001a). Through their numbers alone, then, women have a right to be reckoned with.

Women remain less well educated than men. Fewer women – especially adult women – than men are able to read and write, although this is changing quite quickly. In 1990 illiteracy among women aged 10–44 years stood at about 6.2 per cent (compared with 3.1 per cent for men), but by 2000 this had fallen to 5.2 per cent (still much higher than the rate for men of 2.7 per cent) (BPS

2001b). The above figures reflect the increased opportunity for women to participate in education, even though their literacy rates continue to lag behind those of men.

The country's development policies on education were not intentionally designed to favour girls, but have proved successful in improving their access to schooling. In early 1974, in line with a Presidential Instruction on primary education, the number of primary schools in each village was increased. This policy resulted in a rise in the number of girls attending school, since parents felt they could now send their daughters to a nearby school without having to worry about their safety. Furthermore, with the introduction in early 1984 of a program to make six years of primary education compulsory for all children, all state primary schools were obliged to offer free tuition, although in fact parents still did pay a small amount in fees. This greatly improved girls' opportunity to participate in education because they no longer had to compete with boys for limited household resources. It can be argued that the government's educational policies stimulated the participation of girls more than it did that of boys. The school participation rate of girls aged 7–12 years old (generally those of primary school age) increased from 58 per cent in 1971 to 95.7 per cent in 1999, a much steeper increase than in the rate for boys of the same age (61.7 to 95.0 per cent). The figures for both girls and boys remained much the same in 2000, at 95.9 per cent for girls and 95.1 per cent for boys (BPS 2001b).

The gender gap in education is also apparent in women's participation in higher education, and in their selection of subjects. In 2000, the enrolment rate in tertiary education of females aged 19–24 years was about 10.7 per cent, whereas the rate for males of the same age was 14.0 per cent (BPS 2001b). Furthermore, female tertiary students were more likely to choose so-called 'soft' subjects over the 'hard' sciences. In the fields of mathematics/natural sciences and technology, the percentages of female students enrolled in 1999/2000 were 43.4 per cent and 18.3 per cent respectively (BPS 2001b). Their tendency to choose 'soft' subjects may be a major reason why women face fewer opportunities than men in the labour market.

The gender gap in the labour force is reflected not only in labour market shares, but also in participation rates, unemployment rates, wages and salaries, and fields of employment. The female labour force participation rate for women aged 15 years and over has always been lower than that of males in the same age group, although over the past 14 years the female rate has grown faster than the male rate. Female participation rose from 44 per cent in 1986 to 60 per cent in 2000 (an increase of 16 percentage points), compared with an increase for males from 70 to 74 per cent (BPS 1986, 2000a).

Unemployment has always been higher among women than among men, although – like labour market shares – the gap has tended to narrow somewhat over time. One implication of this is that relatively more female than male tertiary graduates are unemployed. In 1998, for example, the open unemployment rate among female tertiary graduates was twice the male rate (21.3 per cent compared with 12.3 per cent) (Surbakti, Ahnaf and Iriana 2001). There is also discrimination against women in the workplace, although this may be harder to pin down (see also Cameron, Chapter 12). Women are sometimes recruited as casual workers because this allows employers to pay them at a lower rate. In general all women are assigned unmarried worker status, which means that they are not entitled to the various allowances granted to married employees.

The wage differential between women and men varies according to educational level. Within the same educational band, however, women's pay is invariably lower. For example, in 2000 female primary school graduates received less than 56 per cent of the equivalent male wage, female junior high school graduates around 65 per cent, and female graduates of senior high school or higher 72–78 per cent. In the informal sector in particular, differences in remuneration may be related to the hours worked, but even here the gender difference persists. In this sector, the proportion of men working over 35 hours per week in 2000 was 62 per cent, compared with 39 per cent for women (BPS 2000a). Yet overall, many more women than men are employed in the sector: 71 per cent of female workers in 2000 compared with only 62 per cent of male workers.

Decision-making on matters that concern the public at large is one area where gender gaps can easily be identified. The preponderance of men in decision-making positions contributes markedly to gender bias in public sector policies. The number of female members of the People's Representative Assembly (DPR) has declined over the last three parliamentary terms, a trend that is also evident for the People's Consultative Assembly (MPR). In the present parliamentary term (1999–2004), only around 9 per cent of DPR members are women; the figure is much the same for the MPR. In contrast, the number of women in the civil service, including those holding structural positions, has risen. Between 1977 and 2000 the proportion of female civil servants rose from 35.3 per cent to 37.6 per cent, and the proportion holding structural positions from 14.0 to 15.7 per cent (see Oey Gardiner, Chapter 9). Recently there has also been a slight increase in the number of female village heads. In 1996 the percentage stood at only 2 per cent but in 1999 this rose to 2.3 per cent. In urban areas, where the village head (*lurah*) is appointed by the government, women stand a better chance (4.2 percent) of being appointed to this position than in rural villages (2.1 percent), where the head (*kepala desa*) is democratically elected by the people.

The available sex-disaggregated data on employees of judicial bodies demonstrate that a similar gender gap exists there as in the legislative and executive bodies (BPS 2001b). Currently only one of the 37 members of the Supreme Advisory Council (DPA) is a woman; in the Supreme Court 13 per cent of judges are women.

In 1994, the United Nations Development Program (UNDP) introduced its gender empowerment measure (GEM), an index to rank the status of women relative to men in political and economic decision-making. The GEM draws on several indicators to compile its rankings, including the percentage of parliamentary seats held by women, the proportion of managerial, professional and technical positions they hold, and women's share of income. Table 17.1 shows the GEM ranking of seven Asian countries (drawn from a total of 94 countries ranked by the UNDP). Indonesia occupies a low position, indicating a comparatively poor representation of women in decision-making processes.

A gender gap exists not only nationally but also at the provincial level, where the GEM ranking does not necessarily reflect the level of development. Table 17.2 lists the provinces with the five lowest and five highest GEM rankings.

GOVERNMENT POLITICAL WILL

That the government of Indonesia is in favour of enhancing the status of women is undoubted. Article 27 of the 1945 Constitution states that women and men have the same rights and obligations within the family and society, and in development. Several rulings and regulations have been declared in accordance with this article. For example, the nation's education policy encourages parents to educate both their sons and their daughters. As mentioned earlier, in 1984 the government made six years of primary education compulsory, a policy that has been successful in closing the gap between boys and girls in primary school. In 1994 compulsory education was extended to nine years. This policy may be less successful than its predecessor, for two reasons: first, junior secondary school is not free and parents still have to pay some fees, and second, in several regions of the country early marriage is still a common practice. Each of these has serious implications for girls' education beyond primary school.

The Ministry of Labour has issued several regulations on women workers, among them Per. No. 03/Men/1989 prohibiting termination of women's employment on grounds of marriage, pregnancy or childbirth, and Per. No. 04/Men/1989 setting out conditions for workplaces where women work at night.

Indonesia has also issued laws and regulations as part of its commitment to the ratification of several international agreements, although their implementation remains weak. These include:

- International Labour Organisation (ILO) Convention No. 100 concerning equal payment for equal work, implemented by Law No. 80/1957;
- the Declaration on the Political Rights of Women, brought into effect by Law No. 68/1958;
- the Convention on the Elimination of All Forms of Discrimination against Women, brought into effect under Law No. 7/1984;

Table 17.1 Gender Empowerment Measure, 1994 [a]

GEM Ranking	Country	Value
59	Indonesia	0.373
52	Thailand	0.417
48	Malaysia	0.422
47	Singapore	0.423
35	Philippines	0.459
34	Japan	0.465
28	China	0.481

a   Maximum value = 0.795 (Norway); minimum value = 0.177 (Mauritania).

Source: UNDP (1997).

Table 17.2 Gender Empowerment Measure for Five Lowest and Five Highest Ranked Provinces, 1999

GEM Ranking	Province	Value
Five lowest ranked provinces (high position for women)		
1	DI Yogyakarta	0.592
2	Bengkulu	0.555
3	South Kalimantan	0.549
4	East Java	0.540
5	West Kalimantan	0.527
Five highest ranked provinces (low position for women)		
22	South Sulawesi	0.441
23	Central Kalimantan	0.433
24	West Nusa Tenggara	0.427
25	South Sumatra	0.395
26	Riau	0.335

Source: BPS, Bappenas and UNDP (2001).

- the principles of the 1993 UN Declaration on the Elimination of Violence against Women, under the 1998–2003 Draft National Action Program for Human Rights; and
- the Convention on the Rights of the Child, ratified in 1990.

These laws and regulations are important, but enforcement has been lacking to date. Regular monitoring and evaluation is necessary for the successful implementation of any program, but this part of the task has been neglected. The establishment of a Women's Ministry in 1978 was intended to improve the situation. The ministry should focus its efforts on enforcing gender equalisation laws, and be proactive in the monitoring and evaluation of gender-related programs.

Law No. 25/2000 concerning the National Planning Program (Propenas) for 2000–04 is an expression of the government's efforts to further enhance the role and position of women. This law, which sets out national development priorities for the period, aims to promote gender equality and equity for women both nationally and locally, and to improve the quality and independence of women's organisations. The government has devised a set of development programs to achieve these objectives, including a program to improve women's quality of life; a women's empowerment, development and equity program; and a program to improve the role of women in the community through the introduction of gender mainstreaming.

The most significant step the government has taken in this area is Presidential Instruction No. 9/2000 on gender mainstreaming in national development. Directed at the ministries, armed forces, police force, high court, heads of local government and heads of all other governmental agencies, it aims to mainstream gender in the planning, formulation, implementation, monitoring and evaluation of all national development programs.

GENDER MAINSTREAMING

Gender mainstreaming means not only integrating gender issues into all aspects of development but also endeavouring to make development programs more sensitive and responsive to gender. Development programs to increase people's quality of life can and should benefit all members of the community – women and men. Based on this understanding, gender mainstreaming is a major strategy to ensure that women and men gain equal access to, and participate equally in, the benefits of development.

The UN Economic and Social Council has defined gender mainstreaming as:

> the process of assessing the implication for women and men of any planned action, including legislation, policies or programs, in all areas and at all levels. It is a strat-

egy of making women's as well as men's concerns and experiences an integral dimension of the design, implementation, monitoring and evaluation of policies and programs in all political, economic and social spheres so that women and men benefit equally and inequality is not perpetuated (UN Economic and Social Council 1997, cited in UNDAW 1998).

Development programs to date have been considered gender-neutral in design. In fact, however, differences in levels of education, skills and perceptions between men and women have resulted in a different take-up rate of the opportunities offered by such programs. Women lagged behind men, with less access to projects and lower rates of participation. Had the programs been gender-sensitive, better outcomes might have been achieved.

When gender mainstreaming is put into effect, programs are modified to reduce or, if possible, eliminate unequal effects. Five stages of development have been identified as entry points to achieve success in gender mainstreaming in national policy (Marcoes 2001): policy planning; project formulation; development of a plan of action; project implementation; and monitoring and evaluation.

Planning, Formulation and Action

In the planning and formulation stages, sex-disaggregated quantitative or qualitative data can be used to identify gender gaps. Such data enable decision-makers to recognise gender differences related to access to, participation in, or opportunity to control or benefit from development programs. It then becomes possible to analyse the causes of the gender differences and the reasons for any failure of gender-neutral development policy to improve the status of women. Policy can then be reformulated to be more gender-responsive. This should be followed by an action plan to narrow the gap between women and men. Data are therefore the major input into gender analysis at the policy formulation stage.

Implementation

The implementation of gender-responsive policies and programs may vary according to the local situation. To ensure that implementation takes sufficient account of the needs of women as well as men, both sexes should take part in every activity; both should be involved in the management of activities; and there should be development and coordination of stakeholders at all levels.

Participation
At least three questions need to be asked about each program or project.

- Who is it targeting? To obtain qualitative information on whether women, men or both sexes are targeted, a study of the content of the program or project should be undertaken.
- Who are the participants? The participation rate of women and men should be compiled from administrative records as an important component in understanding the gender responsiveness of the program or project. A gender analysis of the reasons women and men participated differently in an activity could be used to improve its design and implementation.
- Who are the beneficiaries? Careful in-depth study should be carried out in the field to determine who benefits from the activity. Sex-disaggregated quantitative and qualitative data on the number of female and male beneficiaries could then be compared.

Management
The numbers of women and men involved in project design, organisation and supervision are one indicator of women's participation in management. These data should be gathered at both the national and the subnational level. The gender ratio of managers at each stage of the project would show up any gender gaps.

Stakeholders
Efficient and effective advocacy to the agents of gender mainstreaming at all levels – from national and provincial down to the district level – to enhance both their understanding of the process of gender mainstreaming and their ability to coordinate their activities would speed up the execution of gender-responsive programs and projects. Sex-disaggregated data are vital to the implementation of gender-responsive programs and a strategic tool in assessing women's and men's participation.

Monitoring and Evaluation

Gender-disaggregated statistics and indicators are crucial for monitoring and evaluating gender responsiveness. First, the evaluator should make a qualitative analysis of a policy or program's gender responsiveness by examining its content. It should be monitored and evaluated regularly to determine whether there has been any improvement in its sensitivity to women compared to men. Second, at the program or project level, monitoring and evaluation can be done by compiling output indicators – that is, data on how many women and men participated in a particular program or project. Output statistics and indicators broken down by sex should be made available regularly. Third, there is a need for sex-disaggregated impact indicators, to determine whether gender mainstreaming has been effective in narrowing or minimising gender gaps.

DATA SOURCES

As discussed above, sex-disaggregated data are an important element of gender mainstreaming and the formulation of gender-responsive policies, of planning and implementation, and of monitoring and evaluation. The Ministry for the Empowerment of Women has experienced difficulties in collecting information disaggregated by sex. This lack of data has caused policy-makers to make decisions based on less than perfect information. Instead, decisions are often based on intuitive responses.

Under Law No. 16/1997, BPS has the task of providing basic statistics, especially to the government. It also formulates national policies, plans and programs on statistics and serves as the principal national centre for statistical and information systems. Other institutions also conduct their own sectoral or specific statistical activities, if necessary in collaboration with BPS. Three different groups of institutions are responsible for collecting official statistics: BPS, the sectoral ministries and non-departmental government institutions.

BPS has three major sources for the collection of basic statistics: censuses, surveys and administrative records. The various surveys conducted by BPS range from population, large-scale labour force and socioeconomic surveys to surveys of small-scale and cottage industries. Most are based on a sampling or household approach. Through its population census, BPS collects information on the characteristics of the Indonesian population; the 2000 census, for example, asked people about their sex, age, marital status, educational attainment, residence (including migration), occupation, religion, ethnic group and birth date. The agricultural census gathers data on the agricultural activities of selected farm households and all legal agriculture-related enterprises. In the case of the household enterprises, information on the sex of the owner is recorded. The census covers primary agriculture, horticulture, plantations, animal husbandry, slaughtering, marine fisheries, aquaculture and forest products. The economic census is the source of information on non-agricultural business units. Only selected household units – whether run by women or by men – are included in this census, although all legal business units are covered. The economic census provides information on the characteristics of economic units across all sectors – manufacturing, electricity and gas, construction, transportation, finance and banks, hotels and accommodation, and trade. In short, sex-disaggregated data on the demographic characteristics of the population can be derived from the population census, and data on the characteristics of business can be derived from the agricultural and economic censuses. At present, only the population census publications contain comprehensive data disaggregated by sex.

BPS publishes tabulations summarising the results of its surveys by selected characteristic, but not all of these are broken down by sex due to limited space. However, sex-disaggregated data from the surveys have been presented in cross-sectoral publications since 1986 – see, for example, BPS (2000b). This publication also contains secondary data compiled from the administrative records of ministries, presented in tabular form and disaggregated by sex.

Unlike BPS, which collects community-based data, the sectoral ministries compile data from administrative records and reports. These are often registrations of activities, collected for administrative purposes, and the information is not recorded in a gender-specific way. Methods of data processing and filing vary, with some ministries using a centralised data-processing centre and others scattering responsibility for this across several units. Several ministries collaborate with BPS in collecting community-based data. The National Socioeconomic Survey (Susenas) conducted by BPS, for example, includes special questionnaires to accommodate the interests of sectoral ministries in such areas as education, health, housing, social affairs and culture, crime and tourism. The sectoral modules are rotated every three years and data are broken down by sex. Based on the level of statistical activity, sectoral ministries can be divided into three groups (Surbakti 2000):

1   those who do not collect data by sex, such as the Ministry of Justice and the Ministry of Industry and Trade;
2   those who collect but do not process data by sex, such as the Ministry of Health and the Ministry of Social Welfare; and
3   those who collect and process data by sex, such as the Ministry of Education and the State Civil Service Board (BKN).

To date, sex-disaggregated data for use in national planning have been provided mainly by BPS, but the data it provides are not sufficiently comprehensive. Planners need to be equipped with sex-disaggregated data on each sector to allow them to perform sound gender analyses – and in particular to enable them to determine the gender responsiveness of program implementation.

CONCLUSION

The task of developing a gender-responsive statistical system is complex. Such a system would need to take account of the different kinds of data collected by government bodies, in particular registrations, surveys and censuses. This would involve developing a comprehensive framework related to data needs, data bases and other data sources to be used in gender mainstreaming. Sex-disaggregated data in the national statistical system are a vital strategic tool, and a prerequisite for the successful implementation of gender mainstreaming.

18 THE CHANGING INDONESIAN HOUSEHOLD

Gavin W. Jones

The household is the key locus of gender relations in Indonesia. It is formed through marriage, and the way marriages are arranged and the ages at which women and men marry reflect gender relationships. In turn, the dynamics of spousal and parent–child relationships within the household reflect norms of gender relationships and their adaptation to the particular circumstances individual families experience.

This chapter will summarise some of the changes that can be observed in the Indonesian family, and particularly the situation of women within the family. It will briefly examine the evidence on female-headed households, trends in the disruption of families due to widowhood or divorce, and the issue of household composition – who is actually living in the household, and who is away. The chapter then focuses specifically on the changing living patterns of young women – their education, age at marriage and labour force participation – and how these are affecting their relationships and living patterns. Finally, the chapter turns to the relationships between parents and adolescent children.

It is hard to get a statistical fix on how household dynamics are changing in Indonesia as a whole, let alone in different parts of the country. Moreover, regional differences would require a monograph rather than a chapter. Therefore, this chapter does not attempt to differentiate between regions, apart from making broad rural–urban comparisons.

SMALLER HOUSEHOLDS

The size of Indonesian households is gradually declining, as shown in Table 18.1. The figures given in the table are the net outcome of a number of causal factors, some operating to reduce household size and others to increase it.

Table 18.1 Average Size of Household, 1971–95 (no. of people)

Year	Size of Household
1971	4.87
1980	4.81
1990	4.52
1995	4.27

Source: Population censuses of 1971, 1980 and 1990, and intercensal survey of 1995.

Factors operating to *reduce* family size are the decline in fertility over this period, as well as changing conventions about young people sharing accommodation in group housing with peers, or living alone. Factors operating to *increase* family size include delayed marriage (and the norm for young people to live at home until married), and increased longevity, resulting in longer periods during which the elderly live with their children in a joint household. The most influential factor is undoubtedly the decline in fertility, but the importance of offsetting factors is evident in the rather modest decline in average household size in the face of a very sharp decline in fertility.

FEMALE-HEADED HOUSEHOLDS

De jure, males almost always head a household where an adult male is present, even in cases where the husband is old and decrepit and his wife actually taking the decisions and actions needed to run the household. *De facto*, quite a high proportion of households are headed by women.

What do the population census data tell us about *de jure* household headship? The proportion of households headed by women has been declining, from 16.3 per cent in 1971 to 14.2 per cent in 1980, 13.3 per cent in 1990 and 12.7 per cent in 1995. Probably, this results mainly from a fall in widowhood and divorce, a decline in death rates, a narrowing of the age gap between spouses and a decline in divorce rates. In unbroken households, the male is almost always recorded as the head of the household.

Table 18.2 shows the percentage of women who head households, by age group. Not surprisingly, the proportion rises with age, reflecting mainly the increasing proportion of women in older age groups who are widowed or divorced. There are some very interesting time trends. The most notable is the

Table 18.2 Indonesia: Proportion of Women Who Head Households, by Age Group, 1971–95 (%)

Age Group	1971	1980	1990	1995
15–19	0.5	0.6	1.2	1.2
20–24	2.0	1.6	2.4	2.6
25–29	4.1	3.0	2.9	2.7
30–34	7.6	5.4	4.4	3.4
35–39	12.1	8.7	6.9	5.6
40–44	18.3	14.1	11.2	9.2
45–49	22.4	17.7	15.1	12.8
50–54	28.4	23.7	20.8	18.7
55–59	29.9	25.4	23.5	23.1
60–64	34.2	30.7	28.9	28.8
65–69	31.9	29.9	29.3	31.4
70–74	32.7	30.2	30.7	33.0
75+	26.0	24.9	25.8	28.7
All ages 15+	**11.5**	**9.7**	**9.1**	**8.8**

Source: Population censuses of 1971, 1980 and 1990, and intercensal survey of 1995.

sharp fall in the proportion of women in their 30s, 40s and early 50s who are household heads. This is almost certainly the result of the sharply declining incidence of widowhood at these ages, to be discussed later (see Table 18.3). Another is the rise in the proportion of young women aged 15–24 who are household heads (though the proportion remains very low). This may reflect a tendency for more young women to move out from the parental house and live in a boarding house (*kos*), or rent accommodation either by themselves or with friends.

Hetler (1986) shows that in areas with considerable circular migration to the cities, there is considerable *de facto* headship by women that is *not* recorded in censuses and surveys. Even where the household is headed by a male, we know from anthropological and sociological studies that women tend to manage the financial affairs of Indonesian, especially Javanese, households (Geertz 1961; Sullivan 1983). Moreover:

> in the social world of village and kampung ... women largely determine the social relations of their family with the surrounding community through their participation in neighbourhood networks of exchange (Hatley 1990: 180).

In reality, women's roles go far beyond those assigned them by the dominant government ideology: of *pendamping* (companion) of their husbands, the rearing of children and household tasks.

A DECLINE IN DIVORCE AND WIDOWHOOD

In Indonesia, the two main reasons for the termination of marriage have been the death of the husband and divorce. The death of the wife is less commonly the reason for marital dissolution, because of the tendency for men to marry women some years younger than themselves, and because of women's greater longevity.

Divorce is the most common reason for young women to leave the married state, but widowhood takes over as the main reason after the late 30s (Table 18.3). By their late 50s, almost one-third of women are currently widowed. However, the proportion of women widowed by these ages has fallen substantially over time. For example, the proportion currently widowed at ages 35–39 fell from 10 per cent in 1971 to 3 per cent in 1995; at ages 50–54 it fell from 41 per cent to 19 per cent over the same period.

Women are much less likely to remarry after being widowed than after divorce. For men, the pattern is entirely different. Men are not considered capable of looking after themselves, so if they are widowed they tend to remarry quickly, and this is viewed approvingly by the community. Therefore the striking difference in the percentage of older men and older women currently widowed (at ages 60–64, 8 per cent of men and 45 per cent of women) results both from the much lower proportion of men whose wife's death precedes theirs, and the much higher proportion of such men who remarry.

Before the 1970s divorce rates in Indonesia were very high. They have fallen sharply over the past three decades, leaving current divorce rates well below those in the United States and, indeed, in most Western countries (Jones 1996, 1997b). This decline began well before the 1974 Marriage Law, although this law and the tightening of procedures required to obtain a divorce certainly helped to accelerate the trend. After the Marriage Law was passed, a Muslim husband wanting a male-initiated (*talak*) divorce (or wanting to take more than one wife) had to go before an Islamic court and provide a reason (Katz and Katz 1987).

Family life is now disrupted by divorce much less frequently than used to be the case. However, this beneficial outcome of divorce trends disguises an increase in *de facto* separations that does not show up in the official figures because of the increasing rigidity of divorce procedures post-1975. In contrast to the simpler regulations of the past and their often lax enforcement, a Muslim man wishing to divorce his wife now has to go through counselling procedures with his wife and three sittings of the Pengadilan Agama (religious court) before

Table 18.3 Women Divorced and Widowed, by Age Group, 1971–95 (%)

Age Group	1971	1980	1990	1995
Divorced				
15–19	3.8	2.5	1.1	0.7
20–24	5.4	4.8	3.1	2.1
25–29	4.6	5.0	3.7	2.8
30–34	4.3	5.0	4.0	3.3
35–39	4.4	5.0	4.1	3.4
40–44	4.7	5.8	4.6	3.7
45–49	4.6	6.0	4.8	4.0
50–54	4.2	6.5	5.3	3.7
55–59	3.8	6.3	5.2	4.0
60–64	3.7	6.3	5.3	3.8
65+	3.0	5.1	4.3	3.5
All ages 15+	4.3	4.9	3.6	2.8
Widowed				
15–19	1.4	0.2	0.1	0.1
20–24	3.0	0.7	0.4	0.2
25–29	3.8	1.5	0.9	0.6
30–34	6.2	3.0	2.0	1.5
35–39	10.2	5.4	3.9	3.0
40–44	18.7	11.3	8.6	6.5
45–49	25.6	16.9	13.8	10.7
50–54	41.1	28.6	23.7	18.8
55–59	47.1	35.4	31.1	30.3
60–64	63.4	53.1	46.6	44.9
65+	73.0	68.3	65.5	64.7
All ages 15+	15.8	12.3	11.0	10.5

Source: Population censuses of 1971, 1980 and 1990, and intercensal survey of 1995.

the divorce can be finalised. Government servants who apply for a divorce face an interview with their superior at work. This has all made male-initiated divorce a more fraught procedure than before, and provided an incentive to circumvent the regulations.

Female-initiated divorce was always a more complicated procedure, though the marriage contract frequently stipulated grounds under which the wife could sue for divorce and the courts tended to be sympathetic to the woman (Lev 1972). Women wishing to divorce have typically talked their husband into registering a *talak* divorce. Their bargaining power was relatively strong, because of the husband's loss of face, not to mention the trouble involved, if he was forced to go through a court proceeding initiated by his wife.

There is clearly a downside to making divorce too difficult, to the extent that it simply substitutes *de facto* separation for divorce. However, there is little doubt that the total proportion of marriages disrupted by either divorce or *de facto* separation has fallen since the tighter divorce regulations were introduced, not so much because of the regulations, but because the trend was anyway towards less marital disruption than before.

WHO LIVES IN THE HOUSEHOLD? WHO IS AWAY?

The proportion of the population living as a non-nuclear family member of an extended family has declined to some extent, as shown in Table 18.4. What this table does not show us is the proportion of extended households. Interestingly, however, one component of many households – the live-in domestic servant – is becoming a steadily declining presence in Indonesia. Census and survey figures indicate that the proportion of households with a domestic servant fell from a maximum of 4.2 per cent in 1971[1] to 1.7 per cent in 1995.

Many households in Indonesia have missing family members – even, in many cases, a husband or wife. This is because of seasonal and circular migration, usually to the cities, but also for rural-based activities such as seasonal agricultural work or small-scale mining. A notable component is the large numbers of Indonesian workers abroad – mainly in Malaysia, but also in the Middle East (see Hugo, Chapter 13). This has effects on remaining household members. One study of the families of Indonesian mothers absent in the Middle East found that these women normally relied on relatives to look after their children. The role of members of the mother's extended family, especially the maternal grandmother, was dominant. In such families, fathers often increased their participation in domestic work and childcare, sometimes taking primary care of the children, though usually with the assistance of an older child or one of the children's grandmothers (Purwaningsih 1998).

Graeme Hugo (1997) has drawn our attention to issues facing the aged in Indonesia, stemming from changing socioeconomic conditions, the altered structure and functioning of the family in Indonesia and shifts in the role of women. He notes five reasons why the position of the elderly may change.

Table 18.4 Indicators of Extended Families, 1971–95 (%)

Year	Non-nuclear Relatives of Household Head [a]		Households with a Servant
	Not Including Servants and Others	Including Servants and Others	
1971	9.9	11.4	4.2
1980	10.0	11.5	2.6
1990	9.2	10.9	2.2
1995	8.3	9.8	1.7

a Grandchildren, parents, parents-in-law and other non-nuclear relatives.

Source: Population censuses of 1971, 1980 and 1990, and intercensal survey of 1995.

1 The power of the elderly will decline as the control over the means of production is no longer vested in the hands of older family members (in line with a trend away from subsistence cultivation as the economic mainstay).
2 More women will be working outside the home, so care of the elderly will not be achieved as readily as in the past.
3 Improved mortality and reduced fertility will lower the ratio of available, economically active family members to the number of elderly.
4 Increased education and greater individualism will erode the power of the older generation over the younger generation.
5 Greater population mobility may mean that fewer children are available locally to assist with their elderly parents' support.

On the other hand, international evidence does not support the notion of a massive withdrawal of family support for the elderly as modernisation and urbanisation proceed. The lower incidence of elderly parents living with their children may reflect their desire for greater autonomy and freedom, while their improved average economic situation enables them to maintain an independent household as long as their health permits.

At the core of issues about the care of the elderly in Indonesia is the rapid growth projected in the number and proportion of elderly. From 2000 to 2020, the number of elderly (aged 65+) is projected to increase by 89 per cent, compared with an increase of 32 per cent in the working age groups (15–64). The micro-demographic realities of individual families mean that, even now, not all elderly people have close relatives available to care for them when needed. A survey in Java (Sigit 1988) revealed that about 9 per cent of older persons had no living children and 28 per cent had only one or two. These proportions were somewhat higher for older women. Sibling support was also limited: 50 per cent of older urbanites had no brothers still alive and 41 per cent no living sisters. Increased population mobility and the increased involvement of females in the workforce outside the home must serve to reinforce the reality of non-availability of kin for a fairly substantial proportion of the elderly.

With respect to the ability of the elderly to be self-supporting financially, it must be remembered that the majority of them are women, that only a minority of them are literate, and that very few – even of elderly men – have access to pension schemes (Chen and Jones 1988: 32–3). The current generation of elderly people is clearly highly dependent upon the family (particularly its female members) and the local community for support (Ihromi 1989; Rudkin 1994).

LIVING PATTERNS OF YOUNG WOMEN

In the 1960s and earlier, young women lived at home until they married, which was on average by the age of 17. In much of Indonesia, the young couple then typically continued to live with either her or his parents for a year or two before moving into their own home.[2] If they divorced (as happened within about five years in one-third of marriages in Java), the young woman would normally continue to live with, or return to live with, her parents before remarrying.

But trends in a number of important background factors altered this typical pattern. The forces for change were rising education; rising marriage age and self-arrangement of marriages; and rising labour force participation rates. Let us look at each of these factors in turn.

Rising Education of Young Women

Table 18.5 shows the changing educational levels of women aged 15–34 over time, for both urban and rural areas. In just ten years, between 1980 and 1990, the proportion of women aged 20–24 who had not completed primary school fell from 58 to 27 per cent, while the proportion that had completed upper secondary school or had a tertiary education rose from 8 to 26 per cent. Young women turning 20–24 in 1990 had been in primary school in the second half of the 1970s, at a time when primary schooling was expanding very rapidly. Clearly, they continued on into upper secondary education in much greater numbers than the cohorts that had preceded them.

The rise in education was very widespread in both rural and urban areas, and in all regions of the country. In 1993 a policy to make nine years' education compulsory was introduced, although this cannot be enforced because of a lack of school places.

Rising Age at Marriage

In many East and Southeast Asian countries, there has been a trend towards greatly delayed marriage, and increasing non-marriage, of women, particularly in the big cities (Jones 1997a; Retherford, Ogawa and Matsukura 2001). This is apparent in the rising proportion of women still single in their 20s, 30s and 40s.

Table 18.5 Indonesia: Educational Attainment of Young Women, 1971–95 (%)

Age Group	Did Not Complete Primary School			Completed Primary or Lower Secondary			Completed Upper Secondary or Tertiary		
	1971	1980	1990	1971	1980	1990	1971	1980	1990
Urban									
15–19	35.2	30.8	8.8	60.9	65.4	81.9	3.9	3.8	9.3
20–24	33.7	34.3	13.6	48.6	44.3	40.9	17.7	21.4	45.5
25–29	45.2	35.7	24.3	42.1	43.8	41.6	12.7	20.5	34.1
30–34	58.4	40.0	30.2	33.7	42.0	45.4	7.9	18.0	24.4
Rural									
15–19	64.4	59.1	22.0	35.0	40.2	75.0	0.6	0.7	3.0
20–24	68.8	65.9	34.9	29.4	30.2	51.3	1.8	3.9	13.8
25–29	78.8	70.4	51.0	20.3	26.3	41.0	0.9	3.3	8.0
30–34	86.5	76.5	58.9	13.1	21.1	36.4	0.4	2.4	4.7
Urban + rural									
15–19	58.3	51.4	17.1	40.4	47.1	77.5	1.3	1.5	5.4
20–24	61.6	57.8	27.0	33.3	33.8	47.5	5.1	8.4	25.5
25–29	73.3	62.3	42.1	23.9	30.5	41.2	2.8	7.2	16.7
30–34	81.9	68.3	49.6	16.4	25.8	39.3	1.7	5.9	11.1

Source: Population censuses of 1971, 1980 and 1990, and intercensal survey of 1995.

In Indonesia the trend is less dramatic, but quite pronounced nonetheless. The median age at marriage for women rose from 18.9 in 1971 to 20.9 in 1990 (Table 18.6). Among some ethnic groups (notably the Sundanese and Madurese), however, it is still common for women to marry at much younger ages, including below the legal minimum age of 16 (Jones 2001).

The proportion of young women in Indonesia remaining single at any given age is much lower than in surrounding countries. For example, in 1990, among women aged 30–34, 13.4 per cent remained single in the Philippines, 14.1 per cent in Thailand and 15.8 per cent among Chinese in Peninsular Malaysia, but only 4.5 per cent in Indonesia. This suggests that parent-arranged marriage – which generally favours early marriage in order to protect the family reputation – remains more common in Indonesia than in these countries. While the role of parents in deciding marriage partners for their children does indeed appear to be more common in Indonesia, it has declined greatly compared with earlier times.

Jakarta is the pacesetter in delayed marriage. It is important to note the rise in the proportion of women still single at ages 30–34, from 4.2 per cent in 1971

Table 18.6 Indonesia and Jakarta: Indicators of Trends in Marriage Timing and Non-marriage for Women (%)

	1971	1980	1990	1995
Indonesia				
Single at ages 15–19	62.6	69.9	81.8	85.7
Single at ages 20–24	18.5	22.3	35.7	40.1
Single at ages 25–29	5.0	7.4	11.2	15.2
Single at ages 30–34	2.2	3.4	4.5	5.5
Median age at marriage	18.9	19.5	20.9	21.3
Jakarta				2000
Single at ages 15–19	68.5	78.9	91.6	93.9
Single at ages 20–24	26.1	35.7	55.7	63.3
Single at ages 25–29	8.8	15.2	23.1	31.2
Single at ages 30–34	4.2	7.0	8.7	14.3
Median age at marriage	19.6	20.7	23.2	24.4

Source: Jones (1996), Table 3.1; population censuses of 1971, 1980 and 1990, and inter-censal survey of 1995.

to 8.7 per cent in 1990, followed by a sharp increase to 14.3 per cent in 2000. It is clear that it is no longer uncommon for women to delay marriage until they are in their late 20s or even early 30s. The trend is more pronounced for women with more education, and appears to reflect both the emphasis on a career among these women, as well as increasingly independent lifestyles and freedom from the formerly prevalent arranged marriages. This is not to say that marriage does not remain the norm, or that the community has become comfortable with the idea of single independent women. These women are still challenging the social norms, but they are doing so in rapidly increasing numbers, and with many more role models to guide them.

Rising Labour Force Participation in Urban Areas

There is not a great deal of value in trying to tease out the meaning of trends in labour force participation rates for women in rural areas, because of definitional problems. The fact is that in farming households, women are involved in economic activities whether the census data show they are or not. Therefore this discussion will focus on urban women.

Participation in the workforce is closely related to trends in both education and marriage. Increasingly well-educated women in urban areas face greater 'opportunity costs' of not being in the workforce, though participation rates for those with only a lower secondary education tend to be lower than for both the poorly educated and the well educated. This is probably because the work opportunities available to such women are not particularly appealing, and because many of them are from rather conservative lower-middle-class groups.

It is the women with an upper secondary or tertiary education whose workforce participation is high and rising. These women have more appealing job prospects, and in many cases have a servant at home to ease the strain of working and raising a family.

What have been the time trends in labour force participation of women in urban areas of Indonesia? First, to set this in context, female labour force participation rates in urban areas of Indonesia have historically been below those in most parts of East and Southeast Asia. In 1971, they were actually not much below those in urban areas of Korea, Taiwan, Malaysia or Singapore. But in subsequent years, rates in these other countries increased faster, with the result that, by 1990, Indonesia had been left far behind (Table 18.7). This is not to deny that there was a rise in Indonesia, but only to stress that the rise was modest.

Age patterns of change are important, and these are shown in Table 18.8. The changes are revealing. The rise in female participation rates has been concentrated heavily in the 15–29-year age groups. These are the age groups that, in the words of one demographer, are 'demographically dense'. That is to say, in these age groups young people typically leave school, get a job, fall in love, marry and

Table 18.7 Female Labour Force Participation Rates in Urban Areas of Selected East and Southeast Asian Countries, 1970–90 (%)

Country	1970	1980	1990
Republic of Korea	26.3	30.4	44.2
Taiwan	26.7	34.2	42.0
Hong Kong	42.8	49.5	n.a.
Singapore	29.5	44.2	48.4
Peninsular Malaysia	28.2	45.0	57.2
Thailand	45.1	54.4	60.8
Philippines	33.7	32.6	54.5
Indonesia	25.5	27.7	34.2

Source: Singarimbun (1999), Table 2-8.

Table 18.8 Indonesia: Trends in Female Labour Force Participation Rates, Urban Areas, 1971–95 (%)

Age/Occupation	1971	1980	1990	1995
By age group				
15–19	19.2	21.6	27.5	31.9
20–24	24.2	27.5	41.0	50.3
25–29	26.1	28.6	39.8	48.6
30–34	29.6	29.8	39.1	43.7
35–44	33.0	34.1	40.8	45.4
45–64	31.2	32.0	36.7	39.1
By occupation				
Professional & clerical	13.0	16.3	19.5	20.6
Sales	29.1	34.4	32.2	35.1
Services	20.4	21.6	18.1	14.4
Agriculture	8.2	7.2	6.9	7.1
Production	13.9	20.2	21.8	22.7

Source: Population censuses of 1971, 1980 and 1990, and intercensal survey of 1995.

Figure 18.1 Jakarta: Female Labour Force Participation Rates, by Age Group, 1971–95 (%)

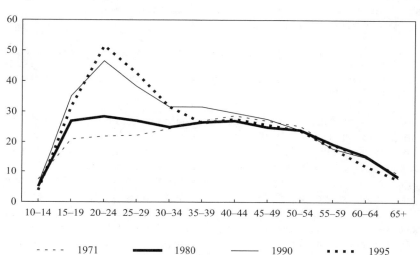

start to have children. The proportion of women aged 15–29 participating in the workforce has risen rapidly. At ages 20–24, the rate rose from just 27.5 per cent to 50.3 per cent in the 15 years from 1980 to 1995; at ages 25–29 it rose from 28.6 to 48.6 per cent. This is a major change, and is no doubt related both to rising education levels and to delayed marriage. More research is needed into patterns of work participation among women of different educational and marital status.

Jakarta is where the greatest changes tend to occur, as Figure 18.1 shows. Particularly for women in their 20s, the increases in participation rates have been relentless and quite sharp. They reflect both the increasing proportion of young women remaining single, and the rising proportion of young married women remaining in the workforce. The pattern does not differ greatly from the changes in urban areas as a whole, just described.

Impacts

Now let me try to relate these three trends – rising education, delayed marriage and increasing workforce participation – to the living patterns of young women and the relationship issues they face. Adolescence has now become an extended period of time between puberty and marriage, raising issues about sexuality and relationships with the opposite sex that simply did not arise in times of early, parent-arranged marriage. Young people are coming into daily contact with the stimulus of sexually explicit material through movies, videos, magazines, books and the internet. Premarital sexual activity is taken for granted in many of these information sources, but the material

> is designed to stimulate and to titillate rather than to educate ... Images of sexuality in the West are at the forefront of this marketing, but this material is not accompanied by Western approaches to sex education and access to information (Utomo and McDonald 1997: 805).

At the same time, traditional influences deriving from religion and ethnicity are still strong. Faced with the conservative forces of idealised morality portrayed through religion, on the one hand, and Western influences promoting a more liberal approach on the other, it is little wonder that many teenagers are confused. Sexual activity is quite widespread: in a 1997 survey in Medan among never-married young people aged 15–24 from a wide range of backgrounds, 18 per cent reported having had sexual intercourse – 27 per cent among males and 9 per cent among females (Situmorang 1998). Other studies on young people in different Indonesian cities show that between 10 and 31 per cent of them have engaged in premarital sex (YKB and BKKBN 1993).

Though adolescents are becoming a more common focus of researchers' attention, more study is also needed of the growing group of single young women in their 20s and 30s. Most of them appear to continue to live at home. But we know relatively little about their relationships with the opposite sex, the extent of comment, censure or even ridicule they receive as a result of their unmarried status, or their role in the household – for example, the extent of their financial and work contribution to the household, or their involvement in household decision-making.

In summary, there is:

- an increasingly long interval between puberty and marriage for most women;
- an increased diversity of living arrangements for single women, although most continue to live with their parents;
- an increasing proportion of young women working outside the home; and
- an increasing proportion of young women having sexual relations before marriage (though mostly with the person they will eventually marry).

RELATIONS BETWEEN PARENTS AND ADOLESCENT CHILDREN

We do not know a great deal about changes in the relationship between parents and adolescent children, but we do know that strong pressures towards Westernisation (witness the changing fare on commercial TV stations, or the popularity of the ubiquitous shopping malls as sites for teenage leisure activities in the cities) and increasing individualism tend to strain the relationship between children and their more conservative parents, particularly in situations in which children are staying longer in the household before getting married and moving out.

Mothers are increasingly out working, making supervision of adolescent children more difficult. Many middle-class parents are worried about clashes between students from different high schools, increasing drug use and possible access to drugs in places where young people tend to congregate. They are also aware of changing sexual mores, and the difficulties this poses for keeping control of teenage girls – and boys. Many parents feel they have 'lost control'. The standard response of authority figures – a focus on *kenakalan remaja* (youth delinquency) and what to do about it – rings hollow to many young people, who in this age of *reformasi* and increased openness in media reporting are well aware that Indonesia is regularly assessed by foreigners doing business there as belonging to the very top echelon of corrupt countries. Much of Indonesia's delinquency is not that of youth, but that of their parents.

NEED FOR MORE INFORMATION

More information is needed on the changing composition of households, intra-familial relationships and, in particular, the changing cultures of young people. Important matters on which there is relatively little information include the incidence of separation between spouses who do not officially divorce, and the attitudes of young men and women towards courtship and sexual relations, whether and when to marry, ideal living arrangements and their responsibility towards siblings, parents and grandparents. In many other countries there are important surveys producing information on matters such as this; the regular National Survey on Family Planning conducted by Mainichi Newspapers in Japan (Retherford, Ogawa, and Matsukura 2001) and the Young Adult Fertility and Sexuality Study in the Philippines (Raymundo et al. 1999) are useful examples. In the past, there was a tendency for officials in Indonesia to place obstacles in the way of studies dealing with adolescent sexuality, resulting in the present lacuna of nationally representative information. Preventing knowledge about a phenomenon does not remove the phenomenon itself. It is time serious efforts were made to obtain better information on adolescent sexuality for planning purposes.

CONCLUSIONS

Family relationships in Indonesia are under considerable strain as the nation modernises, yet continues to struggle with economic weakness and poverty, and with an upsurge of religious extremism in some quarters. The gulf between the urban middle class and the bulk of the population which continues to live in poverty or near-poverty is stark. Generalisations about marriage, divorce, spousal relationships and changing patterns of adolescence for females are hard to reach in a country so complex – whether we are comparing social groups or regional and ethnic groups. Every generalisation has its exceptions. When we talk of rising age at marriage, we need to be aware that marriage below the legal age remains common in certain regions. When we talk of the sharp rise in labour force participation for women in their 20s in Jakarta, we need to realise that, even in Jakarta, some young women remain in traditional confinement in the home. When we talk of widespread exposure of the young to pornographic videos and increasing sexual activity before marriage, we need to be aware that many among the youth are devoutly religious and adhere strongly to traditional teachings about relationships with the opposite sex. Nevertheless, it is possible to discern patterns of change that, though not universal, are widespread. The increasing levels of education and labour force participation of young women, and the exposure to a wide range of influences through the media, are thorough-going, and foster the widespread questioning of many aspects of women's traditional familial roles, and a search for new directions. Whether the political establishment places itself at the forefront of this search, or chooses to be a reactionary bastion, remains to be seen.

NOTES

1   'Maximum', because the proportion is calculated on the basis that all domestic servants worked as the sole such servant in the household. To the extent that some households have two or more servants, the proportion of households with a domestic servant would be lower than that stated above.
2   This pattern resulted from the bilateral kinship system. The proportion of young couples living in the wife's parents' home in this initial period generally exceeded the proportion living in the husband's parents' home, because it was recognized that this would facilitate the young woman's adjustment to marriage. But the decision was generally a pragmatic one, with a number of considerations to be taken into account.

19 WOMEN, FAMILY PLANNING AND DECENTRALISATION: NEW VARIATIONS ON OLD THEMES

Terence H. Hull and Sri Moertiningsih Adioetomo

FAMILY PLANNING IN 1998

If asked to name the New Order program that had the largest impact on Indonesian women, schooling, primary health care and employment generation might all come to mind, but without doubt the national family planning program would eclipse each of these in terms of the proportion of the population affected, the magnitude of the social change involved and the anticipated degree of difficulty faced at the outset of the program.

By 1998 the three decades of development under the New Order regime of Soeharto had produced a family planning program that stood as a model for the developing world. More than contraception, the program promoted income-generating activities, integrated health posts (Posyandu), small credit schemes, and community organisations to cater for the various needs of infants, adolescents and the elderly. By 1992 the National Family Planning Coordination Agency (BKKBN) had motivated sufficient commitment in political circles to develop a basic law on family welfare – UU10/1992. This symbolised a change in the organisation's mandate from population control to the promotion of a broad range of family welfare activities.

By the time the International Conference on Population and Development met in Cairo in 1994, the reputation of the Indonesian program had grown to the status of a model for other developing countries, and a matter of great pride nationally. Haryono Suyono, the chief architect of the family planning mass communications strategies used to overcome resistance and reticence in the nation, had been rewarded for his efforts with a dual appointment as Minister of Population and chief of the BKKBN. From this perspective he could see the need both to promote the story of Indonesia's success in international forums, and to protect the program from growing criticism that its strategies and style

Figure 19.1 Sample Survey Estimates of Contraceptive Prevalence Rates,
1960–99 (%)

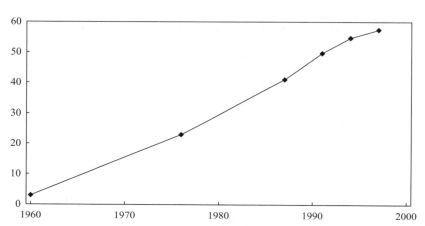

Source: Calculations from the Demographic Institute, Faculty of Economics, University
of Indonesia, based on data from BPS.

were authoritarian. He proclaimed a commitment to quality of care in March
1993 while at the same time moving the core mission of the BKKBN from the
coordination of family planning services to the promotion of family welfare and
poverty alleviation.

In fact this was not a major shift in rationale; from its outset in 1968 the family planning program had contextualised its activities as welfare (*kesejahteraan*).
The difference lay not in the terms, but in the underlying focus and activities.
The term 'welfare' had been a defensive posture in the early 1970s – a way to
put a positive gloss on the controversial goals of fertility control and inherent
social engineering. By the early 1990s the program had become such a success
story that the threat of criticism was overshadowed by the daily reality of social
acceptance. Over half of women of childbearing age were using contraception
(Figure 19.1); fertility was less than half the average six-child family of
Sukarno's times (Figure 19.2; see p. 247); and the program-promoted norms of
small, healthy, prosperous families had become a socially accepted mantra for
virtually all young couples.

A CHANGE OF ERAS

The end of the New Order came faster than many expected, but later than others had hoped. Three decades of authoritarian rule crumbled as the political elite in Jakarta withdrew the de facto legitimacy they had so long invested in Soeharto, and turned to another concept for inspiration. This was the notion of reform, an amorphous desire for change that lacked a concrete program or a specific champion. Instead, the transfer of power to Habibie implied that a reform agenda would be led in the first instance by a person whose very standing was determined by the system he was meant to change.

The goals for change – democracy, good governance, human rights, anti-authoritarianism, decentralisation – were widely espoused but little understood. Students marching in the streets, commentators in the press and middle-class professionals in offices were infused by a combination of euphoria and fear, the one based on hope for greater freedom and equity, the latter fuelled by anxiety over the economic crisis enveloping the country in 1998 and 1999. The community saw reform as a possible safeguard and demanded that the new government take steps to implement change.

President Habibie faced such demands from the community with energy and a fair degree of enthusiasm, but also weighed down by the political baggage of Golkar, corruption and a ministry largely composed of leaders from the Soeharto era. In many essential ways the superstructure of the New Order remained intact, albeit without the resources to carry programs forward. It was the spectre of government budget cuts and the massive changes in the value of the currency that focused attention on government capabilities to meet the needs of a people facing immiserisation.

Under Habibie, Haryono Suyono was the Coordinating Minister for People's Welfare. He continued to run the complex organisational affairs of some of the most important of Soeharto's charitable foundations, but he no longer had a direct interest in the management of the family planning program. In his stead, Ida Bagus Oka, former governor of Bali and a prominent leader in the field of higher education, was given this task. Haryono maintained indirect links, as his office pushed a poverty alleviation agenda and utilised the BKKBN as a vehicle for program delivery. But as reformers in the legislature took increasingly assertive roles in review committees, allegations of financial malfeasance became ever stronger, and Oka felt it necessary to declare that the BKKBN had made a break from the past to take a newer and cleaner path into the future. Obviously Haryono and his supporters regarded this as an unjustified step; before long the tension between the family planning agency and the Coordinating Ministry was palpable. From the viewpoint of ordinary women, though, this conflict had a beneficial side effect. In the effort to move the BKKBN away from its past, Oka declared that it needed to go 'back to basics', paying greater attention to the quality of clinical services and reorienting its activities to focus more closely on client needs. While these two items had been part of BKKBN slogans since before the 1994 Cairo conference, they had not been translated into field operations. Oka saw the reform period as demanding such a change, and at least in rhetorical terms he steered the BKKBN in this new direction.

The challenges of taking a new direction in 1998 soon became apparent. As the newspapers projected the stock images of crisis – hunger, poverty and economic malaise – the economic elite moved to maintain its control over the national institutions. Ominous talk of national disintegration prevented serious challenges to the status quo – the politicians, the military and the conglomerates saw a common interest in maintaining the power networks of the New Order even as they mouthed slogans about democracy, equity and renewal. Stability came above any slogan, and whether seen in the context of secession in Timor, Aceh or Papua, or in the form of protecting the owners of insolvent banks, the elite saw change as something to be hailed but not implemented. This was despite the growing consensus that the 'economic crisis' was actually a product of chronic problems that had built up inexorably over the previous three decades.

THE IMPACT OF THE FINANCIAL CRISIS ON THE FAMILY PLANNING PROGRAM

From the outset of the financial crisis, observers of the family planning program had worried that contraceptive use would collapse. Newspapers headlined fears of a baby boom. This fear was based on a variety of assumptions about the family planning program. Some observers saw inflation and falling real wages as a cost pressure on contraceptive distribution. Others pointed to the fragility of government institutions, saying that it would be impossible to maintain logistical streams and programs to promote contraceptive use. Without government pressure, it was argued, poor women would simply return to historically high fertility. Finally, some observers said that the social depression accompanying the crisis would make childbearing a comforting alternative. Children bring joy. However, these speculations and assumptions had little empirical foundation. They rested on stereotypical ideas about likely patterns of behaviour of middle-class and poor people rather than any surveys or observations based on scientific foundations. In retrospect it is easy to demonstrate that such fears of a baby boom were largely unfounded.

Perhaps 'easy' is not the correct word to use to describe the various approaches taken to show the social impact of the financial crisis. In fact, for a long time before the crisis there were serious concerns about the validity and reliability of survey and registration data related to the family planning program. There are two institutional sources, and a number of different data sets, that can be used to gauge the levels and trend of contraceptive use. The BKKBN produces monthly service statistics (from all public and private clinics distributing program contraceptives), monthly field assessments (collected by a network of field workers) and occasional Demographic and Health Survey (DHS) analyses (carried out in collaboration with the Department of Health and BPS, the central statistical agency). In addition, since 1994 it has carried out an annual family welfare registration program covering all the families in the nation. While primarily designed as a means to measure welfare status, the registration is also used to confirm current use of contraceptive methods. The DHS results are regarded as the most reliable data source among these, but such surveys are carried out only every three years or so, and the results normally take a year or more to emerge. Thus, they are not ideal as a way to investigate short-term changes in trends.

The other institutional source is BPS. As the national statistical agency it publishes data from both government departments and boards, and carries out censuses and surveys (see Surbakti, Chapter 17). The annual National Socioeconomic Survey (Susenas) uses a scientifically designed sample and highly trained interviewers to collect household data relevant to policies and programs. The Susenas is normally held in the early part of the calendar year. Among the data collected are measures of contraceptive use. These data are not immediately comparable to BKKBN estimates because they are based on questions covering a different age range of respondents, and have slightly different definitions of contraceptive use. Also, because the interviewers are not employees of the national family planning program, it is assumed that respondents would have less motivation to give them a 'pleasing' answer. The patterns of response on current contraceptive use among married women under 50 years of age are shown in Table 19.1. They cover the late period of the New Order (1993–98) and the Habibie interlude (1998–99) as well as the initial months of Abdurrahman Wahid's presidency (2000).

The survey results show remarkably stable levels of current contraceptive use, at just over half of the married women (right-hand column). Among the women who are using contraceptives one-quarter use the pill – and this has remained true over the whole period from the time of the Cairo conference in 1994 to the first year of the Abdurrahman administration. At the same time there were declines in the use of IUDs, condoms and traditional methods of fertility control, compensated for by substantial rises in the use of relatively expensive injectables and implants (such as Norplant). These figures do not show any hint of collapse in the family planning program, nor would they lead to an expectation of an increase in fertility levels. If anything this picture raises the question: what crisis? Perhaps a partial response is to be found in Table 19.2. There we see that the year-on-year estimates show a rise until the 1997–99 period followed by minor declines, in both urban and rural areas, but especially so in the countryside.

This pattern fits the history of the international response to the financial crisis in Indonesia. In 1997, as concern about the collapse of the currency and the

Table 19.1 Reported Contraceptive Use among Married Women Aged 15–49, by Method Used (% of users) and Prevalence (% of women), 1993–2000

Year	Pill	Injection	IUD	Implant	Sterilisation	Condom	Other	Prevalence
1993	27.5	32.3	23.7	2.5	8.2	2.2	3.7	53.1
1994	28.4	33.1	23.6	2.5	7.2	1.8	3.4	54.2
1995	29.1	35.0	21.0	2.6	7.7	1.5	3.1	54.2
1996	27.0	37.5	19.8	4.0	7.2	1.6	2.9	54.2
1997	28.1	40.0	17.8	4.6	6.2	1.3	2.0	55.3
1998	27.2	41.2	17.4	4.7	6.0	1.3	2.3	55.4
1999	29.0	39.9	17.2	4.0	7.0	1.0	1.9	55.4
2000	26.9	42.5	16.4	4.4	7.3	0.7	1.8	54.8

Source: BPS (various years), *Statistik Kesejahteraan Rakyat* [People's Welfare Statistics], Jakarta, reporting the results of the Susenas.

Table 19.2 Reported Prevalence of Contraceptive Use among Married Women aged 15–49, by Urban and Rural Residence, 1993–2000 (%)

Year	Urban	Rural	National
1993	56.4	51.6	53.1
1994	57.0	52.9	54.2
1995	56.2	53.3	54.2
1996	55.4	53.6	54.2
1997	56.5	54.6	55.3
1998	56.2	54.9	55.4
1999	55.8	55.1	55.4
2000	56.8	53.5	54.8

Source: BPS (various years), *Statistik Kesejahteraan Rakyat* [People's Welfare Statistics], Jakarta.

tight budget hit the Jakarta newspapers, the donor community worked closely with the BKKBN and the Department of Health to anticipate the impact such events might have on the availability of pharmaceuticals, including contraceptives. This, in part, explained the headlines about possible baby booms. Where many donors had been planning to pull out of Indonesia when it 'graduated' into the middle-income category of nations, the crisis rekindled the motivations for aid. Offices were ordered to work to avoid worst case scenarios of high poverty and low purchasing power. Indonesia had returned to the ranks of the poor countries and donors abandoned all talk of locally sustainable family planning, saying instead that there was a looming crisis of contraceptive procurement that required immediate intervention by traditional friends of the program: the UN Fund for Population Activities (UNFPA), the US Agency for International Development, the Scandinavian and other European countries, and Australia. Offers to contribute contraceptive supplies were made soon after the crash in the value of the rupiah in December 1997, and as the seriousness of the economic downturn increased, so the offers became more generous. Donors attempted to coordinate their contributions, with the UNFPA playing a key role in convening donor meetings and helping to calculate the BKKBN's logistic needs.

However, while this coordination was undoubtedly useful, some of the conditions that donors placed on their contributions had unanticipated impacts on the program. Out of concern for the poor, many donors insisted that any contraceptives they provided be given to women categorised as being in one of the two low-welfare groups identified in the BKKBN's annual family welfare survey. The 'pre-welfare' and 'welfare I' categories covered around 40 per cent of the population – certainly including the very poor, but also including many people that lived well above the official poverty line. Ironically the donors were providing supplies of relatively expensive contraceptives – implants and injectables – as well as the inexpensive pills and intrauterine devices. At the same time that the program was giving these expensive supplies to poor people, the middle classes could not afford to buy their preferred types of contraceptive. This was particularly the case with the implants, which cost US$30–45 per set. Before the crisis the middle classes had readily paid for a substantial part of that cost, with the family planning program subsidising the cost to a greater or lesser degree. After the crisis had pushed the exchange rate for the US dollar from Rp 2,500 to as high as Rp16,000 and had wiped out the government budget needed to provide subsidies, the middle classes found contraceptives very expensive, while the poor, according to the donors, should have obtained them for free.

When researchers from the Demographic Institute at the University of Indonesia went into the field to see how free distribution worked in practice, they met with a number of surprises. They were following the distribution lines of contraceptives supplied by the Canadian International Development Agency (CIDA) program. While it was clear at the central level that all pills were to be donated free to all pre-welfare and welfare I families, in the local clinics they found that medical personnel were routinely charging Rp 2,000–4,000 per monthly packet. The results provoked criticism from donors. This, they said, was typical of the corruption and duplicity of the New Order regime. They called for the rules to be enforced and the poor to be protected.

A different interpretation is possible. The practice of charging for the full or partial cost of contraceptives had been established through the KB Mandiri (Self-reliant Family Planning) program established in the early 1980s and promoted with great vigour by donors and the government alike. The concept was that the program would be less open to criticism if it was clear that the users of contraception voluntarily paid some portion of the cost. Also, the financial vulnerability of a government program dependent on the vagaries of annual budgets would be reduced if there was a flow of funds coming from user fees. Local clinics and providers welcomed the KB Mandiri program because the fees were a welcome supplement to inadequate budgets. Users of contraceptives appeared to be satisfied with the level of fees, and many regarded the payment as a means of ensuring that the goods supplied were of adequate quality. If there was any concern about the quality the purchaser felt empowered to complain or refuse to buy the goods. The demand by donors that contraceptives be given free of all charges severely undermined KB Mandiri and threatened to create a series of perverse consequences. The fact that so many providers (and consumers) ignored the new regulations on free supplies shows how inappropriate donor demands can be, even at a time of crisis.

From the Ministry of Population to the Ministry of Women's Empowerment

When appointed State Minister for Women's Empowerment in 1999, Khofifah Indar Parawansa declared that the BKKBN would have to face a 'new era' in promoting family planning. With a team of 'reformers' drawn from the middle echelons of the organisation, she set out some strategic issues facing the agency at a symposium in March 2000. In addition to the well-known issue of the continuing economic crisis and the impact this might have on the financial viability of the program, she set out a series of propositions that just a year before would have sounded heretical: reproductive rights had not been secured; the program was subject to huge gender bias; the nation faced a moral crisis characterised by human rights abuses; and there was a blindness to the realities of adolescent reproductive health behaviours and needs.

Under other circumstances this transformation of the family planning agency would have attracted national and international attention, but the Gus Dur administration threw up a seemingly endless stream of serious political and economic diversions.

NEW CHALLENGES: DECENTRALISATION AND THE EMERGING POWER OF THE LEGISLATURE

Perhaps the most complex and potentially long-lasting legacy of the Habibie regime was the radical decentralisation policies set out in Laws 22 and 25 of 1999. For the BKKBN, BPS and Ministry of Health, the changes implicit in this form of decentralisation were potentially devastating. Throughout the century the governmental approach to both health and statistics was highly centralised and dependent on a tightly controlled pyramid of authority and vertical flows of information and directions. With decentralisation of a wide range of responsibilities to the district level, bypassing the province in many important ways, these two key government activities faced an uncertain future.

The national family planning movement created in the late 1960s was based on three pillars of government activity – health services, the collection of statistics and the dissemination of information. Regional autonomy has led to differing fates for government bodies. By 2001 the Health Department had largely embraced decentralisation, BPS had successfully fought to remain vertically organised and the Department of Information had been disbanded. During the intense negotiations over the implementation of decentralisation that absorbed the attention of the bureaucracy and the legislature in 1999 and 2000, rumours abounded in Jakarta that 'important interests' were advocating each of these very different outcomes for the BKKBN.

The coming to power of President Megawati Sukarnoputri in August 2001 marked another potentially radical change in the position of the BKKBN in the bureaucracy, with clear consequences for the provision of family planning services and supplies to Indonesian women. The new cabinet was much less committed to decentralisation than its predecessors had been. The new Minister for Home Affairs declared that 'UU22/99 [on regional autonomy] is not a holy book' and in September 2001 laid out a plan for amendment of the law to re-establish rational bureaucratic hierarchies, improve financial systems and ensure that the 'people's' complaints would be heard concerning the range of local regulations that disadvantaged women, ethnic minorities or economic development.

Ironically, just at the time when the government was backpeddling on the issue of decentralisation, the president issued a decision (Keppres 103/2001) on the status and future of non-departmental government institutions, including the BKKBN. Because it was issued on 13 September, when the press in Indonesia, as throughout the world, was totally absorbed by the consequences of the attacks on New York and Washington, this government decision went largely unnoticed. Under it the agency is allowed to maintain its vertical structure only through the end of December 2003, after which time all its responsibilities for program implementation must be handed over to the local governments (clause 114: 60).

Meanwhile the government has dismantled and disbursed many of the policy functions related to population. Consider for instance the following four distinct areas of policy over the past three decades.

1 *Family planning.* In the context of the international efforts to control rapid population growth in the 1960s, at the outset the policy area of family planning focused on the levels and trends of fertility. Over time the demographic policy concerns were transferred to other agencies. As part of the International Conference on Population and Development in Cairo, Indonesia joined other nations in adopting a new policy agenda and program of action. With this, family planning policy came to focus more specifically on the reproductive health of women, and the reproductive rights of all citizens.

2 *Population distribution.* At the beginning of the New Order, the government saw a perceived maldistribution of population as a major challenge, and redoubled efforts to redistribute people under the transmigration program. The Department of Transmigration soon became a large and powerful implementing agency, with a growing mandate to promote regional development and national security. By the late 1990s these activities had become very problematic in a country rent by ethnic and civil conflict, and the word transmigration disappeared from the agenda, to be replaced by 'population mobility'.

3 *Population structure and growth.* While rapid growth was originally seen as the basis for population control measures implemented under the family planning program, by the early 1980s it became clear that the nation needed to consider population in a number of different policy dimensions. The establishment of a Ministry of Population (initially in conjunction with environmental policy) provided a foundation for policy-making on a wide range of issues, including the aging, urbanisation and quality of human resources. To some degree the functions of this ministry overlapped with those of the National Development Planning Board (Bappenas), the BKKBN and the line ministries.

4 *Gender.* The New Order was notable for having a wide range of policies on women, and a shallow agenda of women's policies. Reflecting its policies on women were the institutions built into the government and the community to promote domesticated roles for women, including Dharma Wanita and the many related organisations attached to the military, police and various religious groups, and the PKK (Family Welfare Movement) and related community organisations used as vehicles for the promotion of government programs. Only in the period of President Abdurrahman Wahid could gender policies be said to address 'women's policies' in the sense of empowerment and equality (see Indar Parawansa, Chapter 6).

In each of these policy arenas Indonesia is facing problems of confusion and gridlock. In contrast to the New Order period where state guidelines (GBHN), plans (Repelita), programs and projects were promoted by entrenched interests reflective of a carefully engineered appearance of consensus, the post-1998 political environment has increasingly revealed fissures and conflict. Two sets of dynamics combine to slow policy processes: the jockeying for political power among the newly legitimate political groupings, and the attendant pressure on powerful leaders to protect bureaucratic formations.

An example of the former process is seen in the drawn-out process of determining the leadership of the BKKBN following the accession of President Megawati. It was clear from the time Khofifah lost her position as Minister for Women's Empowerment that she would also be replaced as head of the family planning agency. The options were to make the new minister the head of the agency, to give the position to another minister or to appoint a professional to the post. While some delay in making a decision could be expected as a result of the struggle to determine the position of the BKKBN (see above), once that had been determined it might have been expected that leadership decisions would flow quickly. Instead, debate over potential candidates absorbed the attention of people in the presidential palace, the legislature and the BKKBN itself. A cynical (but perhaps realistic) assessment had it that many political leaders regarded the organisation, with its army of field workers and well-oiled logistics system, as a prize worth fighting for in the run-up to the 2004 elections. At the same time many of the professionals working in the field of women's health care were concerned that the organisation's progressive new mission and vision would be lost if the leadership went to an outside political appointee.

The latter process was exemplified in the attempts to save the fledgling National Population Board (Baknas) from being disbanded. In a flurry of lobbying activities in September and October 2001, the government was asked to save the organisation for the sake of the 1,700 civil servants who staffed it. Given that it had only been formed a few months before President Abdurrahman was thrown out of office, there was no particular program to defend or policy to promote, so the argument that was offered was based on the need to protect a group of administrators. These were people who had been in the original Ministry of Transmigration and then moved, through a series of reorganisations in the Abdurrahman government, to the Ministry of Transmigration and Population. In the second Abdurrahman cabinet they were separated from the restructured Ministry of Labour and Transmigration to form the Administration Board for Population and Population Mobility (BAKMP), which was meant to be attached to the Ministry of Home Affairs. Before this could happen the group was renamed Baknas. In the eyes of outsiders this may seem a very strange bind for the government to be in. However, when seen in the context of Abdurrahman's failure to lay off a single employee of the Department of Information or the Ministry of Social Affairs after he announced the closure of those organisations in his first weeks in office, the case of Baknas points to the way bureaucratic inertia exerts a strong force in Indonesian governance. It could turn out to be a long-term disruptor of the formulation of effective policy relating to population, gender and welfare.

Questions of leadership were resolved when the Minister of Health swore in Professor Yaumil Agoes Achir to become head of the BKKBN. This appointment provided some reassurance to donors and to the professionals in the agency. A psychologist with long experience in the field of population policy before joining the office of the vice-president to serve Megawati, Yaumil seems to have the experience and the connections to promote the interests of the BKKBN in the changing context of decentralisation and political contestation.

RECOGNISING OLD CHALLENGES

High numbers of births continue even as fertility declines. The number of births each year in Indonesia will continue to climb long after the fertility rates (or the number of births per woman) has fallen to levels approaching replacement fertility. This is due to the demographic phenomenon known as population momentum. In the case of Indonesia fertility has been declining since before the inception of the family planning program (Figure 19.2), initially because of the rise in the average age at marriage of Indonesian women, and later as women adopted more efficient means of controlling fertility within marriage through the adoption of modern forms of contraception.

As part of its evaluation of the potential impact of the economic crisis on population numbers, the Demographic Institute of the University of Indonesia carried out a series of population projections using assumptions designed to show 'normal' versus 'crisis' conditions (Rajagukguk 1999). If we look only at the normal scenario, which assumes a steady, modest decline in fertility rates in line with the trends shown in Figure 19.2, the contrast becomes very clear. The annual number of births in the projection continues to rise from the level of 4.8 million births on average in 1995–2000 to a peak of 5.0 million in 2005–10, at which time a decline sets in. However the number of births does not fall precipitously after that. Instead there are still more births in 2020–25 than there were at the end of the 1990s. At that time fertility is assumed to be at levels at which each couple would essentially just replace themselves on average.

While future trends will undoubtedly differ from the assumptions of this simple exercise, the general pattern will hold. Despite 'success' in controlling fertility levels, the responsibility of caring for increasing numbers of children remains substantial, and poses important challenges to the providers of all the services needed by children – education, health and care. As those children grow up they will form their own families, and even as the family size becomes smaller, the total community of children will continue to grow, because of the momentum of population growth. It is this momentum that presses governments to continue to

Figure 19.2 Sample Survey Estimates of Total Fertility Rates, 1968–97 [a]

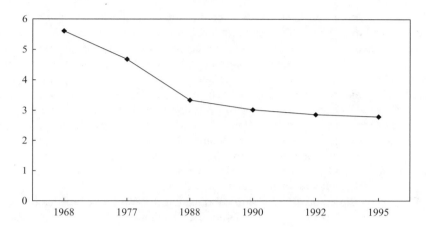

a   The total fertility rates represent the average number of children women would bear
if they maintained childbearing throughout their reproductive lives at levels prevailing at the time of the survey.

Source: Calculations from the Demographic Institute, Faculty of Economics, University
of Indonesia, based on data from BPS.

work to reduce population growth rates even as they plan for increasing population sizes. The need to create places in the labour force, to add to the housing
stock and to provide health and education services is sharpened as these demographic trends work through.

While governments may continue to be committed to family planning programs, there is a possibility of a re-emergence of public challenges to the legitimacy of fertility control. Already in 2000 and 2001 members of the legislature
have challenged the need for a 'small, healthy, happy family' policy, saying that
the 'small' should not necessarily apply to people of particular ethnic, religious
or social groups. Their message seems to be not so much one of promoting personal preferences in family size, but rather to promote primordial interests
through crude demographic measures. This type of argument has taken on new
force with the implementation of decentralisation policies that easily take on
the dimensions of ethnic and other rivalry. Overall there may be a strong feeling among ordinary women and men that larger families will be an economic
burden, but community leaders do not always share this perception, and they
are the people most likely to be at the forefront of new local government initiatives.

CONCLUSION

Women in Indonesia have adopted contraceptive methods to a remarkable degree, and over the past three decades their fertility rates have displayed a clear trend to small family sizes. Surveys and direct observation indicate that the motivation for women to have fewer children is based on a desire that each child should have a better life, as reflected in good health, good education and opportunities for advancement. At the early stages of the family planning program it was clear that many women were subject to various forms of pressure to get them to adopt specific forms of contraceptives. Over time the example of peers, and the acceptance of new sets of community norms about birth control and family responsibilities, changed the environment for family decision-making, and women in particular were more open to the message of fertility regulation. By the time of the International Conference on Population and Development in 1994, Indonesia could fairly claim to be leading the way to a broader family planning agenda, with emphasis on choice of methods, and widespread access throughout the community. At that stage, too, the leadership of the family planning program had begun to realise that the key to voluntary birth control was the improvement of the quality of services, and the promotion of a client-centred approach to program administration.

Old habits were not displaced automatically, and even as late as 1996 some critics of the family planning program were sceptical about the sincerity of the new quality-based message. It took the fall of the New Order regime, and the transformation of the leadership of the family planning program before the message could be transformed into a new 'vision and mission' with a coherent attempt to change the culture of the providers and revise the administration of the program. While this occurred Indonesia was living through the multiple crises of economic downturn and political reform. The changes in family planning, which would have been front page news at any other time, were overshadowed by the threat of national disintegration and the continuing stream of bad economic news that undermined the confidence of the elite and the commitment of foreign partners.

In 1999 and 2000 the domestic agenda was dominated by the re-emergence of decentralisation as a theme of governance, but this time with a radical new departure: the transfer of authority would go from the central to the district, rather than the provincial, governments. For the highly centralised family planning program, this posed a serious challenge just at a time when reform had been accepted at its central levels. The transfer of presidential power from Abdurrahman to Megawati in 2001 raised a further set of challenges, since the latter was an avowed centrist who did not trust the district governments with so much notional power. Almost immediately the decentralisation debate was reopened (though to a large extent behind closed doors), and it became unclear whether the family planning program would remain centralised or, if it did, how it would work in future.

For the women of Indonesia these issues could have serious consequences, though it is unclear how they will be manifested. There seems little likelihood that the family planning program will ever return to the centralised, authoritarian ways of the past, but local governments may display authoritarianism of a different sort if ethnic jingoism or religious zealotry emerges in some regions. It is also likely that the governments (both central and regional) will need some time to work out new modes of service delivery. In the meantime some women may have difficulty getting the supplies they obtained so easily in the past.

20 MEN, WOMEN AND COMMUNITY DEVELOPMENT IN EAST NUSA TENGGARA

Ria Gondowarsito

Poor communities in geographically remote areas of Indonesia have been neglected both by local and national authorities and by aid agencies, and have hence developed specific self-reliance strategies. However, their local resources are limited and intervention by outsiders has become crucial to development within these communities.

This chapter discusses the ten-year, community-based development experience in Semau and other parts of East Nusa Tenggara of the Nusatenggara Association Incorporated (NTA), an Australian non-government organisation (NGO).[1] It reveals how a key activity proposed initially by informal leaders to outsiders led to multiple development activities spread throughout several communities, attracting increasing community participation. It demonstrates what outsiders can provide in terms of technical advice, supported by limited funds, to materially poor and isolated communities living in subsistence conditions in a harsh environment where rainfall is uncertain and food security crucial.

Indonesia has, since the implementation of its first Five-year Development Plan (Repelita I, 1969–74), undertaken vast integrated development efforts in the major sectors. These endeavours were supported by bilateral and multilateral cooperation through the relevant government departments. The goals of the Indonesian government were to achieve economic stability through poverty alleviation and improvements in people's quality of life. Since the early 1990s it has given priority to development in eastern Indonesia, an emphasis justified by the region's annual per capita income of just A$156 (approximately US$78) per head in 1995 – the lowest in Indonesia (Kantor Statistik BPS Propinsi NTT: 442).

Indonesians and foreign donors have increasingly realised that a centralised approach to delivering development packages in designated communities has little relevance to local needs. The intended beneficiaries were often scarcely consulted, and local participation rarely went beyond the employment of contract workers. The centralised, top-down approach did not foster a sense of belonging and accountability among the beneficiaries. Project authorities dealt primarily with provincial and regency officials rather than working directly at the subdistrict (*kecamatan*) or village (*desa*) level, and development activities were operational only during the life span of the project. There were few systems in place to ensure the ongoing maintenance or sustainability of activities established through external inputs.

Aid donors have always faced the challenge of ensuring adequate local participation. In the current environment of *otonomi daerah* (regional autonomy), whereby authority and responsibility for local development have been substantially decentralised, the challenges are new and greater. Aid donors must now find ways of working effectively within bureaucratic arrangements that are still evolving.

Groups outside the government have sought to assist the isolated communities of East Nusa Tenggara province, where material poverty and weak infrastructure prevail. The experience of the NTA shows that, given an appropriate community-level approach, minimum external inputs can achieve maximum results. This requires long-term dedication by aid donors to establish a rapport with the beneficiaries, empowering men and women to identify their primary needs and determine their life quality within local social groups.

BACKGROUND: EAST NUSA TENGGARA'S ECOLOGY, SOCIAL AND GENDER DYNAMICS, AND RESOURCES

The multi-island province of East Nusa Tenggara mirrors the nation's multi-ethnic, multi-linguistic and multicultural character at a micro level. It is the driest province in Indonesia. West Timor is characterised by dry, mountainous areas and short rainy seasons; Flores has similar terrain although it is considerably wetter in the west. Water shortages are common, especially during the dry season from May to October. Most men and women are resilient near-subsistence farmers growing root crops as well as maize and groundnuts as their main crops; these provide crucial food security under the province's harsh ecological conditions. Land access per household unit is two hectares or less, and there are large tracts of collectively owned land under native pasture for cattle grazing.

Collective land ownership is common in most of East Nusa Tenggara. Historically, the local ruler who owned the land distributed it to various clan groups, who further divided it among their members. The *tuan tanah* (literally, lord of the land) is normally a man, the traditional leader who controls the distribution of land and its use for farming or customary (*adat*) purposes. The *tuan tanah* is expected to be an authority on *adat,* but is not automatically regarded as an informal leader in the context of contemporary politics.

Rural community members are exposed to the demands of several leaders. The informal leaders are the advocates for local traditions and tend to be ancestor-oriented. The formal leaders (*lurah* or *kepala desa*) represent the interests of the government, while religious leaders – the ministers (*pendeta*)[2] in most of Protestant West Timor and the Catholic priests (*pastor*) in most of Flores – act as moral watchdogs and are often the motivators for change and development. The teachers and school principals create neutral forums such as parent–teacher associations to accommodate the concerns of the various leaders and their people.

These leaders are usually able to harmonise the interests and goals of their communities. Men and women in these communities have developed adaptive skills to adjust to their leaders' demands while also developing their own material and non-material survival strategies. People live within a collective paradigm of action, but we also find a dynamic tension with radical individualism. People are encouraged to be self-reliant and resilient in coping with various life challenges.

Irrigated rice is a main cash crop. Cattle are another major product. They have always been vital in providing social status, as well as providing an economic buffer against unexpected emergencies. At weddings they are offered as bridewealth (*belis*) to the bride's family; at funerals they are offered as a gesture of solidarity to the clan of the deceased or as a means of settling an incomplete *belis*. The cattle are usually slaughtered and the meat then distributed to guests by the women and girls.

Men dominate politics and public life in East Nusa Tenggara. Land is inherited in the male line. Even though both men and women are involved in farming, on the whole women work longer daily hours than men. They are especially involved in domestic tasks or subsistence production that brings no direct cash return, but also support other household members in performing tasks that do bring immediate cash returns (Table 20.2).

Outsiders (including women) have little access to the women living in some communities except when they bring food to their guests. Women effect a reticent public persona and, in accord with local etiquette, are generally not seen at meetings and do not take part in public discussions or decision-making. This is gradually changing, however. As the local economy improves through expanded agricultural activities and the opening of small kiosks, more women are earning cash by running local shops or selling their crops in West Timor. Through these expanded activities women have become more visible, and more approachable by outsiders. Both men and women are physically active, walking long distances to their communal agricultural lands. The men fish, hunt, and buy and transport cattle.

A feature almost universally observed in rural and urban poor communities – including East Nusa Tenggara – is that women allocate food to their husbands and guests first, then to their children and only last to themselves, even when some of them are sick, pregnant or lactating (Mboi 1996: 181). Hence the women and girls tend to consume food that is inferior in quantity and in quality. This has serious repercussions during pregnancy, childbirth and breastfeeding, and to some extent explains the high infant and maternal mortality rates in East Nusa Tenggara.[3]

The NTA has been working with communities on the island of Semau for the past ten years, and in West Timor for five years. In 2001 a preliminary visit was made to Maumere and Sikka in Flores, and activities are now in train. I will now discuss in more detail the development experiences in Semau and other areas.

SEMAU AND OTHER REMOTE COMMUNITIES IN EAST NUSA TENGGARA

The island of Semau is located three kilometres from the West Timor mainland in the Timor Sea. At its widest points it measures 30 kilometres by 10 kilometres. The island's population of 13,000 people lives in 12 villages, each divided into approximately five hamlets or *kampung*. Different ethnic groups live side by side, and are mostly Helong and Rote, and some Savu. Like most parts of West Timor, Semau is quite dry. It has one of the lowest living standards in East Nusa Tenggara: the annual per capita income is A$50–80, one-quarter of the level in the provincial capital Kupang. However, some residents make much more or much less than this. At one extreme are the rich cattle owners and the merchants who sometimes own the boats running between Semau and Kupang, have houses in Kupang and send their children to school outside East Nusa Tenggara. Then there are the extremely poor, who can afford only a single meal daily, rely on their own produce and survive on the fringes of local societies.

Public facilities and services such as health centres, roads and schools are generally poor. Malaria, cholera, respiratory diseases and allergies are widespread. In the rural areas of West Timor roads are scarce, and those that exist were built largely by the local communities themselves. Most public and private schools have leaking roofs, broken walls and dilapidated floors, tables and benches. Households commonly have a limited daily water supply and no toilet. Such hardships are even more pronounced in isolated and remote settings. Villages in such areas are seldom accessible by vehicle because there are no proper tracks from the main road, located 5–25 kilometres away. It requires a tremendous effort for outsiders such as teachers, paramedics and extension workers to reach these villages. Walking is the main means of transport, except for a minority who own horses or motorcycles.

The above conditions also typify the isolated villages in Besi Pa'e in South Central Timor, the former location of the AusAID Livestock Development

Project and its successor, the Nusa Tenggara Timur Integrated Agricultural Development Project (NTT-IADP). Sharp stony roads make it almost impossible for vehicles to pass, and severe dust characterises the area during the dry season. Water is scarce and sanitation lags even behind Semau. The dominant linguistic groups are the Amanuban and Amanatun. Land is communally owned, and while there are local groups which have high social status acquired by descent, this does not usually translate into political power.

Semau is too close to West Timor to have an air service and the boat trip is considered hazardous. The provincial authorities therefore prefer to focus on other islands such as Rote and Savu. There is also a belief that sorcery is practised on Semau. Such superstitions still persist among a diverse group of people in West Timor who refuse to visit Semau and even refrain from negotiating with the island's traders.

THE *MUSYAWARAH* AND *KELOMPOK* SYSTEMS

In keeping with tradition, men and women in the isolated, remote communities of East Nusa Tenggara undertake activities in groups (*kelompok*). A typical *kelompok* effort would be a labour exchange arrangement to clear land, plant and harvest crops, or build houses. In rural East Nusa Tenggara this cooperation is clan and gender-based, resulting from a *musyawarah* – a consensual, group decision-making process. Gatherings at this level tend to be informal and informative. *Musyawarah* usually ensures the efficient use of local material and non-material assets.

This local system of decision-making is utilised in project activities. In the context of a development initiative, the *musyawarah* occurs at the *kampung* level, where members identify the main needs of the community and determine the kinds of participation required. *Kelompok* are then formed on a consensual basis. Once local leaders have identified a proposal, they put it to a multi-village *musyawarah* at which the needs of the village are discussed and prioritised for submission to the external donor.

Men and women do not normally come together in *kelompok*, preferring to form their own single-sex groups. Within male-dominated societies, this provides a culturally acceptable way for women to be able to voice their concerns and participate in community matters. The acknowledgement of women's *kelompok* by the NTA and other donors has helped reduce the communication gap between women and outsiders, who previously thought that working *kelompok* consisted primarily of men.

Development projects are chosen by local groups according to need, and in line with the commitment to contribute labour, time and local resources to the *kelompok* to achieve the identified goals. This system ensures that projects are both cost-effective and sustainable.

OUTSIDE CONTRIBUTIONS TO POOR, ISOLATED COMMUNITIES [4]

There is a tendency for people in poor, isolated communities to view inputs by regional government officials as stale, uninspiring and patronising. There is also distrust of government, which is considered weak in delivering promises. Outsiders who do *not* represent the government provide greater stimulus to communities to solve their immediate problems. The general support outsiders bring to these communities promotes the formation of new dynamics at the grassroots level – as long as they refrain from promoting consumer values that are inappropriate to local economic conditions. In most cases the local people are already aware of the solutions to their problems but need external assistance (such as additional capital and technical expertise) to implement them.

A commitment to community-level development by external donors entails long-term exposure to build up mutual trust and confidence. Ultimately it is the local people who must remain in charge of their own lives, with outsiders offering support in the form of technical expertise and modest financial help. The will of the people, their resources and the local conditions should determine the kind and size of this assistance. In this way communities can avoid being dictated to by outside aid agencies with their own development agendas.

THE FIRST DEVELOPMENT ASSISTANCE BY THE NTA

After extensive discussions with officials and researchers in Kupang, in 1990 the NTA identified effective water systems close to homes as a high priority for people living in dry, arid areas. Much to the NTA's astonishment, the subsequent *musyawarah* process in Semau identified the principal need as walls to protect agricultural areas from livestock invasion and secure the staple crop, maize. The people affirmed that they had always survived on limited water. Their main concern was how to protect their crops and thus enhance food security. A *kelompok* was soon organised in each village to participate in wall building.

How best could outsiders help? It was found that collecting rocks from the surrounding mountains was highly labour-intensive, and that a truck would be useful. The NTA therefore provided a second-hand truck to the local partner NGO (*yayasan*), which provided the driver. All members of the community, irrespective of age and sex, are now able to utilise the truck for transport and to carry goods to neighbouring villages for barter. The truck has promoted greater inter-action between the generations and between different ethnic groups and clans. As each *kampung* wanted the truck to pass through its area, the residents organised road building. When mechanical trouble arose, the truck got prompt attention due to the communal sense of ownership.

This was the entry point for NTA assistance to East Nusa Tenggara. The association's activities on Semau and elsewhere have expanded greatly since then.

GENDER ASPECTS OF CURRENT PROJECTS

By 2001 the NTA was funding over 70 small projects scattered across Semau island and West Timor. It also set up nurseries to develop and distribute animal forages at Naibonat Research Station (just outside Kupang) and Besi Pa'e (in South Central Timor). Table 20.1 shows the main activities conducted by the NTA in East Nusa Tenggara and local participation in these projects according to gender.

In the case of projects that provide a public facility – such as an effective, locally maintained water supply – men provide the physical labour. For instance, during the construction of stone walls described earlier, the men formed three *kelompok* to collect stones, pile them and load them onto the truck. The women formed a *kelompok* to prepare food for the men. The completed public facilities bring benefits to men and women alike.

Some activities tend to be more gender-specific than others, as Table 20.2 shows. Traditional weaving (*tenun ikat*) is performed by women, who ensure continuity within the clan by passing on their skills to their daughters. As in most parts of Indonesia, in rural East Nusa Tenggara both men and women wear sarongs. The designs on the hand-woven material show the wearer's ethnicity and place of origin. The *ikat* cloth serves as both clothing and blanket, as well as providing one of the principal items of exchange in the gift economy and a means for women to generate cash. The tops worn with the *ikat* complement the costume: sewing these is an additional source of income for women. For practical reasons, women in most of rural East Nusa Tenggara wear the Javanese printed batik sarong, which is cooler and easier to wash, and save the *ikat* for special events. A woman's proficiency at weaving affects the *belis* that the groom negotiates with the bride's extended family.

The women tend to raise goats and smaller animals, while both men and women manage the cattle. Cash crop production and transport to markets is carried out jointly. Men mostly perform the heavy manual labour of clearing trees, shifting stones and building, but men and women cooperate in land cultivation, planting and harvesting. Under challenging living conditions in impoverished, remote, isolated areas of rural East Nusa Tenggara, the flexibility shown by men and women in sharing domestic and non-domestic chores is a useful survival strategy. In villages far from a source of water, for example, men and women as well as their adolescent sons and daughters fetch water daily. The labour division between the sexes and age groups determines the management of the household economy (Table 20.2).

Most households consist of a couple and an average of five children, and commonly also the wife's relations. The extended family pattern is common in Semau as in rural East Nusa Tenggara. Even though men are formally the household heads, women take charge of the family's health and economic welfare, and securing the food supply. Married women and mothers appear to have an ability to maintain and establish rapport within and outside the household: they seem particularly inclined to resolve family, neighbourhood and clan conflicts and handle delicate matters concerning the extended family. Due to the vital position of women within the family, a girl's labour is considered an asset, especially during exchanges of services and goods (such as food and *ikat*) among relatives and neighbours at major events such as a birth, wedding or funeral.

THE NTA APPROACH TO DEVELOPMENT ASSISTANCE

During the ten years in which the NTA has provided external assistance to isolated communities in West Timor, it has adopted a community-based approach where needs are clearly identified and understood by both sides and labour is contributed by the people. Community needs and the commitment to participate therefore determine the form of aid, and *not* vice versa.

Several preparatory visits are essential before the implementation of each project to ensure mutual understanding of the assistance package. Most recipients realise that external assistance is available only if local participation is secured in the form of labour and resources. Subsequent development assistance is considered upon completion of the agreed project. Regular monitoring of past and present activities is crucial to ensure sustainability of the assistance, and value for money, while promoting community self-reliance.

As NTA projects and their funding expanded over the years, it became increasingly important to monitor the disbursement of funds closely. This was done by selecting an independent third party (a reputable retired official) to oversee the progress of projects and disburse or withhold funds from the partner *yayasan*. Subsequently, in 1999, a locally recruited woman was appointed as regional director in Kupang to undertake the monitoring, with an independent third party as financial controller.

The NTA's partner *yayasan* has, over the years, played an indispensable role as intermediary between village communities and the foreign NGO. At the same time it has provided essential moral support to community leaders and their

Table 20.1 Gender Participation in Project Activities

Activity (Place)	Men Only	Women Only	Men and Women
Infrastructure development			
Construction of stone walls to keep livestock away from crops (Semau)	Collecting, piling and loading stones onto truck	Food preparation to support activities, assisted by girls	–
Rehabilitation of old primary schools and provision of facilities for a new primary school (Semau, West Timor)	Labour input	As above	Membership of parent–teacher associations
Education and training			
Program to train 75 primary school teachers (Semau, West Timor)	Trainers	Food preparation to support activities, assisted by girls	Trainees
Island-wide training in livestock and water management (Semau)	Trainers	As above	Trainees
Garment-making classes and assistance for traditional weaving (Semau)	–	Trainees and as above	Trainers
Income-generating activities			
Installation of well pumps for cash crop irrigation (Semau, West Timor)	Heavy labour input at all stages	Food preparation to support activities, assisted by girls	–

Table 20.1 (continued)

Activity (Place)	Men Only	Women Only	Men and Women
Income-generating activities (*cont.*)			
Distribution of cattle and pigs for fattening (Semau)	Beneficiaries (including boys)	–	Beneficiaries in some cases
Development of improved animal forages at nurseries (Semau, West Timor)	Watching over their growth and development	–	Beneficiaries
Seaweed production (Semau)	Cultivation	Dry the crop	Beneficiaries
Capital grants for small village shops (Semau)	–	Beneficiaries	–
Health and sanitation			
Water schemes: water reticulation, installation of tanks and wells (Semau)	Heavy labour input at all stages	Food preparation to support activities, assisted by girls	–
Construction of wells (Semau, West Timor)	As above	As above	–
Provision of materials for toilets in households and schools (Semau, West Timor)	As above	As above	–

Table 20.2 Gender Participation in Daily Activities

Activity	Mostly Men	Mostly Women	Men and Women	Boys[a]	Girls[a]
Cleaning		X			X
Cooking		X			X
Washing		X			X
Bathing and feeding infants		X			X
Looking after infants		X			X
Fetching water			X	X	X
Land clearing	X			X	
Planting			X	X	X
Weeding			X	X	X
Cattle & pig slaughtering	X			X	
Chicken slaughtering		X			X
Food preparation		X			X
Marketing			X		
Weaving		X			X
Village politics	X				
Feeding livestock			X	X	X

a   Ages 5–15 approximately.

Source: Gondowarsito (1998: 4).

people in mobilising group activities. This stresses the importance of collaborating with partners who can create mutual trust and support over the years.

The NTA works either with a local organisation or directly with the community. In West Timor it cooperates with the Protestant GMIT church group, while in Flores it is partnered by a local NGO and the Catholic SVD group. The bulk of the contribution provided by the communities is labour, materials and project management through the *kelompok* system. The essence of development assistance at the grassroots level is to consolidate 'wants and needs' into something concrete and feasible where entire communities take part in doing something together for future common ownership.

Contradictory though it may seem, although projects were designed in partnership with, and based on, people's expressed needs and commitments, it has proved essential to maintain direct and regular contact with the communities to consolidate long-term mutual commitment and trust. The communities need to understand how external assistance functions and realise that accountability is expected from them.

GOOD AND POOR PROGRESS: THE UNDERLYING FACTORS

With good community cooperation and leadership, development work is likely to proceed well; otherwise it will not. Time and extensive consultation with users and regular contact with the community are therefore essential.

During its initial involvement in Semau, the NTA found that one community was particularly progressive. It had an outstanding formal leader who was the prime mover in the village. The situation provided a ray of hope in otherwise impoverished surroundings. A few years later, following a dispute among leaders about the mismanagement of funds, all activities initiated by the people collapsed. Conditions deteriorated and it became difficult to persuade the different groups within the village to work together to achieve a common goal. The people mistrusted their old leaders but were suspicious of their new ones. These circumstances have made it difficult for outside organisations like the NTA to function.

In another part of Semau, the NTA was faced with a local dispute over a large water scheme that would have benefited over 100 households, 1,000 cattle and one secondary school. Despite achieving consensus on labour, material inputs and the installation of equipment, the project ground to a halt. The people refused to contribute their time and labour because they believed that a wealthy land and cattle owner would be the main beneficiary of the project. The land owner and his family responded by offering to do most of the work and to donate cattle to volunteer workers. The dispute continued, with one side presenting very strong arguments for having the water scheme completed, and another group resisting this. The matter was eventually resolved through the intervention of the religious leader and the village headman.

The above two cases illustrate how political dissension can threaten a project. However, there are other elements which are simply outside human control, including:

1 a rapidly spreading bacterial disease which killed goats;
2 failed seaweed production when the crop was eaten by large turtles just before harvest;
3 failed maize harvests due to either too much or too little rain during the growing season; and
4 livestock theft by outsiders.

Some groups have done particularly well. The performance of one coastal village has been excellent in all of the activities proposed: a forage demonstration plot, a school repair project and a toilet installation project. The group leader is a progressive farmer whose family provides a role model for others due to its success both in business and in adopting new farm techniques. The family maintains good contacts with neighbours by sharing food and services. A water reticulation scheme has been proposed for the village and will soon be implemented. Unfortunately, the success of this village has attracted the envy of a nearby *kampung*. The tensions resulting from this are a matter for locals to resolve.

LESSONS LEARNED

Within micro-level development efforts in East Nusa Tenggara, the social dynamics of rural communities indicate the importance of consulting and working with women as much as with men. However, as noted above, local etiquette can make it difficult for outsiders to consult directly with women. These communities already have systems in place to resolve conflicts and maximise resources. Any assistance therefore needs to identify how best to integrate the support provided into these systems.

Both the local government and NGOs have helped to raise the quality of life in the province's remote, isolated communities. Enhanced economic independence for women has increased their confidence in contributing to public discussion. There are avenues for government and other groups to contribute to the community in a complementary way. The regional government has contributed by providing basic infrastructure requiring large public funds, such as roads, schools and health centres. The NGOs have demonstrated ability in small, targeted projects focusing on community participation. It is not a question of competition or even of overlapping activities, but rather of partnership with institutions focusing on community-level development. There is still much work ahead, but a start has been made.

NOTES

1   Based in Canberra, the NTA is a volunteer, non-political, non-religious organisation. It was founded in 1991, when a group of Australians and Indonesians decided to focus on community development in the Nusa Tenggara region, building on previous experience working with projects in West Timor. The NTA is accredited by AusAID and is a member of the Australian Council for Overseas Aid (ACFOA). Its main goals are poverty alleviation, strategy testing and implementation of rural development project activities.

2   About half of the *pendeta* in West Timor are women educated and residing mainly in the cities. This relates to education: the gap in literacy between urban and rural

women aged 10 and over is greater than the literacy gap between urban men and women (BPS 1993: 80).

3   In 1984 the infant mortality rate for mothers who had not completed primary school was 160 per 1,000 live births. For those who had completed their primary school education it was 127, and for those who had a secondary education or better it was only 63 (UNICEF 1984: 62). Maternal mortality rates in 1993 were 45 per 1,000 births for Indonesia as a whole, but over 80 per 1,000 in rural East Nusa Tenggara (Mboi 1996: 184).

4   Under the program based on the Presidential Instruction regarding 'backward villages' (Inpres Desa Tertinggal) initiated in 1993, 'poor' people and villages were defined according to (a) the degree of isolation of the village and nature of the available infrastructure; (b) type of housing and physical environment; and (c) local birth and death rates.

REFERENCES

Abdullah, Hamid (1985), *Manusia Bugis Makassar* [The Bugis and Makassar], Inti Idayu Press, Jakarta.

Adi, R. (1996), The Impact of International Labour Migration in Indonesia, unpublished PhD thesis, University of Adelaide, Adelaide.

Andaya, Barbara (1994), 'The Changing Religious Role of Women in Pre-modern Southeast Asia', *Southeast Asian Research*, 2(2), September, pp. 99–116.

Andaya, Leonard Y. (1979), 'A Village Perception of Arung Palakka and the Makassar War of 1666–1669', in Anthony Reid and David Marr (eds), *Perceptions of the Past in Southeast Asia*, Asian Studies of Australia, Singapore, pp. 360–78.

Anderson, B. (1983), *Imagined Communities: Reflections on the Origins and Spread of Nationalism*, Verso, London.

Anderson, B. (2000), *Doing the Dirty Work? The Global Politics of Domestic Labour*, Zed Books Ltd, New York.

Anon. (1997), 'Indonesia's Overseas Workers: Problems and Solution', *Review Indonesia*, 17, pp. 6–10.

Appadurai, Arjun (1990), 'Disjuncture and Difference in the Global Cultural Economy', *Public Culture*, 2, pp. 1–24.

Asmaudi, Nuryana and Putu Wirata Dwikora (1999), '"Parade Monolog 1999" Rangda Ing Dirah Itu Kambing Hitam Politik?', *Bali Post*, 5 September.

Aspinall, Edward (2001), 'Mother of the Nation', *Inside Indonesia*, 68 (October–December), pp. 23–4.

Atkinson, Stephen (1993), Sadisme, Seks dan Suzanna: Aspects of Gender Representation in the Indonesian Horror Film, unpublished honours thesis, Department of Asian Studies, Flinders University, Adelaide.

Bianpoen, Carla (2000), 'The Family Welfare Movement: A Blessing or a Burden?', in Mayling Oey-Gardiner and Carla Bianpoen (eds), *Indonesian Women: The Journey Continues*, Research School for Pacific and Asian Studies Publishing, Australian National University, Canberra, pp. 156–71.

Bird, Kelly (2001), 'The Economy in 2000: Still Flat on Its Back?' *Indonesia Today: Challenges of History*, Institute of Southeast Asian Studies, Singapore, pp. 45–66.

Blackburn, Susan (1999), 'Gender Violence and the Indonesian Political Transition', *Asian Studies Review*, 23(4), pp. 433–48.

Blackburn, Susan (2001), 'Gender Relations in Indonesia: What Women Want', in Grayson Lloyd and Shannon Smith (eds), *Indonesia Today: Challenges of History*, Institute for Southeast Asian Studies, Singapore, pp. 270–82.

Blackburn, Susan and Sharon Bessell (1997), 'Marriageable Age: Political Debates on Early Marriage in Twentieth Century Indonesia', *Indonesia*, 63 (April), pp. 107–41.

Boellstorff, T. (2001), The Gay Archipelago: Sexuality and Nation in Postcolonial Indonesia', unpublished book manuscript, forthcoming.

Boellstorff, T. (2002), 'Political Homophobia in Indonesia: Masculinity, Islam, and National Belonging', submitted to *Journal of the Royal Anthropological Institute*.

BPS (Biro Pusat Statistik) (1986), *Keadaan Angkatan Kerja di Indonesia 1986*, BPS, Jakarta.

BPS (Biro Pusat Statistik) (1992), *Indikator Sosial Wanita Indonesia 1991* [1991 Social Indicators for Indonesian Women], BPS, Jakarta.

BPS (Biro Pusat Statistik) (1993), *Indikator Sosial Wanita 1992* [1992 Social Indicators for Indonesian Women], BPS, Jakarta.

BPS (Biro Pusat Statistik) (1994), *Indikator Sosial Wanita Indonesia 1993* [1993 Social Indicators for Indonesian Women], BPS, Jakarta.

BPS (Biro Pusat Statistik) (2000a), *Keadaan Angkatan Kerja 2000*, BPS, Jakarta.

BPS (Biro Pusat Statistik) (2000b), *Indikator Sosial Wanita Indonesia 1999* [1999 Social Indicators for Indonesian Women], BPS, Jakarta.

BPS (Biro Pusat Statistik) (2001a), *Hasil Sementara Sensus Penduduk 2000* [Interim Results of the Population Census], BPS, Jakarta.

BPS (Biro Pusat Statistik) (2001b), *Gender Statistics and Indicators 2000*, BPS-UNIFEM, Jakarta.

BPS, Bappenas and UNDP (2001), *Indonesia Human Development Report 2001: Towards a New Consensus: Democracy and Human Development in Indonesia*, BPS, Bappenas and UNDP, Jakarta.

Brenner, Susan (1999), 'On the Public Intimacy of the New Order: Images of Women in the Indonesian Print Media', *Indonesia*, 67 (April), pp. 13–37.

Buchori, Binny and Ifa Soenarto (2000), 'Dharma Wanita: An Asset or a Curse?', in Mayling Oey-Gardiner and Carla Bianpoen (eds), *Indonesian Women: The Journey Continues*, Research School for Pacific and Asian Studies Publishing, Australian National University, Canberra, pp. 139–55.

Budianto, Melani (2002), 'Plural Identities: Indonesian Women's Redefinition of Democracy in the Post-*reformasi* Era', *Review of Indonesian and Malayan Affairs*, Winter, forthcoming.

Cameron, Lisa A. (2001), 'The Impact of the Indonesian Financial Crisis on Children: An Analysis Using the 100 Villages Data', *Bulletin of Indonesian Economic Studies*, 37(1), pp. 43–64.

Chen Ai Ju and Gavin W. Jones (1988), *Ageing in ASEAN and Its Socio-economic Consequences*, Institute of Southeast Asian Studies, Singapore.

Chin, C.B.N. (1997), 'Walls of Silence and Late Twentieth Century Representations of the Foreign Female Domestic Worker: The Case of Filipino and Indonesian Female Servants in Malaysia', *International Migration Review*, 31(2), pp. 353–85.

Chudori, Leila (1989), *Malam Terakhir*, Pustaka Utama Grafiti, Jakarta.

Clancy, Anna (1988), The Cultural Construction of Javanese Women in Modern Indonesian Literature, unpublished honours thesis, University of Sydney, Sydney.

Coté, Joost (1992), *Letters from Kartini: An Indonesian Feminist 1900–1904*, Monash Asia Institute in association with Hyland House, Melbourne.

Coté, Joost (1995), *On Feminism and Nationalism: Kartini's Letters to Stella Zeehandelaar 1899–1903*, Monash Asia Institute, Clayton, Victoria.

Cribb, Robert (1992), *Historical Dictionary of Indonesia*, Scarecrow Press, Metuchen, NJ, and London.

CSIS (Centre for Strategic and International Studies) (2001a), Economic and Political Developments in Indonesia, Quarterly Report, Jakarta, September, mimeo.

CSIS (Centre for Strategic and International Studies) (2001b), Agenda Penyelamatan Ekonomi Indonesia [Agenda for Rescuing the Indonesian Economy], Jakarta, 11 October, mimeo.

Danareksa Research Institute (2001), 'Consumer Confidence', *Monthly Report*, Jakarta, November.

Dee (2000), *Supernova: Ksatria, Puteri dan Bintang Jatuh* [Supernova: Knight, Princess and Falling Star], Truedee Books, Bandung.

Departemen Tenaga Kerja (Department of Labour) (1998), *Strategi Penempatan Tenaga Kerja Indonesia Ke Luar Negeri*, Departemen Tenaga Kerja, Republic of Indonesia, Jakarta.

Dian, Intan Ungaling (2000), 'Kala "Calon Arang" Gugat Pembelokan Sejarah', *Kompas*, 28 November

Dini, N.H. (1976), *La Barka*, Pustaka Jaya, Jakarta.

Dorall, R.F. and S.R. Paramasivam (1992), Gender Perspectives on Indonesian Labour Migration to Peninsular Malaysia: A Case Study, paper presented at the Population Studies Unit's international colloquium, 'Migration Development and Gender in the ASEAN Region', Kuantan Pahang, 28–31 October.

Drakeley, Steven (2000), *Lubang Buaya: Myth, Misogyny and Massacre*, Working Paper 108, Monash Asia Institute, Monash University, Clayton, Victoria.

Fealy, Greg (2001), Gus Dur's Downfall: A Critical Reflection on the Constitutional and Political Issues, unpublished paper presented to the Indonesia Study Group, Australian National University, Canberra, 15 August.

Florida, Nancy (1996), 'Sex Wars: Writing Gender Relations in Nineteenth Century Java', in Laurie J. Sears (ed.), *Fantasizing the Feminine in Indonesia*, Duke University Press, Durham and London, pp. 207–24.

Geertz, Hildred (1961), *The Javanese Family: A Study of Kinship and Socialization*, Free Press, Glencoe, IL.

Gilligan, D., H. Jacoby and J. Quizon (2000), The Effects of the Indonesian Economic Crisis on Agricultural Households: Evidence from the National Farmers Household Panel Survey (PATANAS), unpublished paper, Center for Agro-socioeconomic Research, Bogor, and World Bank, Washington DC.

Gondowarsito, R. (1998), 'Some Aspects of Tradition and Gender Roles', *Nusatenggara Association Newsletter*, September, pp. 4–5.

Graham, P. (1997), Widows at Home, Workers Abroad: Florenese Women and Labour Migration, unpublished manuscript, Monash, Clayton, Victoria.

Gramsci, A. (1971), *Selections from the Prison Notebooks*, International Publishers, New York.

Hafidz, Tatik S. (1993), 'Seandainya Suami Anda Dihukum Karena Memperkosa Anda' [If Your Husband Is Sentenced Because He Raped You], *Editor*, 6(24), March, pp. 18–20.

Hall, S. (1988), 'Gramsci and Us', *The Hard Road to Renewal: Thatcherism and the Crisis of the Left*, Verso, London, pp. 161–73.

Hatley, Barbara (1990), 'Theatrical Imagery and Gender Ideology in Java', in Jane Monnig Atkinson and Shelly Errington (eds), *Power and Difference: Gender in Island Southeast Asia*, Stanford University Press, Stanford, pp. 177–207.

Hatley, Barbara (1997), 'Nation, "Tradition" and Constructions of the Feminine in Modern Indonesian Literature', in J. Schiller and B. Martin Schiller (eds), *Imagining Indonesia: Cultural Politics and Political Culture*, University Center for International Studies, Athens, OH, pp. 90–120.

Hatley, Barbara (2002), 'Post-coloniality and the Feminine in Modern Indonesian Literature', in K. Foulcher and A. Day (eds), *Clearing a Space: Post-colonial Readings of Modern Indonesian Literature*, KITLV Press, Leiden, forthcoming.

Hellwig, Tineke (1994), *In the Shadow of Change: Images of Women in Indonesian Literature*, University of California, Berkeley, CA.

Heraty, Toeti (2000), *Calon Arang: Kisah Perempuan Korban Patriarki* [Calon Arang: The Story of a Woman Victim of Patriarchy], Yayasan Obor, Jakarta.

Heryanto, Ariel (2000), 'Perkosaan Mei 1998: Beberapa Pertanyaan Konseptual' [The May 1998 Rapes: Some Conceptual Questions], in Nur Iman Subono (ed.), *Negara dan Kekerasan Terhadap Perempuan,* Penerbit Yayasan Jurnal Perempuan, Jakarta, pp. 57–97.

Hetler, C.B. (1986), Female-headed Households in a Circular Migration Village in Central Java, Indonesia, PhD thesis, Department of Demography, Australian National University, Canberra.

Hetler, C.B. (1989), 'The Impact of Circular Migration on a Village Economy', *Bulletin of Indonesian Economic Studies*, 25(1), pp. 53–75.

Hetler, C.B. (1990), 'Survival Strategies, Migration and Household Headship', in L. Dube and R. Palriwala (eds), *Structures and Strategies, Women, Work and Family*, Sage, New Delhi, pp. 175–99.

Heyzer, N. and V. Wee (1994), 'Domestic Workers in Transient Overseas Employment: Who Benefits, Who Profits?', in N. Heyzer et al. (eds), *The Trade in Domestic Workers: Causes, Mechanisms and Consequences of International Migration*, Zed Books Ltd, Kuala Lumpur, pp. 31–102.

Hugo, G.J. (1993), 'Indonesian Labour Migration to Malaysia: Trends and Policy Implications', *Southeast Asian Journal of Social Science*, 21(1), pp. 36–70.

Hugo, G.J. (1995a), 'Labour Export from Indonesia: An Overview', *ASEAN Economic Bulletin*, 12(2), pp. 275–98.

Hugo, G.J. (1995b), 'International Labour Migration and the Family: Some Observations from Indonesia', *Asia Pacific Migration Journal*, 4(2–3), pp. 273–301.

Hugo, G.J. (1997), 'Intergenerational Wealth Flows and the Elderly in Indonesia', in

Gavin W. Jones, Robert M. Douglas, John C. Caldwell and Rennie M. D'Souza (eds), *The Continuing Demographic Transition*, Clarendon Press, Oxford, pp. 111–33.

Hugo, G.J. (2000), 'Labour Migration from East Indonesia to East Malaysia', *Revue Européene des Migrations Internationales*, 16(1), pp. 97–124.

Hugo, G.J. (2001), Effects of International Migration on the Family in Indonesia, paper *Asia Pacific Migration Journal*, mimeo.

Hugo, G.J. (2002), Information, Exploitation and Empowerment: The Case of Indonesian Overseas Contract Workers, *International Migration Review*, forthcoming.

Hugo, G.J. and W.R. Bohning (2000), 'Providing Information to Outgoing Indonesian Migrant Workers', *Seapat Working Paper 7*, Southeast Asia and the Pacific Multidisciplinary Advisory Team, International Labour Office, Manila.

ICG (International Crisis Group) (2001a), *Indonesia's Presidential Crisis: The Second Round*, ICG Indonesia Briefing, Jakarta/Brussels, www.crisisweb.org, 21 May.

ICG (International Crisis Group) (2001b), *Indonesia's Presidential Crisis*, ICG Indonesia Briefing, Jakarta/Brussels, www.crisisweb.org, 21 February.

Ihromi, T.O. (1989), 'Social Support Systems in Transition in Indonesia', in J.M. Eekelaar and D. Pearl (eds), *An Aging World: Dilemmas and Challenges for Law and Social Policy*, Clarendon Press, Oxford.

Jones, Gavin W. (1996), *Marriage and Divorce in Islamic South-east Asia*, Oxford University Press, Singapore.

Jones, Gavin W. (1997a), 'The Demise of Universal Marriage in East and South-east Asia', in Gavin W. Jones, Robert M. Douglas, John C. Caldwell and Rennie D'Souza (eds), *The Continuing Demographic Transition*, Clarendon Press, Oxford, pp. 51–79.

Jones, Gavin W. (1997b), 'Modernization and Divorce: Contrasting Trends in Islamic Southeast Asia and the West', *Population and Development Review*, 23(1), pp. 95–114.

Jones, Gavin W. (2001), 'Which Indonesian Women Marry Youngest, and Why?', *Journal of Southeast Asian Studies*, 32(1), pp. 67–78.

Jones, S. (1996), 'Women Feed Malaysian Boom', *Inside Indonesia*, 47 (July–September), pp. 16–18.

Jones, S. (2000), *Making Money off Migrants: The Indonesian Exodus to Malaysia*, ASIA 2000, Hong Kong, and Centre for Asia Pacific Social Transformation Studies, University of Wollongong, Wollongong, NSW.

Kantor Statistik BPS Propinsi NTT (1996), *Nusa Tenggara Timur Dalam Angka 1995* [East Nusa Tenggara in Figures 1995], Kerjasama Kantor Statistik Propinsi dan Bappeda Tingkat I NTT, Kupang.

Kassim, A. (1997), International Migration and Its Impact on Malaysia, paper presented to the 11th Asia–Pacific roundtable, 'Labour Migration in Southeast Asia: The Impact (Political, Economic, Social, Security)', Kuala Lumpur, 5–8 June.

Katz, J.S. and R.S. Katz (1978), 'Legislating Changes in a Developing Country: The New Indonesian Marriage Law Revisited', *American Journal of Comparative Law*, 26(2), pp. 309–20.

Kaukus Ornop 17 (2001), Draft Naskah Akademis untuk Penyempurnaan UU No. 22, 1999 dalam Aspek Partisipasi [Ornop Caucus Draft Academic Paper to Improve Law 22 1999], unpublished paper produced by 17 NGOs for advocacy purposes, funded by the Ford Foundation.

Kayam, Umar (1975), *Sri Sumarah dan Bawuk*, Pustaka Jaya, Jakarta.

Laclau, E. and C. Mouffe (1985), *Hegemony and Socialist Strategy: Towards a Radical Democratic Politics*, Verso, London.

Lev, Danial S. (1972), *Islamic Courts in Indonesia*, University of California Press, Berkeley, CA.

Liddle, R. William (1973), 'Modernizing Indonesian Politics', in R.W. Liddle (ed.), *Political Participation in Modern Indonesia*, Monograph Series No. 19, Yale Southeast Asia Studies, New Haven, CT.

Lindsey, Tim (2001), Constitutional Law and the Presidential Crisis in Jakarta: Some Preliminary Observations, Asian Law Centre, University of Melbourne, http://www.law.unimelb.edu.au/alc/wip/constitutional_crisis.html, accessed October 2001.

Mangemba, H.D. (1977), Siri' Dalam Pandangan Orang Makassar [Siri' from the Perspective of the Makassarese], paper presented at a seminar on the 'Problem of *Siri'* in South Sulawesi', Komando Daerah Kepolisian XVII Sulawesi Selatan and Tenggara in collaboration with Hasanuddin University, Ujung Pandang, 11–13 July.

Mantra, I.B., T.M. Kasnawi and Sukamardi (1986), *Mobilitas Angkatan Kerja Indonesia Ke Timor Tengah* [Movement of Indonesian Workers to the Middle East], Final Report Book 1, Population Studies Centre, Gadjah Mada University, Yogyakarta.

Marcoes, Lies (1992), 'The Female Preacher as a Mediator in Religion: A Case Study in Jakarta and West Java', in Sita van Bemmelen et al. (eds), *Women and Mediation in Indonesia*, KITLV Press, Leiden, pp. 203–28.

Marcoes, Natsir Lies (2001), *Pengarusutamaan Jender: Suatu Strategi Dalam Pembangunan* [Gender Mainstreaming: A Development Strategy], CIDA-Kantor Meneg PP-WSP II, Jakarta.

Mboi, Nafsiah (1996), 'Health and Poverty: A Look at Eastern Indonesia', in Colin Barlow and Joan Hardjono (eds), *Indonesia Assessment 1995: Development in Eastern Indonesia*, Research School of Pacific and Asian Studies, Australian National University, Canberra, and Institute of Southeast Asian Studies, Singapore, pp. 175–97.

McQuail, Denis (1994), *Mass Communication Theory: An Introduction*, 3rd edition, Sage, London.

Mernisi, Fatima (1991), *Women and Islam: A Historical and Theological Enquiry*, Basil Blackwell, Oxford.

Mietzner, Marcus (2001), 'Abdurrahman's Indonesia: Political Conflict and Institutional Crisis', in Grayson J. Lloyd and Shannon L. Smith (eds), *Indonesia Today: Challenges of History*, Institute for Southeast Asian Studies, Singapore, pp. 29–44.

Millar, Susan B. (1983), 'On Interpreting Gender in Bugis Society', *American Ethnologist*, 10 (August), pp. 477–92.

Mohamad, Goenawan (2000), 'The King's Witch', in Frank Stewart (ed.), *Silenced Voices: Manoa* , University of Hawaii Press, Honolulu, pp 65–70.

Mydans, Seth (2001), 'The People Will Return Me to Power, Declares Confident Wahid', *New York Times,* 22 October.

Nasution, M.A. (1997), Aliran Pekerja Indonesia Ke Malaysia: Kes Tentang Pekerja Indonesia Dalam Sektor Pembinaan Di Kuala Lumpur, Malaysia [Flows of Indonesian Workers to Malaysia: The Case of Indonesian Workers in the Service Sector of

Malaysia], PhD thesis, Faculty of Social Science and Culture, Universiti Kebangsaan Malaysia, Bangi.

Nilan, Pam (2001), Young Indonesian Women and the Discourse of Romance, paper presented at the 6th Women in Asia Conference, Australian National University, Canberra, 23–26 September.

Noerdin, Edriana (2000), Women against Islam-based Nationalism in Aceh: A Discourse Analysis on Language, Social Institutions and Subjectivity, MA thesis, Institute of Social Studies, The Hague.

Oetomo, Dede (1999), 'Gender and Sexual Orientation in Indonesia', in Laurie J. Sears (ed.), *Fantasizing the Feminine in Indonesia*, Duke University Press, Durham and London, pp. 259–69.

Oey-Gardiner, M. and N. Dharmaputra (1998), The Impact of the Economic Crisis on Women Workers in Indonesia: Social and Gender Dimensions, unpublished paper prepared for the AIT/ILO Research Project on the Gender Impact of the Economic Crisis in Southeast and East Asia, Insan Hitawasana Sejahtera, Jakarta.

Oey-Gardiner, Mayling and Sulastri (2000), 'Continuity, Change and Women in a Man's World', in Mayling Oey-Gardiner and Carla Bianpoen (eds), *Indonesian Women: The Journey Continues*, Research School for Pacific and Asian Studies Publishing, Australian National University, Canberra, pp. 1–23.

Pangestu, Mari and Miranda Swaray Goeltom (2001), 'Survey of Recent Developments', *Bulletin of Indonesian Economic Studies*, 37(2), pp. 141–71.

Pangestu, Mari, Tubagus Feridhanusetyawan and Kurnya Roesad (2001), Managing Indonesia's Debt, Research Report for CIDA, Jakarta, September.

Pelras, Christian (1996), *The Bugis*, Blackwell Publishers, Cambridge.

Philpott, Simon (2000), *Rethinking Indonesia: Postcolonial Theory, Authoritarianism and Identity*, Macmillan, London.

Pujiastuti, T.N. (2000), The Experience of Female Overseas Contract Workers from Indonesia, unpublished MA thesis, Department of Geographical and Environmental Studies, University of Adelaide, Adelaide.

Purwaningsih, Sri Sunarti (1998), Childcare Strategies of Javanese Families with Mothers on Overseas Labour Contracts, unpublished PhD thesis, Demography Program, Research School of Social Sciences, Australian National University, Canberra.

Pusat Penelitian Kependudukan (Population Studies Institute) (1986), *Mobilitas Angkatan Kerja ke Timur Tengah,* Pusat Penelitian Kependudukan, Gadjah Mada University, Yogyakarta.

Radjab, Muhammad (1969), *Sistem Kekerabatan di Minangkabau* [The Minangkabau Kinship System], Center for Minangkabau Studies Press, Padang.

Raharto, A., G. Hugo, H. Romdiati and S. Bandiyono (1999), *Migrasi dan Pembangunan di Kawasan Timur Indonesia: Isu Ketenagakerjaan* [Migration and Development in Eastern Indonesia: Labour/Human Resource Issues], PPT-LIPI, Jakarta.

Rahim, A. Rahman (1981/82), *Sikap Mental Bugis: Berdasarkan Lontarak-Lontarak Latoa dan Budi Istikarah* [Bugis Mentality: Based on the Traditional ManuscriptsLatoa and Budi Istikarah], Universitas Hasanuddin, Ujung Pandang.

Rajagukguk (1999), Proyeksi Penduduk Indonesia, 1995–2025 [Population Projections for Indonesia, 1995–2025]. Skenario Normal dan Krisis, unpublished report, Demographic Institute, Faculty of Economics, University of Indonesia, in collaboration with University Research for Graduate Studies, Directorate General of Higher Education, Ministry of Education.

Rammage, Douglas E. (1995), *Democracy, Islam and the Ideology of Tolerance*, Routledge, London and New York.

Raymundo, M. Corazon, Peter Xenos and Lita J. Domingo (eds) (1999), *Adolescent Sexuality in the Philippines*, Office of the Vice Chancellor for Research and Development, University of the Philippines, Manila.

Retherford, Robert D., Naohiro Ogawa and Rikiya Matsukura (2001), 'Late Marriage and Less Marriage in Japan', *Population and Development Review*, 27(1), pp. 65–102.

Robinson, Kathryn (1991), 'Housemaids: The Effects of Gender and Culture on the Internal and International Migration of Indonesian Women', in G. Bottomley et al. (eds), *Intersexions: Gender/Class/Ethnicity*, Allen & Unwin, Sydney, pp. 31–51.

Robinson, Kathryn (1998), 'Indonesian Women's Rights, International Feminism and Democratic Change', *Communal/Plural*, 6(2), pp. 205–23.

Robinson, Kathryn (2000a), 'Indonesian Women: From Orde Baru to Reformasi', in L. Edwards and M. Roces (eds), *Women in Asia: Tradition, Modernity and Globalisation*, Allen & Unwin, Sydney, pp. 139–66.

Robinson, Kathryn (2000b), 'Gender, Islam and Nationality: Indonesian Domestic Servants in the Middle East', in K. Adams and S. Dickey (eds), *Home and Hegemony: Domestic Service and Identity in South and Southeast Asia*, Michigan University Press, Ann Arbor, pp. 249–82.

Rodgers, S. (1995), *Telling Lives, Telling History: Autobiography and Historical Imagination in Modern Indonesia*, University of California Press, Berkeley.

Romdiati, H., T. Handayani and S. Rahayu (1998), *Aplikasi Jaring Pengaman Sosial Bidang Ketenagakerjaan: Beberapa Isu Penting Dari Hasil Kajian Cepat Di Propinsi Jawa Barat*, PPT-LIPI, Jakarta.

Röttger-Rössler (2000), 'Shared Responsibility: Some Aspects of Gender and Authority in Makassar Society', in Roger Tol, Kees van Dijk and Greg Acciaioli (eds), *Authority and Enterprise among the Peoples of South Sulawesi*, KITLV Press, Leiden.

Rudkin, L. (1994), 'Dependency Status and Happiness with Old Age on Java', *Gerontologist*, 34(2), pp. 217–23.

Rural Development Foundation (1992), *Trade in Domestic Helpers, Indonesia (with a Micro Study from East Javanese Domestic Helpers)*, Final Report, Rural Development Foundation, Indonesia.

Rusmini, Oka (2000), *Tarian Bumi* [Dance of the Earth], Penerbit Indonesia Tera, Magelang.

Scalabrini Migration Centre (2000), *Assessing Population Movement and HIV Vulnerability: Brunei–Indonesia–Malaysia–Philippines Linkages in the East ASEAN Growth Area*, UNDP South-east Asia HIV and Development Project, Bangkok.

Schuman, Michael (2001), 'Megawati's Moves Disprove Many Doubters in Indonesia', *Asian Wall Street Journal*, 12 August.

Sen, Krishna (1982), 'The Image of Women in Indonesian Films: Some Observations', *Prisma: The Indonesian Indicator*, 24 (March), pp. 16–29.

Sen, Krishna (1993), 'Repression and Resistance: Interpretations of the Feminine in New Order Cinema', in V. Matheson-Hooker (ed.), *Culture and Society in New Order Indonesia*, Oxford University Press, Kuala Lumpur, pp. 116–33.

Sen, Krishna (1998), 'Indonesian Women at Work: Reframing the Subject', in Krishna Sen and Maila Stivens (eds), *Gender and Power in Affluent Asia*, Routledge, London, pp. 35–62.

Sen, Krishna (2002), Gendered Citizens of the New Indonesian Democracy', *Review of Indonesian and Malay Affairs*, Winter, forthcoming.

Sen, K. and D.T. Hill (2000), *Media, Culture and Politics in Indonesia*, Oxford University Press, Melbourne.

Sidel, John T. (2001), 'It Takes a *Madrasah*? Habermas Meets Bourdieu in Indonesia', *Southeast Asia Research,* 9(1), pp. 109–22.

Siegel, James T. (1998), *A New Criminal Type in Jakarta: Counter-revolution Today*, Duke University Press, Durham.

Sigit, H. and S. Surbakti (1999), 'Social Impact of the Economic Crisis in Indonesia', Paper prepared for the conference on 'Assessing the Social Impact of the Financial Crisis in Selected Asian Developing Economies', ADB Auditorium, Manila, 17–18 June.

Sigit, Hananto (1988), *A Socio-economic Profile of the Elderly in Jakarta*, BPS, Jakarta.

Singarimbun, Nima (1999), Changing Female Labour Force Participation and Work Patterns in Jakarta, PhD thesis, Demography Program, Research School of Social Sciences, Australian National University, Canberra.

Singhanetra-Renard, A. (1986), The Middle East and Beyond: Dynamics of International Labour Circulation among Southeast Asian Workers, Gadjah Mada University, Yogyakarta, mimeo.

Situmorang, Augustina (1998), Virginity and Premarital Sex: Attitudes and Experiences of Indonesian Young People in Medan, paper presented at the Ninth National Conference of the Australian Population Association, 29 September – 2 October, Brisbane.

SMERU (Social Monitoring and Early Response Unit), Regional Autonomy and the Business Climate, Field Report, Jakarta, May, mimeo.

Soekanto, Santi W.E. (1999), 'Megawati a Boon for Women', *Jakarta Post*, 29 October, p. 4.

Spaan, E. (1999), *Labour Circulation and Socioeconomic Transformation: The Case of East Java, Indonesia*, Report No. 56, NIDI, The Hague.

Stephen, Michele (2001), 'Barong and Rangda in the Context of Balinese Religion', *Review of Indonesian and Malayan Affairs*, 35(1), pp. 137–94.

Sudaryanto, Kiayati Y. (1996), 'PKK: Gerakan Perempuan Dikendalikan oleh Laki-laki' [PKK: A Women's Movement Steered by Men], in Mayling Oey (ed.), *Perempuan Indonesia Dulu dan Kini* [Indonesian Women: In the Past and the Present], Gramedia, pp. 410–31.

Sullivan, Norma (1983), 'Indonesian Women in Development, State Theory and Urban Kampung Practice', in Lenore Manderson (ed.), *Women's Work and Women's Roles: Economics and Everyday Life in Indonesia, Malaysia and Singapore*, Development Studies Centre Monograph No. 32, Australian National University, Canberra.

Sullivan, Norma (1991), 'Gender and Politics in Indonesia', in M. Stivens (ed.), *Why Gender Matters in Southeast Asian Politics*, Monash University, Centre of Southeast Asian Studies, Clayton, Victoria, pp. 61–86.

Sumardi, Sandyawan (1998), 'Rape Is Rape', *Inside Indonesia*, 56 (October–December), pp. 20–21.

Sumardjo, Jakob (1982), 'A Peaceful Home: Women in Indonesian Literature', *Prisma: The Indonesian Indicator*, 24 (March), pp. 40–52.

Sunaryanto, H. (1998), Female Labour Migration to Bekasi, Indonesia: Determinants and Consequences, unpublished PhD thesis, Department of Population and Human Resources, University of Adelaide, Adelaide.

Sunindyo, Saraswati (1993), 'Gender Discourse on TV', in V. Matheson-Hooker (ed.), *Culture and Society in New Order Indonesia*, Oxford University Press, Kuala Lumpur, pp. 134–48.

Surbakti, Soedarti (2000), *Evaluasi Kebutuhan Sistem Statistik Yang Responsif Jender di Indonesia* [Evaluation of the Need for a Gender-responsive Statistical System in Indonesia], Kantor Meneg PP dan JICA, Jakarta.

Surbakti, Soedarti, Arizal Ahnaf and Nona Iriana (2001), 'Matriks Indikator Kesenjangan Repelita VI', in Dra. Nina Sardjunani and Lenny N. Rosalin (eds), *Indikator Gender Untuk Perencanaan Pembangunan* [Gender Indicators for Development Planning], Bappenas and WSP II-CIDA, Jakarta.

Suryadi, Linus (1981), *Pengakuan Pariyem*, Penerbit Sinar Harapan, Jakarta.

Suryakusuma, Julia (1996), 'The State and Sexuality in New Order Indonesia', in Laurie J. Sears (ed.), *Fantasizing the Feminine in Indonesia*, Duke University Press, Durham and London, pp. 92–119.

Suyono, M. (1981), 'Tenaga Kerja Indonesia di Timur Tenagah Makin Mantap', *Suara Karya*, pp. 2–6.

Tio, M. (ed.) (2001), *Megawati Dimata Politisi* [Megawati in the Eyes of Politicians], Garuda Ijo, no place of publication given.

Tiwon, Sylvia (1996), 'Models and Maniacs: Articulating the Female in Indonesia', in Laurie J. Sears (ed.), *Fantasizing the Feminine in Indonesia*, Duke University Press, Durham and London, pp. 47–70.

Ulil, Abshar Abdallah (1999), 'Megawati dan Islam' [Megawati and Islam], in Muin Kubais Madzin et al. (eds), *Menolak Politik Anti-Nurani*, Bigraf Publishing, Yogyakarta, pp. 155–8.

UNDAW (United Nations Division for the Advancement of Women) (1998), *National Machineries for Gender Equality: Expert Group Meeting Report*, UNDAW, Santiago.

UNDP (1997), *Human Development Report 1997*, UNDP, New York.

UNICEF (1984), *Situation Analyses, Jakarta*, Singapore.

UNICEF (1999), *State of the Children Community Report*.

Utami, Ayu (1998), *Saman*, Kepustakaan Populer Gramedia, Jakarta.

Utami, Ayu (2001), *Larung*, Kepustakaan Populer Gramedia, Jakarta.

Utomo, Iwu Dwisetyani and Peter McDonald (1997), 'Religion, Culture and Sexuality: A Study of Young People in Higher Income Families in Jakarta', in International Union for the Scientific Study of Population (ed.), *International Population Conference, Beijing 1997*, 2, pp. 803–28.

Wageman, Mildred L.E. (2000), 'Indonesian Women between Yesterday and Tomorrow', in Mayling Oey-Gardiner and Carla Bianpoen (eds), *Indonesian Women: The Journey Continues*, Research School for Pacific and Asian Studies Publishing, Australian National University, Canberra, pp. 303–31.

Wanandi, Jusuf (2001), 'Hopes, Fears about Cabinet', *Jakarta Post*, 13 August, p. 4.

Widodo, Amrih (1995), 'The Stages of the State: Arts of the People and Rites of Hegemonisation', *Review of Indonesian and Malayan Affairs*, 29(1–2), pp. 1–36.

Wieringa, Saskia (ed.) (1995), *Subversive Women: Women's Movements in Africa, Asia, Latin America and the Carribean*, Kali for Women, New Delhi.

Wieringa, Saskia (1998), 'Sexual Metaphors in the Change from Soekarno's Old Order to Suharto's New Order in Indonesia', *Review of Indonesian and Malayan Affairs*, 32(2), Summer, pp. 143–78.

Wilson, I. (1999), 'Reog Ponorogo: Spirituality, Sexuality, and Power in a Javanese Performance Tradition', *Intersections: Gender, History, and Culture in the Asian Context*, 2, http://wwwsshe.murdoch.edu.au/intersections/issue2/Warok.html.

Wolf, Diane L. (1990), 'Factory Daughters, the Family and Nuptiality in Java', *Genus*, 46(3–4), pp. 45–54.

Woodcroft-Lee, Carlien Patricia (1985), 'Profiles in a Crowded Mirror: Some Perceptions of the Role of Women in Society in Contemporary Indonesian Popular Fiction', in Wang Gungwu, M. Guerrero and D. Marr (eds), *Society and the Writer; Essays on Literature in Modern Asia*, Research School of Pacific Studies, Australian National University, Canberra, pp. 261–80.

World Bank (2001a), *Indonesia Country Brief*, Jakarta, October.

World Bank (2001b), *Indonesia: The Imperative for Reform*, Jakarta, 2 November.

YKB (Yayasan Kusuma Buana) and BKKBN (National Family Planning Coordination Agency) (1993), *Hasil 'Need Assessment' Reproduksi Sehat Remaja di 12 Kota di Indonesia*, Jakarta.

YPP (Yayasan Pengembangan Pedesaan) (1992), *Trade in Domestic Helpers, Indonesia (with a Micro Study from East Javanese Domestic Helpers)*, Final report, YPP, Indonesia.

INDEX

women's participation, 145–7, 230–31
women's rights, 89–90
see also overseas contract workers
exchange rate, 41, 42, 43, 47, 48, 49, 50

family planning, 6, 7, 11, 72, 74, 77, 78,
103, 190, 193, 194, 235–49
Family Welfare Movement, now Family
Welfare Empowerment Movement
(PKK), 8, 9, 12n, 70, 76, 83, 89, 103,
111n, 187–91, 195, 196–7, 202, 244
Fatayat NU, 89, 192, 193, 194, 196
feminism, 80–91
Five-year Development Plan
see Repelita
financial crisis, 3, 41, 42–4, 145–53,
238–42
FN-P3M
see Organisation for the Development
of Pesantren and Society
Forum for the Study of Classical Islamic
Texts (Forum Kajian Kitab Klasik
Islam), 194
Forum Kajian Kitab Klasik Islam
see Forum for the Study of Classical
Islamic Texts, 194
Fourth World Conference on Women, 71,
102
FPMP
see Women's Forum
FWPSS
see Women Journalists Forum for
South Sulawesi

gay and *lesbi* Indonesians, 92–9, 131
GBHN
see Broad Guidelines on State Policy
GDP, 44, 45, 46, 47, 48, 50, 52
GEM
see gender empowerment measure
gender empowerment measure (GEM),
212, 213
gender ideology, 132–3
gender mainstreaming, 6, 67, 73, 74, 79,
214–18

Gerwani, 70, 102, 133, 138
see also Communist Party
Golkar, 17, 21, 23, 30, 31, 181, 189, 202,
237
Gus Dur
see Abdurrahman Wahid

Habibie government, 6, 10, 33, 103, 106,
237, 243
Haz, Hamzah, 1, 12n, 15, 17, 18, 186n
health services, 75, 188–91, 196–7
see also family planning; Posyandu
HIV/AIDS, 177, 190
homosexuality, 7–8, 92–9, 131
Hong Kong, 159,
households, 219–34
size, 220
human rights, 6, 19, 31, 32, 37, 39n, 75,
87, 90–91, 194

IAIN
see State Institute for Islamic Studies
IBRA, 51, 54, 56, 58, 64
ILO
see International Labour Organisation
IMF
see International Monetary Fund
Indar Parawansa, Khofifah, xiv, 4, 5–6, 7,
11, 66, 78–9, 105–6, 168, 205, 242,
245
India, 38, 39, 80, 185–6
Indonesian Consumers' Association
Foundation (YLKI), 105
Indonesian Democratic Party of Struggle
(PDI-P), 3, 8, 13, 22, 23, 35, 65, 104,
107
Indonesian Women's Coalition (KPI), 3,
110
Indonesia Women's Congress
see Kowani
inflation, 2, 47–9, 51, 62–3, 64, 70
Institute for the Study of Coastal Commu-
nities (LP3M), 200
Institute of National Information (LIN),
19–20

INDONESIA ASSESSMENT SERIES